BECOMING
REAL

RECLAIMING YOUR HEALTH
IN MIDLIFE

D0802111

Rose M. Kumar M.D.

Medial Press • Pewaukee, Wisconsin

Medial Press
www.medial-press.com
www.becoming-real.com
www.ommanicenter.com
The Ommani Center for Integrative Medicine
1166 Quail Court, Suite 210
Pewaukee, WI 53072

The Four Body System™ is trademarked to Kalpana (Rose) M. Kumar M.D.

ISBN: 978-0-9833521-1-2 softcover

Cover design by Kathi Dunn, www.dunn-design.com
Interior design by Dorie McClelland, www.springbookdesign.com

Second edition
Printed in the United States of America

*This book is dedicated to
my daughter, Nisha, and my son, Matthew.
May you always live from Truth and Integrity and
honor only what is Real.
With my love to you forever.*

Contents

List of Figures

Acknowledgments

The creation of this book emerged in the "middle" of my life. The process leading up to its birth was nothing short of alchemical. I have been burned in many fires which have honed my soul and my truth. My journey was midwifed by many whose guidance helped me become "real." I will be forever grateful for their love and support.

My parents, Adarsh and Mahendra Kumar, have been amazing role models and mentors. Their commitment to integrity, truth, and hard work has had a profound impact on my character and resilience. Their generous gifts throughout my life will carry forward through me into future generations. Their love and support through my midlife process has helped me to stay rooted in this real and sacred place.

I thank my beautiful children, Nisha and Matthew, for their unconditional love and their ability to see the truth beneath illusion. They have been amazing examples of resilience, love and integrity and are clearly here to make a positive contribution in our world. They are my continual source of inspiration and hope.

I am deeply grateful for my husband, Jerry, my best friend and *true* life partner who continues to support what is real within me. With him, I have learned about the power of healthy love. Thank you for your sincere and endless support and the sacrifices you have so willingly made to help me complete this book.

I thank my stepchildren, Hannah and Nicholas, for their love and belief in me and for embracing the path of transformation as we have grown together as a blended family.

I am deeply grateful for my animal companions, Jazmine, Boosie, and Starlight, who have powerfully and unconditionally supported me with their love and loyalty.

I am thankful to Diane Herold an extraordinary energy healer who taught me the value of boundaries and facilitated the connection to my "real self."

My practice manager, Sherris Corby, arrived in my life at a precise time to aid the vision and mission of The Ommani Center. Her loyalty, dedication and commitment to seek are invaluable gifts that support the continued manifestation of Ommani's vision.

I offer my humble gratitude to the practitioners and staff at The Ommani Center who loyally and faithfully serve it's vision with love and commitment.

And last but not least, I would like to acknowledge and thank my patients—past, present, and future—who make my life's work possible and are continual catalysts for my own healing and awakening process. I am forever indebted to their courage and love that has added immense joy and fulfillment to my work. I am deeply honored to serve you.

Kathi Dunn and Dorie McClelland gave this book the beautiful form you are holding in your hands. I am grateful for their support of my vision for healing.

While writing this book, I felt guided by my Muse who took residence in me and did not rest until our work was completed. I am but her humble scribe.

I am awed by the Feminine and Masculine energies of the Universe which compassionately and continually unfold us towards healing and wholeness. May we always stay open to their grace and power.

Dragonfly Medicine

Dragonfly is a symbol that represents our ability to discern illusion from reality. We are conditioned to believe we are less powerful than we are. Dragonfly Medicine is the medicine that heals this wound.

It is said Dragonfly was once a mighty dragon with magical powers who was tricked into believing she was a tiny dragonfly. Dragon changed form into a dragonfly due to this false belief.

Too often we allow our failures, shortcomings and limitations to define us. We are conditioned to believe we are less powerful than we really are. If we accept these illusions as real, we become disempowered. We can choose to wield our intrinsic power and wisdom to dismantle these false beliefs and transform into our Real self. Dragonfly Medicine empowers and guides this sacred process.*

My blessing to all who read this book is for you to become your Real self through Dragonfly Medicine that graces these pages.

May you heal the world as you connect with your intrinsic power and wisdom.

~ Rose M. Kumar M.D.

*adapted with permission from Sharon George
www.fantasy-goddess-art.com

Introduction

Medicine is not only a science; it is also an art.
It does not consist of compounding pills and plasters;
it deals with the very processes of life, which must be
understood before they may be guided.

~ Paracelsus

The processes of life are rarely understood by the current medical system, least of all, midlife. Midlife arrives, heralding changes at all levels, changes we were never prepared for. Imagine what would it be like to be prepared for this time, to wait in anticipation for the transformation it holds, to consciously engage in caring for ourselves as we approach this powerful and sublime stage of life when our body, mind, and our very being can transform in ways that express our wisdom and essence like never before.

Both men and women go through midlife somewhat blindly and without guidance. It is often accompanied by needless fear and suffering. Men, unlike women, are socialized to withhold their feelings. They rarely understand or even acknowledge the changes underway in their bodies and minds. Unacknowledged fear and confusion builds, expressing itself in symptoms like never before. The medical system does not recognize their need for process or framework and most often, men muddle through midlife blindly, carrying outdated emotional baggage into the second half of their lives.

Midlife women endure powerful shifts in their bodies often overlooked by physicians who merely replace receding hormones with synthetic ones. This is a dangerous and weak solution for their multifaceted process. A great majority of "modern" societies in the world ignore midlife and superimpose their pervading yet ineffective paradigm of "quick-fixing" with superficial solutions to cope with its symptomatology, ignoring its powerful potency and potential for growth and wisdom. Being part of a society that merely copes and devalues indigenous wisdom and natural rhythms, we are all left alone through this unprecedented gateway, to make peace with our losses, our newly changing bodies and the explicit lack of meaning that many of us fear we will carry into the second half of our lives.

As a physician, having worked with thousands of patients going through midlife, I feel it necessary to offer a framework for this time that not only guides, but provides an understanding of its many facets. Midlife is so full of potency yet endangered if not navigated from a place of radical truth and self-care. The framework presented in *Becoming Real* is intended to guide you through this time with direction and hope to help you restore and reclaim a level of health and meaning you may never have thought was possible.

In the three years since the first edition of *Becoming Real* was published, I have even more keenly observed midlife patterns in both men and women. Many men who read the first edition felt strongly that the transformational processes I described for women, applied to them as well. In fact, a few stated that although the book addressed changes women experience through menopause, simply replacing the female with male gender would describe what they too experience during this time. Menopause no longer refers simply to the cessation of menses, but is associated with the myriad of changes that accompany its presence.

The root of the term *menopause* is derived from the Greek word "meno" meaning month or moon and "pause" meaning cessation. It's pure meaning refers to the changes women experience during and after the cessation of menses. Although, this stage is marked by profound shifts in physiology it is also marked by an emotional, mental and spiritual recalibration that makes itself known throughout this gateway.

Women's bodies go through dramatic shifts during menopause, as menstrual cycles change alongside emotions with a deepening of feeling function which in turn, informs them of the hormonal shifts underway.

In fact, under the influence of hormones, women's brains rewire and recalibrate and parts of their neuronal wiring down-regulates while other parts gain prominence. Men undergo biological shifts as well, but these are poorly understood and hardly studied.

In men, testosterone levels drop, stress hormones rise, and the male psyche begins to deepen in an attempt to evoke more meaning and awaken them to their neglected and forgotten parts, previously suppressed through socialization and adaptation. The dramatic shifts that occur in both men and women are dealt with differently by each. Men are not socialized to express any level of their process. They hold their feelings in, sharing snippets with their wives, partners or confidants. The medical system fails to address their real needs. Prescriptions for Viagra and Cialis are limited offerings only, prescribed commonly for men and not worthy substitutes for the intimacy and meaning that they are really seeking.

What both men and women long for is a way to live from a depth of meaning, creativity and intimacy, while cultivating a deeper relationship with life itself.

Our society has severely neglected to value the need for a framework to understand the hows and whys of transformation and individuation during this time. It does not provide us with needed guidance, safety or sacred space through this gateway, which can be likened to a death and rebirth process of the most intense kind. Many even call midlife "the death before death."

For women, menopause holds a promise for transformation at all levels. Many women enter midlife when their children leave home, when their very identities are called into question. They are called to examine their relationship with themselves and explore the depths of their sacred purpose, different than what was defined for them in the first half of their lives. Their very souls demand this. They seek sovereignty and a new identity, one that calls their previously adapted selves into question.

For many, this is a time of intense creativity, heralded by the death of their distorted relationships with themselves and their youthful bodies they are now leaving behind. They are called from within to reinvent themselves, to weave wisdom and discernment gained from their past.

Midlife is full of power and purpose and brings with it its own "medicine" offering a deeper level of health for both men and women. Its power and potential must be harnessed for both to become real and no longer serve the world at the cost of themselves.

The midlife gateway often expresses its uncompromising demands in men through a heart attack or some crisis that seals their fate. Even then, they can only marginally process the urgings from their souls without a framework for guidance.

My hope is that this book will offer a framework and understanding of the potential and possibilities the midlife gateway holds. I have reframed "menopause" from being seen as a time of degeneration as it currently is, to one of regeneration filled with power and purpose with the potential for core healing. I have used the female gender as the voice of this book as I am able to write authentically about midlife and menopause from a woman's perspective.

In the nearly three decades that I have practiced medicine, I am sorry to say that traditional medicine has not made much progress in the area of Women's Health. In my late twenties, as a practicing internist, I was naive about the need for context and framework when working with women in a health care setting. I was taught by reputable teachers that women's symptoms resulted from pathology—hormone deficiency simply requiring management. I was taught to medicate them with antidepressants and synthetic hormones and settle for this as standard-of-care. Medicine did not hold much else for them. More than twenty years later, women continue to seek comfort for symptoms they try to understand, after being placed on medications that do not serve their needs. Now in my fifties, having gone through menopause myself and the transformation it carries, I am saddened to see the continued absence of framework and guidance for women (and men) in medicine today.

Women, as cyclic beings, are well-versed in transitions. Their monthly menstrual cycles accompanied by changes in their bodies, emotions and intuitions pose a challenge when living in a world where emotional intensity is pathologized. Midlife and menopause can be a precarious passage, when the longing for meaning crescendos as women awaken and yearn to connect with who they really are. They often remain alone with their feelings, adapted in a world that no longer resonates with their truth. They feel lost without framework, afraid they may be losing their minds, believing what their physicians tell them about their patho-psychological states that now define them. Many succumb to medications prescribed to help them cope with their symptoms. What they need is a safe space to honor their alchemy and balance their hormones with framework and presence.

What women experience is not pathological. It is a normal, sacred and powerful transition from being adapted to becoming real. This transition causes an eruption of symptoms at all levels of the body/mind as the soul rises up to claim its place in the world. This precise yet powerful process begins with hormonal shifts that occur in the late thirties and continue into their fifties. During this 12 to 15 year process, the task before women is to truly understand themselves and learn how to balance their lives at all levels.

Providing hormone balance is a critical part of their journey towards wholeness. Its methodology is yet to be fully understood and utilized by traditional medicine and essential for not only emotional well-being, but physical and mental health as well.

Hormone balancing is an intriguing and precise science that requires artful mastery. In working with women for nearly thirty years with natural hormones, I have learned techniques to balance their hormones precisely and effectively. They work for the majority of patients with minimal side effects and maximal benefit. As a scientist who is true to my vocation, I continue to fine tune my approach to make it understandable to my patients so they can learn to heal their symptoms while using my guidance. Every woman with her unique physiology will respond uniquely to natural hormone therapy. There is no one protocol for all, as is so common in traditional medicine. Hormone balancing must be tailored to suit how each woman's body responds with consistent monitoring of blood levels to insure safe dosing. After working with close to a hundred thousand women in my career, I have been able to design a method of hormone balancing that is safe and effective. It is important to help women understand when adjustments are needed for continued balance. A minimalist at heart, I have discovered the formula for dosing that uses the smallest doses for the best outcomes. This has kept patients safe from side effects and potential risks that even natural hormones may carry.

Women have the right to understand their cycles, menopause and their midlife process. Keeping them in the dark and dismissing them with expertise does not serve what they really need. In fact, it perpetuates the patriarchal patterns of the Dark Ages. Midlife (menopausal) women have a wealth of intrinsic power within them. Not only are they now fearless to make their truth known, the very act of speaking their truth is a necessary part of emancipation into their wisdom years. Our hurting world can only be healed when midlife women and men become real. Only then, can they lead the way with their clarity of truth to restore the integrity missing in our world systems today.

Corporate health care has endangered the soul of medicine in its true essence. By ignoring *process*, the practice of medicine has ignored its true intention to heal. Currently, it is going through a death of its own making, a crisis that calls for the birth of a new paradigm of medicine, from which it can truly serve its patients. Integrative Medicine holds this promise, but, in its infancy, it is confusing and commonly offered as a potpourri of treatments, ill-defined and lacking in framework.

In the chapters that follow, I present a cohesive framework for a higher standard of Integrative Medicine. One that can serve as a guide for both physicians and patients and deepen the practice of medicine while it individuates to embody its true purpose. Without this, physicians will continue to unknowingly hold an unsafe space for patients, and patients unknowingly, will settle for superficial solutions, relying merely on symptom management, ignoring the wisdom contained within illness and missing the opportunity for consciousness and awakening.

My intention for both men and women in the pages of this book, is to help dispel the fear that midlife can evoke, replacing it with understanding and awe. My hope is that the framework I offer will help you replace adapted patterns with real ones that resonate with your truth and your soul's very purpose.

As we embrace midlife and menopause as the gifts that they are, we can reclaim our health and access our true destiny with clarity and meaning.

Becoming real may be our only hope to honor what is truly sacred as we ascend into the second half of our lives with the promise of our authentic presence.

1

Uncovering the Feminine

Transformation is the pivotal process that defines midlife. Anybody who has gone through midlife with some level of consciousness will agree that the process itself is sublime and can strip us of *who we think we are* and replace it with *who we really are*. This is the work of the Soul. The nature of the Soul is said to be Feminine and the nature of the mind, Masculine. The Soul steps ahead of the mind in midlife and balances the Feminine and Masculine energies to restore health and make us whole. The Soul's agenda overrides all others during this powerful time. The transformation catalyzed by the Soul transforms us into larger versions of ourselves. Through this gateway, we grow our "inner eye" that enables us to see through the darkness of illusion into reality.

My heart has always longed for a world that lived from love and compassion, one where health and relationships were inclusive of the feminine qualities of collaboration and process, transformation, and balance—one in which truth could be freely expressed and where the voice of integrity was honored as a core value. As a physician, I also searched for the presence of these qualities within our health care system. I worked within corporate health care after completing my medical training. I tried all the ways I could to fit into this system, but was unable to without paying a grave price. This price was the compromise of my soulful connection to medicine's sacred vocation. True service to its vocation was missing in corporate health care. The corporate environment lacked the Feminine Principle. It lacked all the qualities of the feminine I cherished, such as collaborating, loving, listening, healing, and feeling. These missing elements were like oxygen for my heart. Without their presence, I was unable to practice the medicine I loved from a place of soul.

I spent my childhood in India, a country where stories and myths are important elements in the cultural fabric and where the Goddess is worshipped and revered. As my perspective matured, I realized that I was living in a paradox. The culture, on one hand, spiritualized the feminine and, on the other, suppressed and repressed women. I was unable to understand the reasons for this and could not find an explanation for the dissonance. It seemed hypocritical. How could people who revered the Goddess as a deity treat women with disrespect? How could they tout spiritual principles that honored the Divine Feminine, yet dismiss the needs of women? My family expected me to conform to these cultural norms, despite my confusion about this paradox. I was not allowed to question it.

During my medical training in the U.S., I witnessed the same dissonance. I observed that women in medicine were not treated equally. But they adapted to be accepted. They normalized inequality. Women patients were treated the same way, especially if they expressed any emotions or feelings.

Feminine qualities were disregarded in many organizations across America. I realized that this was a global wound that transcended culture. Despite differences in its outward appearance, this wound affected everyone in similar ways.

The feminine in medicine

As an employee of corporate health care, I witnessed the many ways in which the feminine was dishonored both covertly and overtly, yet many women in medicine did not consider it a problem. They continued to adapt to being treated with disrespect and denied the pain it caused. Some felt angry, but many felt paralyzed and did not understand this as their reaction towards disrespect.

For them, denial was easier than rocking the boat. When I worked for corporate health care, some women physicians became intolerant of this injustice. They demanded equal treatment to no avail. I took a stand to end the discrimination and advocated for fair and equal treatment on behalf of women physicians. After a year of vigilant effort, the corporate medical system I worked for made the needed changes I requested.

My ability to advocate for myself in my marriage was in sharp contrast to my professional life. At home, I had no voice, and was conditioned to second-guess myself and my truth. This part of my life was dissonant with my integrity as a woman who honored the Feminine Principle and practiced it at work. Most often, when I expected respect and honor, I was dismissed and undermined. I felt powerless in my attempts to change how I was treated and adapted to survive, denying my pain in ways similar to my colleagues at work. I experienced the disempowerment one feels when adapting to the *power principle*. I found myself disconnected from my real self at home, yet able to live from it at work. My life was out of balance. I was living the all too familiar paradox. Since I was imprinted as a child to not question dissonance, I continued to second-guess myself, yet felt anguish for how I was dishonored. I thought that somehow *I* was the cause of the disrespect and abuse I received.

I needed to heal the disparity between my personal and professional lives. Because of the dissonance that was present, I felt tossed between two worlds—one where I had courage and clarity around how women deserved to be treated, and one where I felt intense fear and paralysis. I began to examine why I felt anguish in my marriage. I needed to awaken to how I was being treated and why I was allowing this. This was the beginning of my personal awakening.

Personal recovery opened my eyes to what was *really* happening to many women in medicine. I noticed that they were reluctantly adapting to a disrespectful system as a method of survival. This left them with little to no connection to their real selves. Although I had strongly advocated on their behalf, my personal process awakened a deeper perspective regarding their dishonor by the medical system. Compromising their truth for acceptance was a form of self-betrayal. This was the unseen reason that also perpetuated their disrespect by the medical system. I had done the same thing in my personal life. These adapted patterns were now becoming clear. I was finally able to see through the fog of illusion into the reality of my situation.

It was clear that the medical system made women (both patients and physicians) second-guess themselves when they adapted to patterns of treatment that dishonored both them and their process. This system was neither heart-centered nor respectful to the Feminine Principle. It did not serve the soul nor the true vocation of health care. On the contrary, it perpetuated a fear-based system that disempowered all.

Integrative Medicine

Around this time, Integrative Medicine was becoming the new buzz word. It seemed like a better approach to health which was confirmed by health care data. It made sense to integrate complementary (alternative) and traditional medicine. It appeared to be a more complete model for health care. The medical system began to open clinics that offered both traditional and complementary medicine and called it integrative medicine. The intent of this form of medicine was logical in theory, and corporate health care wanted to capture market share. Patients began swarming to these clinics expecting humanistic, less fragmented and less pathologically focused health care, in short health care that honored the Feminine Principle. Over a relatively short period of time, many left disappointed, as they experienced the traditional model practiced beneath a new label, one that still saw illness as a breakdown of the body that could be fixed now through "alternative" rather than traditional means. Focus on the *cause* of illness was still not a part of this system. Experiencing a potpourri of modalities in conjunction with traditional symptom management without a causal focus provided only a limited level of healing. Patients continued to feel disempowered within this new model. They found that this form of medicine was not truly integrative, but was the traditional medical model that now utilized complementary methods from its limited framework. They were actually spending even more for complementary methods in addition to traditional ones for mere symptomatic relief.

In addition, around this time, a number of "holistic" doctors emerged in an effort to meet these needs. Many were not practicing standard-of-care medicine and were implementing medical practices that were neither safe nor scientifically proven to be effective. Patients were still searching for a better and more effective way to heal. The open system they sought was not found in either traditional or integrative medicine within the current health care model.

I was becoming increasingly restless as I continued to feel the critical and meaningful essence of healing missing in health care. I felt that the current medical model was too limited to truly heal its patients. I began to envision a health care model that would be invested in healing rather than merely managing symptoms; where the Feminine Principle, when integrated, could also heal the health care system itself. This could potentially heal the deep wounds of feminine suffering present in corporate health care.

It was time to create a health care model that honored the vocation of medicine, one that was inclusive of process and committed to educating patients. I felt that the medical system needed to integrate the Feminine Principle at all levels of its infrastructure, both as a business and therapeutic model. This was the crucial piece missing in corporate health care. I began to realize that my life's work was to create a medical model that included the qualities of collaborating, listening, feeling, and expertise. It would not compromise standard-of-care in favor of the Feminine Principle. It would be inclusive of both. This could reframe health care into a working model where its intent and mission included the facilitation of wholeness. It would be integrative at its very foundation.

I attempted to practice medicine from this perspective within corporate health care. The response from management was not encouraging. They felt threatened by this "open system" of practice. They asked me to down play my approach and accommodate what was familiar and normalized by the current system—sick care. They informed me they would not support a medical practice that did not maintain sickness, as it compromised hospital dollars. Supporting *health* did not work for their business model which relied on costly diagnostic procedures and hospital admissions. My low admission numbers were not matching their projected profits as my patients were healing. This was a conflict of interest for the corporate system. I was disheartened. But, I was not willing to compromise my soul to increase their quarterly profits.

I left corporate health care to create a new medical model, one where I could practice what I loved: a form of medicine that maintained a high standard-of-care and *healed* its patients. It would integrate the wisdom and expertise of traditional medicine with the wisdom of complementary healing traditions that had been scientifically proven. I felt that this could reframe the current health care model and transform it into a truly integrative one. This would be inclusive of the Feminine Principle. This would offer patients the experience of a medical system that validated and empowered them as they journeyed through life's difficulties. This inclusive framework could help them make sense of their suffering. As they learned to live from heart and meaning and explore the causes of their illness, they would be able to reclaim themselves and restore wholeness. This was my deepest calling.

The process of creating this model was itself a powerful "medicine" in my recovery from working in corporate health care. At its foundation, it contained the elements of both the Masculine and Feminine

Principles. Both were needed for true healing. High standard-of-care would be maintained in the search for the causes of illness. This is where symptoms originated that my traditional tools could fix. I found that when patients uncovered this, their health improved as they used their new found awareness to make healthier choices. This prevented the recurrence of symptoms and future illnesses. This also made them self-responsible. This form of health care was an educational model committed to exploring process, where both biology and biography were considered as critical components for healing and standard-of-care was not compromised. This model evoked the "seeker" in patients—where curiosity guided them towards the answers they sought. This added depth to their life experience. Here, illness was seen as a catalyst for awakening. This health care model carried the possibility for transforming patients *before* the manifestation of a life crisis by teaching them how to live more consciously. This could truly prevent illness. This could connect patients to their intrinsic power and wisdom. I realized this model could actually awaken their consciousness.

This would be a more patient-centered model of health care, and reform the current ailing medical system and heal its mission. A health care system based on the integration of process and expertise could both heal and fix patients. This model, I believed, could finally restore the soul of medicine, the soul that had been buried underneath the mechanical and heartless system that medicine had become.

This integrative model also needed to be a healthy business that did not compromise patient care in favor of profit. Unlike corporate health care's business model, this model would be sustainable, regenerative, profitable, and cost-effective.

I realized this was my opportunity to recalibrate my life's work. My personal recovery had invoked a powerful turn in my life. The process of reclaiming myself from abuse also served as a catalyst for healing the health care system, where the feminine was also undermined and neglected, disrespected and dismissed. It was time to bring heart-centered care back into the medical system and create a medical model that operated from its sacred mission to heal. This had the potential to restore the soul of medicine that lay buried underneath the closed corporate system that it was.

Open and closed systems

Therapist and author, Virginia Satir, categorizes systems as being either *closed* or *open*. A system consists of individual parts that are essential and related to one another. These parts interact to fulfill the goal or purpose set by rules defined by the system. Power is distributed among a few members who maintain the system's working patterns to deal with outside influences.

In a closed system, the people in power separate it from outside influences to maintain its internal dynamics. This maintains the system's "status quo." This system values its members based on their performance that perpetuates the patterns of the system. The "power principle" is the means by which its members are monitored to make sure the systems' rules are being followed. If they aren't, they are dealt negative consequences. The rules are made by the few members who maintain power within the closed system. This is a classic example of patriarchy.

An open system is one in which intrinsic worth rather than performance is considered as primary. Performance is related to worth, but does not define it. Change within the system is welcomed and is seen as necessary for its growth. In fact, it is encouraged. Communication is an important element in an open system that keeps its dynamics healthy.

Lack of communication is the hallmark of a closed system. In closed systems, people are secretive and defensive when questioned. Here, secrecy is the unwritten rule, and a lack of trust is prevalent among its members.

Often, when people second-guess themselves and feel fearful, confused or disempowered, they are part of a closed system. A closed system does not communicate to clarify intent or interact from integrity or truth. Its primary focus is to maintain its rules or the "status quo."

Many of us can agree that we grew up in closed systems. The "code of conduct" was determined by the people in power and we adapted to their rules. The larger system that influenced the family was the cultural system within which the family existed. Questioning unhealthy cultural norms was often not permitted. A family can become a closed system if it follows the rules and code of conduct normalized by the culture. Open communication is not present and problem solving is not valued. Rules are followed to maintain the system's status quo.

I lived within in a closed system as a child and then in my marriage as an adult. When I questioned the unhealthy dynamics that I was expected to normalize, I was silenced. At that time, I had no understanding of the concepts described above. I lived mostly in fear. I lacked safety and trust in relationships. In my marriage, I walked on eggshells, afraid of punitive consequences I would suffer if I communicated my needs or longings. I was living within a closed system as an adult, where I had no power or voice, and adapted with learned behaviors from the closed system I grew up in.

By my forties, I was unwilling to live from what felt familiar, but was unhealthy. I needed to reconfigure my relationship to myself. I needed to reclaim my personal and intrinsic authority and reevaluate myself through my heart and feelings. I knew when I was not being true to myself and also knew how I deserved to be treated in my marriage. As a child I had been taught that I had no intrinsic authority to assert my will, and that my instincts were wrong. This was reinforced in my marriage as an adult and also by the medical system where I received my training. I was taught, as many of us are, by the rules of the power principle, to override my instincts and inner voice and conform to the rules of the closed system to maintain the status quo.

I did not feel any difference between the closed system of my culture, my personal life, or corporate health care. All evoked fear and punitive consequences when the rules were questioned or disobeyed. There was no room for growth or change. I adapted to survive. This made me vulnerable to abuse. I second-guessed myself frequently as the result of my cultural and familial imprinting. My relationship to my intuition, instinct, and inner wisdom was wounded. I did not feel safe in my own skin.

Are physicians and patients victims of a closed system of health care?

In the thirty years I have been a part of the medical system, I have observed that most physicians choose a career in medicine to help and heal others. They enter the medical system to serve patients from its sacred mission and vocation. The framework from which corporate medicine operates sets physicians up for adapting to the rules of its closed system. They leave their medical training in significant debt, severely fatigued from working long hours with lack of sleep for nearly a decade. They are wounded, as they have had to adapt for survival. They complete their residencies and seek employment within corporate health care in an attempt to pay off debt, regain balance, and utilize their learned skill set. They quickly realize that the closed system requires them to conform to its next and new set of rules. Questioning these results in punitive consequences. Since they are conditioned to adapt, they compromise their souls to keep their jobs within the corporate (closed) system of medicine.

When we adapt to closed systems that are based in fear, we often incorporate its elements into our behaviors. Since fear disempowers us, we unknowingly project it onto others, in an attempt to compensate for our loss of personal power. Fear becomes a central and insidious part of our relational dynamics and contaminates our life in both subtle and overt ways. When we are fearful, we often evoke fear in others. The majority of physicians who work within the current system of health care are fearful. The conditions of medical practice today evoke fear, and the rules of the closed system of corporate health care also evoke fear. Patients are almost always fearful when they see their physicians. Fear is the primary feeling present within health care. This undoubtedly confirms that both physicians and patients are operating within a closed system.

Is the current health care system a closed system?

Within an open system, the Feminine Principle fosters the qualities of connection and collaboration. While functioning within it, it is possible to bear witness and hold space for truth and feelings. Speaking one's truth without the fear of rejection takes courage yet supports and empowers sovereignty and individuality.

In contrast, in a closed system, codependency is the operating principle. A few members, in positions of power and authority, dominate subordinate members who adapt to being dominated, and compromise their truth and sovereignty to maintain the system's internal dynamics. Dominators require subordinates to dominate, and subordinates adapt to being dominated. This dynamic wounds and disempowers both. The elements of the "power principle" that dominators engage regulates behavior through fear. In this dynamic, intrinsic power cannot be accessed, and collaboration is not valued. The system's goal is to maintain its status quo. If any members within it begin to outgrow its dysfunctional dynamics in favor of health, other members manipulate them to continue engaging the system's familiar, yet unhealthy, dynamics. Their intent is to maintain the system's status quo. Authority cannot be trusted, and members walk on eggshells while compromising their real needs. They do this to avoid being punished if they are too afraid to leave. Over time, this pattern becomes the governing dynamic between its members. It becomes incorporated into their psyches and reflected in their behavior. They lose the relative position for health. All of their relationships operate from the dynamics of a closed system. This is prevalent in corporate health care today.

In an *open* system, its members can be true to themselves and feel assured that they will be treated with respect and honor as long as they behave with integrity. Self-responsibility is the core element in relationships within an open system. This system stays open to growth and change and evolves as its members grow within it. As they seek health, the open system grows healthy. This is the kind of system I longed for. I had not experienced dynamics like these in my training, as an employee of corporate health care or in my marriage. I too, did not have a relative position from which to choose healthy relationships. At an intrinsic level, however, I knew they existed. I imagined what it would be like for health care to function from these dynamics. I felt it would promote health and growth, and even support healing. I believed corporate health care needed to become an open system.

The Ommani Center for Integrative Medicine

After many years of working within corporate health care, I realized that in this system, health was a conflict of interest; it didn't generate hospital profits. As people stayed healthy, hospital admissions, diagnostic and pharmaceutical interventions all decreased. This did not serve corporate health care's financial objectives. In fact, it threatened them. An open system of healing could not function within the closed system of health care if it relied on the sickness of patients. I realized I had to leave this system in order to practice *true* health care. I needed to create an open system of my own that resonated with the soul of my vocation.

I created The Ommani Center for Integrative Medicine as a prototype of an open system of health care. Its vision was committed to health, education, and transformation. Medicine practiced from this framework quickly began to heal its community of patients. This open system was in stark contrast to the closed system of corporate health care that I had left.

A few years after opening The Ommani Center, I awakened to the reality of my personal life. I had adapted to closed system rules in my marriage and was blind and numb to how disempowered I felt. I was living from the familiar paradox of my childhood. At this juncture, I could not function in an open system at work and live in a closed system at home. The Ommani Center was based on the principles of transformation and wholeness, and required me to live its vision authentically. Soon after I awakened to this, my personal life imploded, marking my midlife gateway.

After years of being treated with dishonor and disrespect, my marriage hit a new low. This time through adultery. This activated my midlife transformation. I had to face my blindness caused from my chronically adapted state. I needed to examine all the ways I had held my marriage together by remaining compliant for years. I needed to dismantle my negative self-talk and conditioned way of being that expected me to adapt to being dishonored and disrespected. This was my opportunity to reweave myself and reconstruct a life of health and honor that resonated with the Feminine Principle. I had the responsibility to dismantle all the ways my feminine energy had been degraded, and powerfully redefine my worth. This was my midlife juncture point. This was my task at hand.

After I filed for divorce, I found myself amidst the energy and chaos of an intense death-and-rebirth cycle. I needed to create a new life from the rubble of the old. I needed to find a path to transform and transmute myself from an adapted woman who had tolerated abuse into a woman who lived from self-respect and "walked her talk." I needed to embody this as my work was committed to the facilitation of true healing. Through this gateway, I needed to reclaim my integrity and self-worth and reframe my relationship to my intrinsic self, and align it with the vision of the open system of health care I had created.

Through this process, I realized the immense responsibility that we all have in midlife. This gateway expects much of us. The journey I undertook would not only be valuable for me, but for my children, my patients, and everyone I would encounter. It would connect me more deeply with my life's work. Only by courageously aligning myself with this process could I earn the trust of women and men who relied on me for guidance. They were seeking a path through the treacherous territory of their own gateways. They were seeking a way to transform their compensated and adapted selves into their real selves. Unless I knew this territory and navigated my way through it, I would lack the insight to guide them through their transformational journeys; in fact, it could be dangerous for them to entrust my help through their process.

When I realized that my inner work required this level of personal transformation, I discovered the voluminous amount of material that had been written about this process. In fact, I had collected many books and articles on this topic for five years prior to this juncture point. My instinct had already been guiding me without my conscious awareness, in preparation for what was to come. This material was my solace and offered me much needed guidance. In addition, mentors appeared as if by magic, who midwifed and oriented me through my journey. I had an insatiable hunger to rediscover myself and to dismantle all of my parts that were compensated, adapted and inauthentic. My intent for recovery and reclamation manifested a safe container within which I could feel supported and healed as I engaged in this difficult, powerful and deeply intense work. It provided me with solace and safety through the terror of deconstruction that my identity was going through and that my soul expected me to complete.

Looking back over the years, I could see that a theme had been prevalent throughout my personal and professional life. I had frequently felt profound loneliness which I was not able to understand or heal. Through my transformational process, I began to see that this resulted from my pain of separating from the Feminine Principle as I adapted to the closed systems of which I had been a part. I needed to reintegrate the elements of the feminine I had compromised by adapting. I began to see all the ways in which our collective culture dismissed the sacred feminine and how we all unconsciously participated. If our world was beckoning a paradigm shift, healing this wound would be critical. As I reconstructed my identity to include elements of the Feminine Principle, I was able to reframe all of my relationships to include respect, honor, love, and integrity. This healed my relationship to the sacred feminine. It also enabled me to practice medicine more authentically.

Awakening to our inner truth is catalyzed by the suffering caused from deep wounding. This is actually the means by which we regain the inner-sight we previously lacked due to our fear of rejection. We need this to access our intrinsic power. The price we pay for our blindness is enormous and grave. The midlife process does not support this way of living. The relationships in which we choose to stay blind invariably fail us. We suffer deep wounding through this alchemical process of "failure." *The blessing from the deep wound is the powerful "medicine" it holds.* This medicine permeates our lives and eventually graces us with a clarity of vision that can no longer be fooled by adaptations or cover-ups. This medicine reconnects us to our real selves and uncovers the vulnerabilities that conditioned us to adapt and compromise our truth. Once awakened, we are finally able to reclaim our intrinsic power.

The value of being heart centered

Our heart is the seat of truth, honor, integrity, and love, yet many in today's world do not live from these qualities. These have been replaced by competition and greed, resulting in duality and our separation from one another. A framework based on duality separates. It functions from "either or" or "us versus them" concepts. When these define our paradigm, they lead to violent behaviors common in our world today. These inflict pain and weaken us at deep levels as they lack the heart-centered qualities of the Feminine Principle. These have been prevalent throughout the history of the human race and have caused great suffering.

The heart cannot relate through duality. On the contrary, it relates through connecting and collaborating. Its intent is to unify. The heart also does not relate through "either or" and "us versus them" concepts that our culture normalizes. Instead, it relates through inclusive "both and" concepts. This is the heart's natural state. The heart resonates with the dynamics of an open system. The heart aches in the presence of duality. Duality generates fear; unity generates love. Love is powerful, resilient, fierce, and uncompromising. However, our culture defines love differently. Its definition confuses *codependency for love*. This distortion resonates with the dynamics of a closed system. We have normalized these distortions. We must redefine and reframe our definition of love to include the strong elements of the Feminine Principle. We need to restore it to its original and purest root.

As we awaken to the power present in healthy love and begin to behave from it, our life can transform. When we replace what is real with distortions, we pay a heavy price. Our adaptations make us vulnerable to doing this. The powerful elements of the Feminine Principle that are necessary for health and happiness lay buried underneath this normalized façade. By midlife, our adapted self feels hollow and superficial. It does not evoke meaning. When we awaken to this, we feel disillusioned. Disillusionment is painful, yet it helps us gain clarity. Through it, we can see what is real, but covered by illusion. Our society lives according to the rules of a closed system. This disconnects us from the sacred feminine resulting in a loss of meaning and purpose. We are collectively experiencing this. It takes courage and consciousness to integrate the feminine into our relationship with our self. This is our holy task through midlife.

The medial place

It takes strength and endurance to swim upstream, to not feel like a victim and to connect to and live from one's real self. Story teller and Jungian analyst, Dr. Clarissa Pinkola Estés, describes midlife as the "medial place." It is the midpoint in our lives when we release the "world of expectations" in favor of the "world of soul." It is the gateway between the ages of 42 and 49 where we have to choose between what feels familiar, but adapted (for which we have compromised our truth) and what feels real, requiring no compromise. The medial place requires us to be radically honest and make important and powerful choices to live authentically. This is the personal paradigm shift evoked by midlife, an initiation necessary for our journey towards wholeness. *This gateway holds the potential for us to transform our lives so we can live from a place of heart and meaning.* Our world itself is in a gateway, a "medial place." Our normalized and adapted ways are no longer working. We must choose to live from our souls through this gateway to help our world transform.

Midlife crisis and Women's Health redefined

If the closed system of corporate health care sets the definition of Women's Health, we cannot expect it to heal women, or even offer them direction through midlife.

As women enter midlife, they straddle the time between peri-menopause (the time surrounding menopause) and menopause. The health care system sees this transition through its lens of pathology, and physicians manage and fix the symptoms that accompany it. Menopause is viewed as an illness, a disease of hormone deficiency, not the powerful transformational process that it is. The traditional health care system negates process and finds ways to numb feeling function and the emotive power of women. It dismisses the questions they ask about their changing bodies and emotions as their powerful midlife process unfolds. They are now seeking a way to reclaim themselves and their worth from a culture that has normalized their disempowerment.

Corporate health care is unable to meet their needs. The number of hysterectomies, synthetic hormone prescriptions, antidepressants, and sleep-aids climaxes in midlife women. The health care system has defined its protocol to "treat and medicate" to eliminate symptoms of perimenopause and menopause. Symptom control is big business for health care. Physicians are not allowed to question these treatments and many are required to fulfill quotas of diagnostic tests and surgical procedures to maintain employment within the corporate system. The field of Women's Health suffers deep soul loss within this closed system of medicine. The midlife gateway loses power and purpose when women are pharmaceutically numbed with a dismissal of their process. As a result, they second-guess themselves and fear this process and its powerful potential for transformation.

Midlife and the health care system

Midlife is a time when we must listen to and obey our longings and inner callings. This alone can restore our self-respect and self-worth. Currently, our society does not have a framework for this. To facilitate this, it would need to be an open system. If health care was an open system, it would be supportive of the transformational process evoked by our changing bodies. It would help us evolve and grow in this gateway that offers a second chance for us to live authentically. It would be committed to promoting health as we passed through our "medial place." We would be guided and supported as we dismantled our adapted and fearful selves to restore meaning and become real.

This gateway is a time when we must begin to ask the deep and crucial questions about our worth and purpose in life. In order for the health care system to facilitate this process, it must be open to a framework that supports health and transformation. Biological manipulation and symptom management alone do not fulfill a woman's needs. The closed system of corporate health care does not offer support for personal growth. Instead, it encourages the masking of physical symptoms, sabotaging the alchemical purpose necessary for transformation.

In order to appropriately treat the biological causes of physical symptoms, we must understand and also explore the deeper questions they evoke to facilitate intrinsic health and uncover meaning in midlife.

Why is the menopausal transition so difficult for women in America? Why are women currently afflicted by an increase in menopausal symptoms? How can women be empowered to transform through their midlife transition and not be dismissed with merely synthetic hormones and psychiatric medications?

As a physician, I am fascinated by the physiological changes that accompany menopause. It has biologically precision, with patterns common to all women. In this book, I explore the physical aspects of menopause in addition to the inner life of the midlife woman to widen its context. Her truth and power arise through feelings that facilitate her connection to her real self. I have illustrated this through stories of women whose symptoms and feeling function led to a "course correction," by aiding a shift from an adapted to an authentic life. I have also described my medical framework for diagnosis and treatment that I have termed the "Four Body System™." This framework provides an understanding of how physical symptoms have their origins at emotional and energetic levels. Understanding these levels is critical to seeking the appropriate care needed for healing. This can accelerate the restoration of well-being through the midlife journey.

Women's health is currently defined by the traditional medical system through its pathological lens. I have replaced this with a transformational lens, emphasizing the need for an open system for safe guidance through the midlife gateway. The stories presented demonstrate the courage needed for healing, and the power that a framework and safe space can provide for transformation. During their midlife transitions, the women presented, redefined and reframed themselves from feeling like victims to feeling empowered and whole.

As midlife women, we have an important and sacred opportunity to help our hurting world. Our world-systems need to transform from closed into open ones to heal the chaos and separation that causes suffering. Facilitating this transformation will require our collective effort.

My hope is that you awaken and begin to question your adapted lives bereft of meaning and feel empowered enough to redefine your understanding of health. We need to heal the cultural wounds that normalize and perpetuate the *illusion of health* and, instead, live from its true definition. We need to engage our courage to transform our closed systems based in fear into open systems committed to growth and empowerment. This powerful work transcends race, color, religion, gender, and nationality. It is the sacred and true work of our time.

My intent is to evoke creative thought which encourages us to question the "status quo" as defined by the current and prevailing paradigm of the "power principle" whose presence is central to the perpetuation of closed systems. This is essential for the restoration of personal and organizational health.

My hope is to facilitate a dialogue that transforms our current definition of Women's Health from one that does not value empowerment or feeling function, into one that is inclusive of these elements. At its heart, this redefinition will restore and heal, acknowledging the death-and-life cycle of transformation as a necessary part of personal and collective growth. This reframe can occur only by integrating the Feminine Principle into our relationships and current systems.

This courageous and necessary work has the potential to heal the deep wounds of our culture and transform the shape and feeling of our personal and professional lives. This could also transform the health care system into one that is, at last, worthy of our trust.

2

What Is Real?

Becoming Real

At 45, I awaken a weaver.
As my old self falls away,
I take strong thread and
weave Soul into substance.
For me, it was marked;
I was hollowed out.
This was needed
for me to resurrect,
to come back to life.
For some, it is gentle,
for me, it was alchemical.
By turning lead into gold,
it turned a woman of the world
into a woman of Soul.
After feeling the deepest pain and
crying tears that didn't stop,
I discovered joy in my laughter,
and melody in my song.
The tapestry of my heart,
now sewn with stronger thread,
seeps Soul into Presence.
I am the Medial One,
I have become Real.
I take the next step.

There is a belief in indigenous mythology that our "double" lives within our soul. She is the part of us most connected to our real self. She is not tainted by our wounding and provides us the resilience and strength needed for healing. She embodies our wholeness. She carries the "codes" for our higher destiny. When we are disconnected from our real self, we can miss Her call and fail to manifest our higher destiny. The call from our "double" is the loudest during midlife. This is a time when the veil between the unconscious and conscious selves is thin. When our hormones shift and the gateway to the second half of life beckons, our soul moves closer to us than any other time in our lives. Many of us were not able to access our truth before the arrival of this gateway, as we mistakenly identified our wounded for our real self. Our "double" calls us from within as a reminder that there is more to life than how we have been living. She carries within Her our deeper and more meaningful life.

Our "double" always carries us towards our highest destiny. We are frequently presented with choices to upgrade or downgrade our life's course. Midlife is an important gateway where we need to choose between familiarity or authenticity. It takes courage to be authentic. When we are, we embody our real self during the second half of our life. We can then manifest our highest destiny.

Alice

One of my friends, Alice, was a 66-year-old attorney. For many years, she was bedridden with a neurological illness. She told me that while in her forties, she felt that she was in a gateway that presented two doors before her. One felt familiar with the wealthy trappings of corporate law that expected ruthlessness, while the other was unfamiliar leading to an unknown destiny. She chose the familiar door with material trappings. She walked through it into a career of corporate law. She was successful from society's standards but her life of ruthlessness lacked meaning. She deeply regretted having chosen the familiar door.

She admitted that she chose the familiar out of her fear of the unknown. During her career, she often wondered what her life would have been like if she had stepped into the unknown. I also wondered what her life would have been like. Would she have been fulfilled and happy? She played the part expected of her and pursued society's definition of success. Her soul always longed for more meaning. She spent the last days of her life in regret for having chosen familiarity through her midlife gateway. I will never forget her call to me before she died. She encouraged me to follow my bliss. She asked me to promise her that I would not make the same mistake she had. She had spent the last 30 years of her life in pursuit of what was not real. She felt this deep in her being. Her "double" had called to her, but she had chosen to not listen and buried it beneath worldly trappings. In the end, she knew she had not lived from her highest destiny.

The dismantled feminine

As women, we often make errors in judgment like Alice did. We are conditioned to compromise our instincts in favor of adapting to what society expects of us. Approximately 4000 years ago, the feminine was devalued and discarded in favor of the masculine. Since then, our culture has been wounded. Our instinct and feeling function is a part of our feminine energy. We have sacrificed this in favor of thinking and act in accordance to what society values. The results of this are evident in our world today, where lack of meaning results from the lack of feeling.

The lack of meaning triggers feelings of hopelessness and anger that we unknowingly project onto others. Anger, as an emotion, can be used as a catalyst for transformation and direct us back onto a real and more authentic path. Anger can be a powerful call to action. It can also be used as a catalyst for us to reclaim our health.

It can help us reconnect with our truth. Anger can only be effective as a catalyst if we use it consciously with the intent to transform.

Reactive anger is destructive. When used consciously, it can be creative. Our lives are too often driven by the wounds in our unconscious and subconscious minds. Due to our lack of awareness, we risk misusing anger in destructive ways. Living without awareness can disconnect us from our real self. This is the part of us capable of alchemy. It is not contaminated by cultural distortions. It has intrinsic power. If we do not connect with it, we risk trying to find meaning through external means. This leaves us feeling empty and disconnected from our intrinsic power. As a compensation, we may try to dominate others in a futile attempt to restore our sense of power and worth. This perpetuates the dysfunctional dynamics common in our society.

Society expects us to obey its rules and protocols. While some are needed for our safety, most of them are separative and oppressive. We are expected to adapt to these mostly patriarchal rules that limit access to our truth. Additionally, society distorts what it defines as "masculine" or "feminine." Its definitions are inauthentic.

For example, society defines success as the accumulation of material wealth. The drive to accumulate wealth can compromise self-care. Normalizing this endangers us to adapt as others do, resulting in the sacrifice of meaning. We often behave this way to fit in and thereby abdicate our true values. If we reject our inner truth for acceptance, we risk losing the intrinsic connection with our "double." We may justify and normalize our compromises, resulting in deep loneliness and the disconnection from truth and authenticity. This is often difficult for us to identify because the collective normalizes society's definitions and values. Over time, this disconnection can present as physical or mental symptoms.

As we approach midlife, what is normalized by society begins to feel like a façade. Our "double" cannot be fooled. She expresses our disconnection from Her in our feelings of emptiness and lack of meaning. These may present as anxiety or depression. If we heed her call during this gateway, we have the opportunity to transform and connect with our real self. Her voice is present in our symptoms, and we must choose to reconnect with our truth to feel whole. This awakens creativity like never before, propelling us in the direction of our bliss towards our higher destiny.

The midlife journey

The transformational journey in midlife is one that we can all choose to make. Many take this journey unconsciously as society lacks a framework for transformation. For many, midlife is marked with what we call a "midlife crisis." A crisis can actually facilitate our connection with our "double." If we lived unconsciously during the first half of our lives, fate can force us to awaken through a crisis to catalyze the connection needed for us to become real. This can then become the gateway through which we choose to reconstruct our lives. For some a "midlife crisis" can present as an illness; for others, it can present as a divorce, or the loss of a job or loved one. For all, it is the call from the "double" to become real. In order to dismantle our unhealthy imprints, we need to individuate from familiarity. It is frightening to leave the known behind, but we must, to finally discover who we really are.

The power of familiarity

We spent the first few decades of our lives in our family systems being imprinted with their dynamics. Our imprints carried over into our relationships as adults. If they were unhealthy, we risked creating the same or similar dynamics in our adult relationships. Many of us are unconscious of the imprinted patterns we carry. We attract relationships that remind us of the dynamics from our families of origin. These dynamics feel like "home." They are familiar. We also live from adapted patterns that we learned in our family systems. Many of us adapted to their dysfunctional dynamics for acceptance. This required us to suppress what we truly felt and compromise our truth by remaining silent. When we were young, we did not realize that we were being conditioned to do this. Some of these behaviors were necessary for our socialization, but many were not healthy and were adaptations for survival. Since our family was our safety, we adapted to survive. As we used these strategies, we moved further away from our real feelings. This often resulted in feelings of loneliness and loss during the first half of our lives. These feelings were difficult to understand. We felt wounded. We felt invalidated and sometimes not even seen or heard. This manifested as depression and anxiety.

As midlife approaches, these wounds call for healing. It becomes difficult for many to be around their families of origin during their midlife gateway. Many midlife patients come to see me before family gatherings. After newly connecting with their real selves, they feel vulnerable as their patterns of adapting still hold traction. They are afraid of losing contact with this connection while around their families of origin. Within a few days with them, many find themselves behaving from the familiar and adapted patterns they learned as children. This causes stress and anxiety. A sense of relief accompanies the end of the family gathering. The pressure to adapt lifts and they can safely return to healthy patterns, which resonate with their newly discovered selves that no longer want to adapt.

The familiar dynamics we recreate from the first half of our life often resonate with those present in a closed system (based in fear). In midlife, our soul calls us to deconstruct these and replace them with those of an open system. This evokes a deeper level of meaning. It takes great courage for us to live from our truth. We often risk being rejected by others when we undergo the alchemical process through the midlife gateway. As we dismantle our adapted and inauthentic behaviors to uncover our real self, we no longer resonate with those who behave from patterns we are leaving behind. They often reject us. Transforming into our real self releases our need for external validation and restores our integrity. It also strengthens our capacity for self-reliance and heals the anxiety caused by low self-worth. It connects us with our intrinsic power.

Individuation

Carl Jung was a well-known psychiatrist who coined the term "individuation." Individuation is a process during adolescence and midlife, of separating from family of origin in favor of identifying with the real self, hidden underneath the familiar and adapted one. The "double" guides the individuation process. She awakens our ability to become aware of our unconscious and hidden agendas present in the part of us called the "shadow." These agendas are based in fear and reinforced by society. This process is frightening, yet powerful. It holds within it the potential to open our inner-eye. It exposes the rules and operating principles we may be unconsciously living from. It requires us to dismantle those that are inauthentic. It is profoundly difficult to do this in adolescence, especially since our society lacks a framework to facilitate this process in a healthy way. As a result, many adults miss individuating as adolescents and are hence unable to guide adolescents safely through the individuation process. In indigenous cultures, individuated mentors take adolescents on vision quests where they are led through a series of rituals to make contact with their "double" for wisdom and insight. They are then able to incorporate what they learned into their lives to unfold their higher destinies with consciousness awakened through this process. This is viewed as an *initiation* and is considered deeply sacred. It can only be facilitated by mentors who have become real through their own midlife gateways, and hence can initiate adolescents through individuation.

Our society sadly lacks awareness around the power and purpose of individuation. In our culture, we often pass through the gateways of adolescence and midlife unconsciously and attempt to fill our emptiness with superficial and material trappings. Many of us currently in midlife had the chance to individuate during adolescence, but due to lack of mentorship, we missed connecting with our real self during that gateway. In midlife, we get a second chance to individuate so we can connect with our real self.

The complacency in our society towards living unconsciously endangers individuation. We normalize our adapted ways of living and often medicate our emptiness. The price we pay for this is *soul loss* which results in a loss of connection with our truth and sovereignty. We need to reevaluate our choices and use the midlife gateway as our opportunity to transform and individuate. This is the sacred task of our generation. This can restore our sense of meaning and self-respect. In fact, it can have a profound effect on future generations. It may even heal many of the challenges we face today that result from our attempts to solve society's problems with ineffective and superficial solutions that are often due to our lack of individuation.

The dilemma in parenting

We have experienced how our imprinting has impacted our destiny track and compromised our sense of meaning and fulfillment. When we remain unindividuated, we are not able to engage with our children from adult behaviors that are necessary to facilitate their movement towards their higher destinies. When we are unindividuated as parents we may unconsciously expect our children's choices to fulfill *our* unmet needs. We can get caught in the loop of using their performance to define our self-worth. We are often unaware that this is our projection. It is heavily influenced by our culture and our conditioning, as well as our adapted self, that we may have mistaken for our real self. When we do this, our children feel the imposition of our projections and often push back against our expectations if they do not resonate with them. If they are punished into fulfilling them, they risk losing contact with their truth and their real self. They risk losing a connection to the voice of their "double." They risk integrating *our* projections into their thought patterns and being intrinsically controlled by them. In this way, we risk perpetuating our adapted patterns onto our children. Awareness of this is critical for parents of adolescents. In midlife, we must realize how we were wounded when not mentored through this gateway. The generation before us was not aware of these dynamics. We adapted as they did and lost contact with our "double" like they did. This is how the cycle perpetuates itself through generations. For our children to make contact with their real selves in adolescence, *we* must individuate in midlife.

If we do not heed the call to live authentically, we risk living from our adaptations and *pretending* to be real. The symptoms of this are pervasive in our society. Over-consumption is a compensated behavior that we engage in to fill our emptiness when we are disconnected from our real self.

We may be unaware of this until our forties. At this juncture, the physiological changes uncover and unleash the unindividuated and unprocessed parts of our psyche through our feeling function and bring them to consciousness. Feelings of anger and sadness may surface. This can be confusing for many. Our bodies mark this powerful time of detoxification when it becomes necessary to release the life patterns that have caused our suffering.

The depth of the midlife process

For women, this time is usually marked by hormonal changes that unleash a torrent of emotions and intense feelings that can be overwhelming. Many women feel like they are "going crazy" when their hormones begin to change.

In my own life, I felt a rustling inside that indicated my life as I knew it would soon be coming to an end. I was 42 and had been in an unhealthy marriage for years. I was unable to leave it due to my imprinted and conditioned patterns. A few years after this feeling surfaced, my life was blown to pieces.

31

This was an intense process that flooded me with deep feelings of grief and loss. I needed to reconfigure my thinking from the inside out. I was betrayed in a relationship that I held sacred even after years of abuse. My conditioning directed me to adapt to tolerating abuse. I unknowingly allowed this, as many of us do. Sometimes we adapt by growing numb to the pain of being disrespected and dishonored. By adapting over time, we become desensitized to escalating pain to "keep the peace." This process is called *learned helplessness*. We become the proverbial "boiling frog." If the system we live in feels familiar, we are fearful to leave it. The pain we imagine from losing the relationship may feel worse than the pain of the abuse within it. Fear distorts our perceptions and we become willing to adapt to abuse. Sometimes the abuse is emotional and sometimes it is physical. Sometimes it is both. Emotional abuse is often harder to acknowledge as it does not leave physical scars, but can be just as damaging as physical abuse. Often it is harder to leave relationships that are emotionally abusive due to our degree of adaptation over time. If we are unable to leave a relationship that causes us pain, it means we are deeply disempowered. These are the effects of living in a closed system. Sometimes, when abuse and pain escalate to a great degree, the system ruptures. Betrayal ruptured mine. I was no longer able to adapt to this level of disrespect.

It was my time to sort through the rubble that contained my imprinted and conditioned parts and examine who I really was. I needed to individuate from my adapted self and reinvent myself from an intrinsic place. I began to consciously dismantle all the parts of my adapted self resulting from my familial imprinting that I had mistakenly identified for my real self. I offered myself choices between who I thought I was and what felt authentically true to me. I was making contact with my "double." Wholeness had beckoned, and I chose to step in.

To my surprise, as terrified as I was to leave the abusive relationship, its rupture unraveled a process that felt richer and more meaningful in many ways than anything I had experienced before. The gates of hell had opened, and with intense fear and courage, I fell into the abyss. In that moment of pure anguish, my "double" spoke to me with a deep inner voice I recognized as my own. I felt that my life would somehow be reborn from the bottom of the abyss. In fact, it really was.

I surrendered my tired and broken self that could no longer adapt and fell into the abyss with profound grief and despair. The deep shock of betrayal dismantled my adapted life. Despite false voices from the culture that told me to "get over it," I chose to feel every feeling to its true depth. This was the only way my wounded instinct and feeling function could heal while I reconnected with the voice of my soul, my real self. As I continued to heed this voice, I grew stronger and my instinct was able to guide me in directions that I would have never considered before.

Synchronicities began to occur, and I felt as though I was embarking on a higher destiny directed by my soul. It felt unfamiliar compared to the one that I had lived from before. My "double" had charted a course correction and directed me back on a path to becoming real. I was finally healing after four decades of being wounded. I began to trust in my process and heal my fear of being authentic. My instinct and feeling function became key elements of my inner guidance from that moment forward.

Through this process, my intense love for my children served as a constant source of strength. My commitment to them held the deepest meaning and offered the greatest courage for me to move along this difficult path when I felt tired and hopeless. In these moments, I had to take responsibility for *my* role in the wreckage that had occurred in their lives resulting from my adaptations. Although I was unaware as an unindividuated woman and felt profound loneliness, I realized that the opportunity to create an authentic life lay before me that could now provide mentorship and support for them. I also needed to forgive myself for remaining unconscious and being adapted for so long.

This was an intense process. I watched my children trying to deal with the rupture of our family by normalizing and adapting in order to survive. I struggled with an almost other-worldly grief. I had repressed my feeling function for years to survive in a relationship that required me to deny my truth and sovereignty. I had learned to project a mask of "happiness" that others expected to see. My grief decimated this mask. My feeling function required me to connect with my feelings of outrage I was expected to suppress. I needed to bring who I really was into alignment with my feelings. This process was profoundly difficult and also profoundly healing. It connected me with women all over the world who were also reclaiming their truth and sovereignty. It also connected me with my ancestors, women who had gone before me, who capitulated to society's expectations of being "a good wife" and tolerated abuse as a mark of "a strong woman." It was as though my feeling function, lying dormant for generations had resurrected, and I was given the opportunity to use the alchemical qualities of my soul to make something of worth and meaning with my pain.

I had to redefine all the ways I had perceived reality. I had to learn how to first connect with, and then validate and honor my feeling function, that I was told for the first half of my life was "wrong" and "too intense" and a threat to the status quo.

I realized that my definitions of love, power, truth, and self-worth needed to be continually reevaluated. I needed to purify them through what felt true for me. The definitions from society felt superficial and distorted. They fostered codependency and made me vulnerable to the type of abuse that I had experienced. I recognized that the wisdom in my feeling function was able to discern what felt healthy and what didn't. It was resurrecting itself after half a lifetime of being wounded. I felt this would help me reconstruct my life from a place of *my* truth. I needed to trust that my truth and feelings were *correct*.

This process was painful and intensely difficult. I lived in constant fear of being rejected by others, of being left alone in a world that normalized dishonesty, adultery, misogyny, and adapted behaviors. As my perception of the world began to change, I realized that the world itself needed guidance. I felt that I could play a part in healing our culture's collective and unhealthy patterns and definitions. My alchemical process catalyzed these insights. My midlife patients were doing this work as well, and I found myself in a community of courageous transformation. I realized this was important work for our generation. We needed to individuate to collectively transform adapted patterns that were normalized, yet profoundly unhealthy and unfulfilling. This could bring powerful and precise meaning to our suffering. If I could consciously individuate through my midlife gateway, and recreate myself through mentorship from my "double," I could earn the ability to mentor my children and future generations from a place that was real. I knew that I needed to live from my truth from that moment forward and behave in ways that honored my feeling function and my instinct.

I realized that this was an important part of my work as a woman, a mother, an Indian, an American, and also a physician. I was being called by my higher destiny to help dismantle the unhealthy and adapted patterns I had normalized that allowed others to treat me with dishonor and to redefine Women's Health through this deeper place that honored the Feminine Principle.

The midlife process in health care

Our motivation to unfold our real self and support each other to do the same has the potential to restore the health of our culture in profound ways.

The field of Women's Health must be redefined to include support and guidance through individuation as a necessary part of its framework. In order for women to bring transformational solutions to the world, they need to connect with their intrinsic power and wisdom. Women's Health has a responsibility to facilitate the reconnection of women with their real selves through the midlife gateway. When offered from this framework, it can have a significant impact on the healing of society at large.

As my perspective deepened, I was able to see more clearly how women were frequently dismissed by the health care system when they sought solutions to their common midlife symptoms. If their feeling function was heightened and expressed, they were often considered pathological, and medicated. They had no voice to speak their truth in this system. What they needed was for physicians to bear witness to their biographies and their stories. Through the limited lens of the current health care system, they felt unsafe in their own skins and frightened by their feelings.

I realized women were looking for something more than what the current health care system offered. Women's Health, defined by that system, was too limited, too physical, too physiological, and superficial. It had no container for women's stories and feelings. These aspects of their lives were integral to their journey towards health. Their stories held powerful "medicine" for them to connect with their real self. The limited space their physicians held did not facilitate their transformation. Women needed a framework that could mirror their greatness and their highest potential back to them to help them connect with their truth. They needed to be received in a sacred space where they could feel safe enough to honestly reckon with who they had become as adapted and wounded women and confront the shame this evoked. They needed a place where they could feel unconditional support through their midlife process. They needed more than just hormone therapy.

Shame is the toxic feeling that contaminates a woman's relationship towards herself. She feels it when she views herself through a critical lens and when she behaves in ways that compromise her truth. Shame is always a sign that a woman's shadow is near. Women in midlife want to purify their relationship to themselves by living from integrity and truth despite the lives they may have created from adaptations and conditioned behaviors. Sometimes shame can serve as a catalyst to transform these patterns. It can be the feeling that awakens women to their inauthentic relationship with themselves. In midlife, they can no longer lie to themselves and pretend that their façades are real.

Women live with shame for most of their lives. For many, it is loud and looming. It manifests in avoidant behaviors that can isolate them from others. It often compromises their ability to speak their truth. It is based in fear. It makes them vulnerable in relationships that operate from the dynamics of a closed system. These behaviors are unfulfilling. We feel shame when we compromise ourselves through adapted behaviors, but we can also feel it when we disappoint others while living from our truth. In the former situation, we feel shame due to self-betrayal; in the latter, shame is inflicted upon us by others for not normalizing their unhealthy dynamics. It can be confusing to differentiate between these feelings of shame. Either one can drive us to behave in compensated ways and self-medicate with food, alcohol, shopping, or disassociation. These behaviors can deplete us and make us ill. We need to remember that the shame we feel due to self-betrayal can serve as a healthy signal that reminds us to live from our truth; the other kind of shame is unhealthy and needs to be processed and released. Many women long for a safe space where their recovery from shame is seen as sacred, allowing them to reorient back to their truth.

When I work with women, the festering wounds caused by shame are often exposed. When I ask crucial questions and bring integrity and truth to the space I hold, they are able to confront their shame and heal it. Women often gain the ability to identify the many faces of shame that exist in their psyches. They gain the awareness they need to prevent them from behaving in the compensated ways that betray their truth. It is difficult to awaken to these in isolation. We often need others to bring our awareness to our unhealthy patterns in order for us to heal them.

In order to safely facilitate another's movement toward what is real, we must first engage in our own personal work of individuation. We cannot help others arrive at a place we have not arrived at ourselves. Physician and therapist offices are filled with wounded and unindividuated practitioners who haven't had the courage to do their own transformational work. As a result, they are unable to help others fully transform as they lack the insight needed to help their clients and patients navigate through the territory of individuation. In fact, being held in this kind of space can be dangerous for a patient through their difficult and confusing process. The practitioner's ignorance can actually sabotage a client's transformation. We need to bring an understanding of this crucial element of necessary process to our professional and cultural framework to guide clients and patients safely through the midlife gateway. This requires professionals to stand in the fire of their own process and individuate so they can be authentic.

What had awakened in me through my own midlife process was deeper and more powerful than anything I could have imagined. I always felt that there was more to the medical model than what I had been taught. I had felt profound loneliness during my medical training since I did not resonate with the limited lens through which I was taught to evaluate and treat patients. This lens did not include the possibility for patients to heal their lives or live from their greatness. I realized how I had suffered as a result of this limited perspective, and how that led to feelings of powerlessness in my own life. Having gone through my own transformation enabled me to hold space for patients who were seeking to transform while under my care.

An authentic medical practice

When I realized that I shared in this collective wound, I knew that I needed to do my part to shed light on it for my own healing.

In my own process, as I grieved the loss of all that I held sacred, I connected with my ability to create my higher destiny. I also con-fronted my fear of being rejected by my family and society when I redefined myself in unfamiliar and healthy ways. At this point, I had nothing to lose. If I were "loved" as a reward for being obedient to familial and cultural definitions, then this love was not healthy or real.

It was a distortion. It was based in fear and a conditioned reward for my obedience to a construct that kept the closed system's shadow hidden. As I transformed into my authentic self, over time I was able to reconnect with my family from a healthier place without compromising my truth.

"Getting over" our feelings

We are often told to "get over" how we feel if our feelings carry depth or intensity. Many in our culture are not comfortable around strong feelings. We have to honor our feelings and not normalize these injunctions. We need to examine what it means to "get over" feelings. Does it mean that we are expected to deny our feeling function and suppress our truth to perpetuate societal patterns of the closed system? In my case, many around me expected me to "get over" my grief and anger towards how I had been treated. These injunctions challenged my process of attempting to connect with my real self and intrinsic power. Furthermore, I had a responsi-bility to myself and my children to live from my truth. They had witnessed the ways I had adapted to abuse and who I had become in an unhealthy relationship. I could not mentor them effectively or honestly if I continued to betray myself this way to perpetuate my façade of "happiness." I could no longer live from this adapted and inauthentic place.

As I questioned these injunctions and refused to obey them, I began to find my voice that connected me to my deep feeling func-tion. We often apologize for our feeling function when it seeps through our tears as we attempt to speak our truth. When we subdue it, it manifests as the neurotic thoughts that keep us awake at night. We try to "keep the peace" to not "rock the boat," but in midlife, our feelings arise in ways that are intense and powerful. They are the voices of our intuition, instinct, and the means through which our inner wisdom communicates. We must not apologize for them.

As I disobeyed the injunctions to "get over" my feelings and practiced being comfortable with my intense feeling function, I made a conscious commitment to myself. I vowed that I would never compromise my feelings in obedience to society's expectations. This was society's attempt at perpetuating the closed system.

This wisdom gave me both the strength and courage to empower other women to do the same. This was the beginning of a personal transformation and a collective awakening within my medical practice. I was "coming into my own." I was individuating.

Healthy love as unfamiliar

A few years after I made this commitment to myself, love reappeared in my life. But this time it was an unfamiliar love that felt undistorted and healthy. I believe that my connection to my truth magnetized it. I was willing to be alone for the rest of my life if living from my truth was not acceptable to others. This love emerged as a result of the healthy definitions from which I was beginning to live. It was strong enough to accept me for who I authentically was. It held space for my process and expected no compromise of my real self. Even though I had never experienced this before and did not have a relative position to define it, it felt real. Previously, I was expected to sacrifice myself to "hold it together" while I compromised my truth and my power. I was driven by my conditioning to keep it together at all costs.

I realized that my "double" had laid out a path for my individuating self to experience the uncontaminated definitions of love, power, and self-worth. She was supporting the choices I was making from a place of courage and truth rather than fear.

A healthy relationship in midlife is one that supports and strengthens our sovereignty and movement toward wholeness. It supports the call from our "double" and mirrors Her back to us when we forget to live from Her direction and guidance. A healthy relationship may feel unfamiliar, yet it can be seen as a powerful sign of our reclamation. Unhealthy relationships before the midlife gateway can also be transformed into healthy ones by both members engaging the consciousness and courage required to uncover authenticity, truth, and sovereignty.

The juncture point in midlife

At the end of our lives, before the final gateway of death, we are guaranteed a life review when we will have to come to terms with whether the choices we made in midlife were from courage or fear. Like Alice, any fear-based choices that took us off course will cause us anxiety. We all hope to die with peace in our hearts. For us to die peacefully, we must connect with our real self and live from our highest destiny for the second half of our life. Serving the expectations of the world at the cost of our truth will never bring us peace.

The process of individuation is also one in which the precision of life reveals itself. This can connect us with the sacred. This helps us see the purpose of our "mistaken" choices and what we needed to learn from them. When seen through this perspective, our life's purpose can be revealed through our recovery from our previously adapted selves. Although this process is alchemical and is often catalyzed by pain, we must feel our feelings fully and deeply in order for them to be able to transform us. Choosing health after being adapted can be confusing. Although healthy choices may feel unfamiliar and counterintuitive, they can heal our wounded instincts and make our inner truth and wisdom more accessible. They can even correct the course of our lives. They can also offer us much needed solace at the end when we can feel comfort for finally having lived authentically.

Hormonal shifts mark the midlife gateway

For midlife women, changes in their bodies begin subtly in their late thirties, hinting of hormonal imbalance before menses, when their feeling function heightens. They may feel agitated and suddenly find themselves unable to tolerate the ways in which they are expected to adapt. During their forties, this intensifies. Hormonal shifts widen, changing biology and uncovering the previously repressed details of biography, bringing them into consciousness for review and reframing. Individuation beckons with deep intensity and often fury.

I became fascinated by the power with which hormonal shifts unleashed intense feelings and alchemical energy in women. I observed this as a part of my own transformation as my early morning awakenings wrought with fear, were followed by intense creativity. This process was deeply personal and I moved through it alone. As my adapted life was falling to pieces, my "double" was unfolding my true destiny. I was learning Her language through my feelings every night. She awakened me with hot flashes and night sweats. I began to furiously journal, weaving my patients' similar stories through the framework I was learning from this deeper part of myself. All parts of my life revealed a precision that I saw for the first time. As I applied this framework to my patients' lives, they were able to see their wholeness through it and become empowered. Women began to leave the victimized place from which they had been living. Their pain and wounding made sense and they were able to use them as catalysts to uncover the parts of themselves they needed to reclaim. They were able to see the wisdom in the chaos they had frequently felt as they recognized the sacred theme that was always present in their lives. When they reframed their perspective, they realized they could release the illusion of their smallness and make contact with the unlimited potential contained within their real selves. They could mobilize their awareness and reframe their role as a heroine in their biography, rather than a victim. They could use the inner pressure caused by their suppressed feelings to alchemically transform into their authentic and real selves. This connected them with their truth and wisdom. They gained access to their potential to activate their intrinsic power and reclaim the joy that had been missing for so long. They became the phoenix rising from the ashes of whom they were leaving behind.

Our body as the initiator

During childhood, our bodies initiate us through menses from children into maidens. They initiate many through pregnancy into motherhood. Our bodies also connect us with a deeper sense of meaning through illness.

Menopause is our body's way of initiating us yet again. First, during the end of our thirties, our feelings begin to intensify. Next, in our forties, our emotions escalate with gusto and added symptoms of hot flashes and night sweats. Our "double" begins to call to us through our bodies due to the parting of our "hormonal seas." As the progesterone level falls, it creates the biological imbalance that calls for the restoration of a *deeper* balance, and our lost self calls us to connect to what is real. We begin to hear the voice of our "double" through the intensity of our feelings. She asks us to now make choices that can connect us to our real self. She offers us the door to the unknown that is frightening and unfamiliar, yet leads to our higher destiny. This is the *other* door, the door that Alice did not walk through, despite promptings from her "double." This is the door we must walk through in order to finally live an authentic life.

It is a great honor and privilege to work with this transformative initiation of midlife. The sacred is acutely palpable in this gateway when the veil between the conscious and unconscious grows thin.

This is where the soul seeps through. It speaks through the feelings and dreams of the courageous people who consciously journey through this portal to connect with their real selves. They are often awed by their new found level of self-worth and capabilities. Fear is replaced with a trust in the process. As they upgrade their choices, they carry an energy that is intensely beautiful in this initiatory state. They are now connected to their inner greatness—a place they had never felt before. They begin behaving as though they embody their holy "double." They begin living from curiosity and wonder, able to utilize the discernment they gained over half a lifetime and can now live from the inner wisdom they finally have access to.

The biological changes women go through in midlife are extremely powerful. The fact that they evoke deeper levels of transformation is a framework necessary for us to acknowledge for Women's Health to be truly effective. Sadly, what physicians have done thus far is to prescribe medications and dismiss and label the symptoms of transformation and rising feeling function as pathological rather than alchemical. Additionally, some physicians who prescribe hormonal balance as a "cure" for menopause, undermine the transformative power contained within imbalance and, inadvertently, disregard the capacity to become real by bypassing this process.

We need to reframe menopause as a sacred initiation. In the same vein, we need to integrate the Feminine Principle into all of our systems in society. Our institutions of medicine, finance, politics, religion, and education all suffer from the lack of the healthy feminine. Our sacred work as midlife women is to awaken to our truth and reclaim it until we feel comfortable in our new and authentic skins. It is only through our transformation that we can bring our real selves through our actions, behaviors, and presence into the world and transform it from illness to health.

We also need to understand our bodies so as to not fear the changes that the midlife gateway brings. What we do not understand causes fear. As a health care provider, it is a part of my vocation and responsibility to educate and reframe the symptoms menopause evokes and help women understand them as catalysts in this transformational gateway. An understanding of the powerful process initiated by biological precision can dispel the fear that often accompanies this transition. It is essential for us to mark our initiatory passages which have been neglected and dismissed by our culture and the current medical system. Many women feel lost and alone, struggling through menopause with no guidance, wishing they could turn back their biological clocks and become young again.

For us to be truly healthy, it is important for us to balance the physical, emotional, and spiritual levels of the body, and remember that this medial time in midlife is one of great power. It calls us to reframe our definitions of health and meaning. Success can no longer be defined by society's standards, but from an inner place that is restless and no longer fulfilled by material and superficial trappings. Our authentic "double" calls us to go within and speaks to us through restless nights and our feelings of longing. We are called to deconstruct our old adapted selves and are given many opportunities to individuate from familiar patterns that have deprived us of meaning, and now evoke the beauty of what is real and authentic.

The holy "double" never rests. Her language is one of "restlessness." Not connecting with Her can keep us awake at night and make us anxious.When we connect and ask questions like "why are we here," and "how can we live authentically and die a good death," She settles and grants us a good night's sleep. Our symptoms heal, and life takes on a deeper level of meaning. We must ask these crucial questions during the midlife gateway. Our answers, behaved through authentic choices, will help us unfold the second half of our lives with added meaning and purpose. We must remember our deep inner guidance, the voice of restlessness within that keeps us loyal company, only settles when we live out the important answers that unfold our highest destiny.

Every woman's journey is unique and sacred. It is deeply influenced by her biography, heritage, and environment. To be able to weave these parts together and gain understanding with this sacred perspective is critical for our connection with our souls' purpose.

Moving through the midlife gateway consciously holds the keys to our joy, health, fulfillment, and success.

Becoming real is necessary and urgent in our world today. We must hold this intention deep in our hearts. If we answer the call from our "double" and transform, we will never feel lost or alone again.

3

The Female Body in Midlife

Carla

Carla is a 48-year-old woman who came to me to find relief from her perimenopausal symptoms. I asked her about her knowledge of the menstrual cycle. She wept, ashamed for not understanding it. She was thirteen when she began menstruating, and every month, she looked forward to the day her periods would end. Her cycles felt like an illness and a nuisance, as her premenstrual symptoms were intense. She did not understand their biological or symbolic meaning. None of her physicians had explained this to her. Since her mother did not understand this herself, she had been unable to educate Carla in this area. Now, Carla was in the perimenopausal transition with daily symptoms of emotional agitation, mental fog, headaches, insomnia, and hot flashes. As I explained what was occuring in her body, she felt relieved. She was never taught how to honor this time as one of great power. With an understanding from a deeper perspective, she felt both a sense of relief as well as loss. For most of her life, she had missed the opportunity to view her cycles from a sacred perspective.

I felt sadness upon witnessing Carla's grief. Despite the vast amount of information available today, many women are ignorant about the biology and meaning of their menstrual cycles. It is important for them to have an understanding of this to care for themselves more effectively. This may seem intimidating for many, but the price we pay for ignorance is fear. A basic knowledge of the menstrual cycle can be a helpful platform for understanding the reasons for symptoms during menses and menopause. Without this, we risk remaining disempowered and dependent upon medical experts who only provide prescriptions to manage our symptoms.

Female hormones

The female ovary produces three main hormones:
1. Estrogen
2. Progesterone
3. Testosterone

Estrogen

Stated simply, estrogen is the hormone that both females and males produce, but females produce it in greater quantities.

Estrogen:
- is responsible for the development of breasts, uterine tissue and vaginal wall thickness
- has effects on multiple other organ systems, including the liver and the digestive system where it decreases motility and increases the absorption of nutrients
- affects bone density, where it decreases the breakdown or turn-over of bone

Estrone, Estradiol and Estriol are the three main estrogens made in the human body. These are referred to in science as E1, E2 and E3.
- **Estrone (E1)** is produced in the ovary and, in large percentage, by fat cells. It is the least abundant of the three estrogenic hormones. It is the primary estrogen produced during menopause, but in small amounts.

- **Estradiol (E2)** is produced by the ovaries and is the estrogen responsible for female cycles and the development of sexual characteristics. It is the culprit in many breast cancers, breast cysts, fibroadenomas, endometriosis, and fibroid tumors. When estradiol levels decline in a woman's 40s, the typical symptoms of perimenopause such as hot flashes and night sweats are present more frequently.

- **Estriol (E3)** is a form of estrogen produced almost exclusively during pregnancy by the developing fetus. Estriol crosses the placental barrier to enter the mother's body. It is largely responsible for maintaining the integrity of the vagina, cervix, and vulva. It has little to no impact on breast or uterine tissue.

Progesterone

Progesterone is a hormone produced by the ovaries, the adrenal glands, and the placenta during pregnancy. Its main role is to maintain the lining of the uterus after ovulation so the fertilized egg can implant onto it to develop into a baby. Progesterone has a profound effect on many other areas of a woman's body.

Progesterone:
- effects mood by increasing the level of serotonin
- promotes muscle relaxation
- stimulates bone growth
- stimulates nerve growth
- promotes healthy skin and hair
- assists in thyroid balance
- has anti-inflammatory properties
- decreases tissue and muscle stiffness, and hence muscle injury
- decreases heavy menstrual flow
- effects the tone of the urinary sphincter, the urethra. A decrease in its level can cause urinary leakage.
- regulates the sleep cycle
- relaxes the digestive system affecting motility (movement) of the gut and intestine
- acts as a diuretic (decreases water retention)
- balances the effects of estrogen

- lowers blood pressure
- decreases coronary spasm

An imbalance between estrogen and progesterone, where the estradiol (estrogen) level is not balanced with an adequate level of progesterone, can cause premenstrual syndrome (PMS) and a myriad of perimenopausal symptoms. The balance of estrogen with progesterone is also protective against breast cancer, breast and ovarian cysts, fibroid tumor formation, and endometriosis.

When the progesterone level falls, the ratio between estrogen to progesterone (E/P) increases, placing women at risk for breast and uterine cancers, stroke, hypertension, and heart attacks. These diseases are prevalent in peri- and post menopausal women in epidemic proportions in the Western Hemisphere.

Testosterone

Testosterone is produced in women in small amounts in the ovaries and the adrenal glands.

Testosterone:
- affects a woman's sex drive
- increases feelings of vitality and energy
- affects the potency of a woman's orgasm and sensitivity of her erogenous zones
- increases muscle tone and muscle mass
- affects the tone of the urinary sphincter

When the ovaries begin to wind down in a woman's late thirties and forties, the testosterone level begins to fall. As a result, she may feel a decrease in her libido and vitality and may also experience urinary leakage and irritation of the urinary sphincter.

DHEA

DHEA (dehydroepiandrosterone) is a hormone produced by the adrenal glands and a precursor of female and male reproductive hormones (estrogen, progesterone, androgens). *A precursor is a protein from which other proteins and hormones are made.* When a woman has adrenal fatigue, her DHEA level can decline. The DHEA level naturally decreases after the third decade of life. Too low of a DHEA level is indicative of adrenal fatigue.

The menstrual cycle

I have attempted to demystify the menstrual cycle and provide a basic understanding of its biological process. Between the ages of ten and thirteen, a girl's pituitary gland (*an endocrine gland in the brain that regulates hormone production*) begins to produce two hormones: Follicle Stimulating Hormone (FSH) and Luteinizing Hormone (LH).

- FSH stimulates a part of the ovary called the follicle to produce estrogen. The *follicular phase* of the menstrual cycle is the phase between menses and ovulation, from days 0 (the first day of menstrual bleeding) to 14 (Figure 1). During this phase, the egg develops and grows under the influence of estrogen until ovulation, when it is released from the ovary and awaits being fertilized by a sperm. Estrogen is also responsible for building the lining of the uterus where the fertilized egg can develop and grow into a baby.

- LH stimulates ovulation together with FSH (around day 12 to 14) in the middle of the cycle when there is an abrupt increase in both FSH as well as LH levels. It marks the beginning of the *luteal phase* (days 14 to 28) of the cycle. In a majority of women, menses frequently begins on day 28 of the cycle.

As soon as ovulation occurs, the egg is released from the ovary and journeys to the uterus to be fertilized by a sperm. The corpus luteum, or sac, that housed the egg inside the ovary begins to produce progesterone.

Progesterone protects the uterus from shedding its lining that estrogen carefully created in the *follicular phase* so that the fertilized egg can implant within it and grow into a baby. If the egg is not fertilized, the progesterone level begins to drop by day 24, and approximately 14 days after ovulation the uterine lining is shed with an abrupt fall in progesterone (Figure 1). This is referred to as menstruation or menses.

The time between ovulation and menses is called the *luteal phase* of the menstrual cycle, when the corpus luteum produces progesterone. This is sometimes the most emotionally difficult time of the menstrual cycle in women who do not ovulate regularly or do not produce enough progesterone upon ovulation. Progesterone has a significant impact on a woman's emotional health and well-being. The balance or imbalance between the estrogen and progesterone is

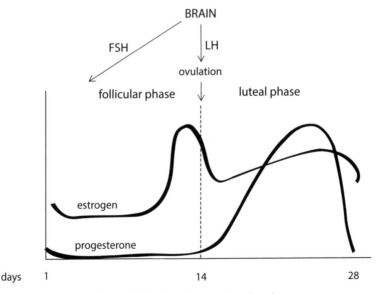

Figure 1: The female menstrual cycle

felt in the Emotional body. Often in their late thirties, women begin to skip ovulation, resulting in a drop in progesterone and an imbalance in the estrogen to progesterone ratio. When the progesterone level falls, estrogen becomes the more "dominant" hormone. This imbalance termed "estrogen dominance," is one of the main causes for premenstrual and perimenopausal symptoms.

Estrogen dominance

In the U.S., as compared to other countries, estrogen dominance is present in epidemic proportions. Our food supply is contaminated with synthetic estrogens, or xenoestrogens, from many different sources. One source is synthetic hormones that animals are fed to increase their yield of meat and milk. When consumed, these hormones become concentrated in our bodies. The concentration of hormones, pesticides, and medications occurs any time humans consume foods containing them as they become more concentrated as they move up the food chain. For example, if a plant eaten by an animal is sprayed with pesticides, they become more concentrated in the animal. If the animal is then given synthetic hormones, the concentrated pesticides together with the hormones the animal was given, become more concentrated in the human. Xenoestrogens are a breakdown product of the many pesticides that are used to spray crops in the U.S. They are also the breakdown product from plastics. These are endocrine disruptors. Synthetic hormones prescribed by the medical system as Hormone Replacement Therapy (HRT) are an additional source of synthetic estrogens. Synthetic estrogens over-stimulate the estrogen receptors present on the surface of cells, and accentuate symptoms of estrogen dominance in humans. A receptor is a protein molecule on the cell surface to which the hormone binds, causing a reaction inside the cell.

In other countries, estrogen dominance is not as significant a problem, as it is in the U.S., due to the lower use of xenoestrogens and the higher number of soy and plant-based foods consumed. Soy contains phytoestrogens or plant based estrogens that protect estrogen receptors from being overstimulated by xeno or synthetic estrogens. Estrogen dominance is more prevalent in women in the U.S. due to the amount of synthetic hormones prescribed and the elevated xenoestrogen load in the foods consumed. One way to minimize this load is to eat organic food.

Stress and estrogen dominance

Stress is an important factor that contributes to an imbalance of the estrogen to progesterone ratio. Stress hormones lower the progesterone level. Much of our stress is a result of the loss of our connection with each other, which contributes to our feeling unsupported and unsafe in the world. Less than thirty years ago, people were valued as a part of their village or community. This provided them with an emotional buffer for life's stressors. Since we no longer have this level of support, we deal with stress alone. This causes a significant increase in stress hormones (produced by the adrenal glands). We live in a chronic state of survival. Survival triggers the "fight-or-flight" response, a biological mechanism designed to either fight or flee, due to real or perceived stress. This causes the production of high levels of adrenalin, the most common stress hormone produced by the adrenal glands. Under conditions of chronic stress, the survival state becomes chronic and triggers the adrenal glands to produce high levels of the stress hormone cortisol. (The adrenal glands also produce other hormones that benefit our health and regulate our bodily functions). Too much cortisol over time can cause unhealthy effects on the body.

Some of these are:
- weight gain
- depression

- fatigue
- increase in stomach acid
- increase in cholesterol
- increase in blood sugar
- increase in appetite
- increase in blood pressure or hypertension
- spasm of the coronary arteries (the arteries that supply the heart with oxygenated blood)
- decrease in memory
- thinning of skin and hair
- suppression of the immune system

Two factors reduce the progesterone level during a state of chronic stress.

1. Cortisol competes with progesterone for the ability to bind to receptors on the surface of the cell. This accelerates a decline in the amount of progesterone that enters the cell. This decline exaggerates the estrogen to progesterone imbalance, contributing to a greater level of estrogen dominance.

2. Cortisol suppresses the production of progesterone. During stress when the cortisol level rises, the progesterone level falls. Both of the factors mentioned, cause a reduction in the progesterone level relative to estrogen, contributing to estrogen dominance.

It is worth mentioning that women who are emotionally sensitive produce higher concentrations of stress hormones while under stress. Since they feel deeply, they also feel stress more intensely. Because of their increased sensitivity, they can also feel restorations in balance with natural hormones more rapidly.

Hormone testing

Hormone levels can be tested in the blood or saliva. Over the past twenty years, I have found blood levels to provide a more accurate correlation with symptoms. Many physicians favor saliva testing. In my experience, this test is cumbersome, expensive, and carries a high percentage of procedural error. The accuracy of saliva testing is unknown when saliva samples are shipped in extreme weather, without proper packaging needed to maintain the sample's stability. When salivary hormone levels are compared with blood, the blood levels correlate more accurately with the clinical response. This provides greater accuracy when adjusting the dose of prescribed natural or bio-identical hormones to provide greater balance and more effective peri- and postmenopausal symptom management.

Depending upon the stage in menopause, an estradiol to progesterone ratio (E/P) of five to ten, is ideal for restoring balance. Women have the greatest level of well-being with hormone levels in this ratio. In menopausal women a ratio of two to five is ideal, as the estradiol level is much lower. For example, if a perimenopausal woman has an estradiol level of 100, a progesterone level between 10 to 20 would provide an E/P ratio between five to ten. In a menopausal woman, for an estradiol level of ten, a progesterone level between two to five would provide a ratio between two to five. These ratios should always be correlated with clinical response or symptomatic relief as some women feel better at the lower end of the ratio and some at the higher end. The goal of hormone balance is to use the least amount of hormone for the greatest clinical response. Hormone balance, not replacement, should be the goal. Balancing hormones is as much an art as a science and must be customized for every woman and correlated with her clinical response.

Estrogen or Estradiol (E2)

Estradiol (E2) is the form of estrogen that is most frequently measured. This is the estrogen that needs to be balanced with progesterone. Estradiol (and progesterone) levels are measured by a blood test between days 21 to 24 (of a 28-day) menstrual cycle to offer an accurate reading of a woman's estradiol to progesterone ratio. If the estradiol level is too high, and a woman is taking natural estrogen, the dose of natural estrogen should be decreased. If she is not taking natural estrogen, but is taking natural progesterone only and blood levels indicate estrogen dominance, this means either her dose of progesterone is too low or progesterone is being converted to estrogen, which occurs in a small percentage of women.

In the latter instance, the timing and mode of progesterone use during the menstrual cycle should be assessed. If a woman is using it during the follicular phase (before mid-cycle), it has a greater chance of conversion resulting in estrogen dominance. Many over-the-counter progesterone creams direct women to begin using it on day seven, during the follicular phase, resulting in this outcome.

Progesterone

Progesterone has a slight estrogenic effect that can abate some of the common symptoms of estrogen withdrawal such as hot flashes and night sweats that are caused by the decreasing level of estradiol. Hormone levels need to be measured every three to four months in a woman using natural progesterone, to check the estradiol/progesterone ratio. A clinical sign of progesterone to estrogen conversion would be an aggravation of the symptoms of estrogen dominance. If a perimenopausal woman takes natural progesterone during the follicular phase of her cycle (day 0 to 14), as described above, she has a greater risk of converting progesterone into estrogen due to the estrogenic influence of the body during this phase of the cycle. The body is geared towards estrogen production during the follicular phase of the menstrual cycle and is more likely to convert progesterone into estrogen during this phase. Natural progesterone taken during the luteal phase is less likely to be converted to estrogen.

The best time to measure estrogen and progesterone levels to assess balance is during days 21 to 24 of a 28 day cycle or five to seven days prior to menses. This provides the most accurate reading to assess the estradiol to progesterone ratio. In postmenopausal women (who are not menstruating), hormone levels can be measured at any time of the month as they no longer have cycles. After starting natural progesterone, a postmenopausal woman's hormone levels should be checked after the first month of use and then every four to five months thereafter. A perimenopausal woman's hormone levels should be checked two cycles after starting the progesterone between day 21 to 24 of a 28-day cycle and every three to four months after balance is achieved.

Testosterone

Free testosterone is testosterone that is freely available to function in the body. *Total* testosterone is the combination of *free* testosterone and testosterone bound to albumin (*a kind of protein*). The *free* testosterone level provides a measure of the active testosterone in a woman's body. Free testosterone can be measured by a blood test to determine if a woman needs supplementation with natural testosterone for symptoms caused by low testosterone such as lack of vitality, libido, or a decline in muscle mass.

Free and *total* testosterone levels can be measured in the blood. If the *free* testosterone level is low, natural or bio-identical testosterone can be prescribed in the form of a cream, gel, or capsule. A woman experiencing chronic urinary tract infections after menopause can also benefit from the application of natural testosterone cream to the urinary (urethral) opening and vulva to reduce the incidence of these infections.

It is important to check the *free* testosterone levels at least every three months after beginning natural testosterone, as its level can suddenly increase, causing acne, facial hair, emotional irritability, and *conversion to estrogen*. Testosterone can also be converted into estrogen, particularly after menopause, through a reaction that occurs in the cells. This can aggravate estrogen dominance, so it is important to manage the prescribed dose with blood levels under the guidance of a physician. Initially, a woman may benefit from daily natural testosterone usage, but once a therapeutic level is reached, she may not need to take the full dose on a daily basis.

The risks of estrogen dominance

A worrisome fact about women in the U.S. compared to other countries is the high concentration of estrogen present in their body fat.

This is due to two factors:

1. A high concentration of synthetic estrogens present in food in the U.S. due to the widespread use of pesticides and synthetic hormones supported by "agribusiness."

2. Moderate use of synthetic hormones ingested by women in the form of oral contraceptives and hormone replacement therapy.

Farming practices in the U.S., which utilize pesticides and synthetic hormones, add xenoestrogens to the environment. These are present in non-organic plants, meat, and the animal runoff that permeates the ground water. In addition, women who take prescribed oral contraceptives or synthetic hormone replacement therapy, excrete synthetic hormone fragments in their urine that also permeate the ground water. This increases the concentration of synthetic and xenoestrogens in ground water that, when consumed, increases the incidence of estrogen dominance.

Estrogen dominance makes us vulnerable to diseases caused by estrogen excess, such as:

- breast cancer
- uterine cancer
- fibroids
- endometriosis
- fibrocystic breasts
- insulin resistance
- increase in blood cholesterol levels
- strokes
- hypertension
- blood clots
- obesity
- infertility
- coronary artery spasm (resulting in heart attacks)
- immune system suppression
- urinary leakage
- thyroid disorders

Some symptoms of estrogen dominance are:

- heavy periods
- intermittent or mid-cycle bleeding
- mood swings
- breast tenderness
- headaches
- water retention
- fatigue
- foggy thinking
- decrease in short-term memory
- abdominal bloating
- irritable bowel symptoms such as constipation and diarrhea
- dry skin
- insomnia
- weight gain
- accelerated signs of aging

- muscle pain (fibromyalgia-like symptoms)
- mild vertigo
- thinning of hair

Many of these symptoms can also be experienced with a declining level of progesterone. Without an adequate blood level (to balance estrogen), we are more vulnerable to these conditions as we age. We feel them with greater vigor in our forties when progesterone levels decline and the imbalance between estrogen and progesterone is greatest. They become less pronounced after menopause as both hormone levels decline. At this time, a small dose of progesterone is protective and can also ease some of the symptoms of estrogen withdrawal (such as hot flashes and night sweats). Estrogen dominance can occur during menopause if a woman is obese and has higher levels of estrogen due to the conversion of estrone (E3) to estradiol (E2).

Perimenopause

Perimenopause is the time surrounding the onset of menopause. It typically ranges from ages 38 to 55 depending upon when a woman stops menstruating or enters menopause. Menopause is defined as the cessation of a woman's menstrual cycles. In their late thirties, many women in the U.S. begin to experience changes in the premenstrual or luteal phase of their menstrual cycles. This time can be marked by an increase in symptoms of emotional sensitivity, breast tenderness, weight gain, and fatigue. Menstrual flow can be heavy due to the buildup of the uterine lining under the influence of estrogen dominance. As the progesterone level decreases, so do its estrogen balancing and protective effects on the body. Mid-cycle bleeding and heavier menstrual flow are early indicators of declining levels as progesterone is needed to maintain and withhold the lining of the uterus.

This is the stage of perimenopause when women typically see their physicians because of an increase in their premenstrual symptoms, only to be commonly treated with oral contraceptives, antidepressants, or both. These can exaggerate their symptoms, as oral contraceptives contain synthetic estrogen and/or progesterone, while antidepressants numb emotions. These synthetic treatments often increase the health risks caused by estrogen dominance. Women in this stage of perimenopause need to know how their lifestyle choices influence their symptoms, what their symptoms mean, and the variety of therapeutic options available for creating balance.

Additional symptoms of perimenopause

When women in their forties are treated with synthetic hormones, this can aggravate estrogen dominance causing an increase in their symptoms of:

- insomnia
- hot flashes
- night sweats
- depression
- anxiety
- hair thinning
- heavy menstrual flow
- bowel spasms, constipation and diarrhea (irritable bowel syndrome)
- dry skin
- joint pain
- joint stiffness
- muscle pain
- weight gain
- fatigue
- hair loss

- loss of libido
- urinary incontinence
- acid reflux
- hypertension
- headaches
- nausea
- food sensitivities
- allergies
- increase in fat production
- increase in abdominal girth
- mental fog
- increase in blood sugar
- mild vertigo (dizziness)

Between the ages of 45 and 55, women begin to experience a decline in estrogen levels as the ovaries continue to wind down. As the estrogen level decreases, hot flashes and night sweats often increase due to estrogen withdrawal experienced at the level of the estrogen receptor. Additionally, women in the U.S., feel a lack of energy and vitality, as they eat more processed than whole foods, which lack nutrtional value.

For most women, dietary changes that include more plant-based and animal-free foods, in combination with natural progesterone, can significantly reduce their perimenopausal symptoms. Often, as stated before, the addition of natural progesterone can help symptoms caused by declining estrogen levels, like hot flashes and night sweats, due to its mildly estrogenic effects. If natural progesterone does not improve these symptoms, a small dose of natural or bio-identical estrogen may be needed to provide balance and symptom management.

Postmenopausal symptoms and replacement
of synthetic estrogen with natural estrogen

Traditional medicine defines a woman as *post*menopausal if she has not menstruated for one year. Women who no longer menstruate and suffer from severe hot flashes and night sweats can be helped with a low dose of natural estrogen if natural progesterone alone does not alleviate their symptoms. In most women, a small dose of natural estrogen will be adequate to decrease menopausal symptoms and offer only minimal risk. It should always be balanced with natural progesterone to decrease estrogen's potential risks.

If a woman is on synthetic hormone replacement (HRT) and wants to switch to natural hormones, the most effective way is to begin natural estrogen at a dose equivalent to the dose of synthetic estrogen she is taking. Natural estrogen has a gentler effect on the body than synthetic estrogen. Initially, a slightly higher dose may be needed if she has estrogen withdrawal symptoms when prescribed the same dose as synthetic estrogen. Once a woman has been on a prescribed dose of natural estrogen for a month or two, and is asymptomatic, she can begin to gradually wean it under the guidance of her physician. The goal is to balance her hormones and not replace them to menstrual levels, as many physicians do, as balance carries less of a chance for estrogen dominance and its associated risks. Moreover, as the estrogen level declines with age, estrogen receptors are less able to process high doses of estrogen. Hormone receptor function declines as hormones are biologically programmed to decrease. Estrogen receptors incorporate estrogen into cells. If menstrual doses of estrogen are administered during perimenopause or menopause, receptors cannot process the excess hormone load, causing increased side effects and potential risks.

The strategy of gradually weaning the natural estrogen dose enables estrogen receptors to "get used to" lower levels of estrogen over time, minimizing the symptoms of estrogen withdrawal. The goal is to use the least amount of estrogen required for symptomatic relief. Plant-based estrogens or phytoestrogens, such as organic soy and preferably fermented soy, are also very effective for treating symptoms of estrogen withdrawal. Pills and bars containing soy are not safe because soy in this form has been modified and may actually stimulate estrogen receptors. If a woman is unable to tolerate natural hormone therapy, phytoestrogens, like soy, can offer relief and protection from the over-stimulation of estrogen receptors, thereby reducing the symptoms of estrogen dominance and its associated risks.

Progesterone and mood

As progesterone levels decline, so do serotonin levels in the brain and body. Serotonin is a chemical produced by the nervous system that regulates mood, sleep, appetite, learning, and muscle contractions in the large muscles and gut. It contributes to feelings of well-being. A decrease in seratonin can cause depression, anxiety, a lack of motivation, abdominal bloating, sleep disturbance, and irritability. Progesterone increases serotonin levels in the brain and nervous system. In contrast, estrogen decreases them. Natural progesterone increases seratonin, increasing feelings of well-being, unlike synthetic estrogen and progesterone that decrease it. Treating symptoms of low serotonin with anti-depressants and synthetic hormone replacement merely masks symptoms without providing hormone balance, that actually increases seratonin levels.

Synthetic progesterone

The traditional medical system prescribes synthetic progesterone or *Progestin*, as a form of hormone replacement therapy for menopause. Synthetic progesterone is manufactured in a laboratory

and does not have the same chemical structure as natural progesterone (Figure 2). Natural or bio-identical progesterone's chemical structure is identical to progesterone produced in the human
body. Synthetic progesterone is not able to correct estrogen
dominance. It is also dangerous for women to take. *A large scale
Women's Health Initiative study, conducted in the U.S. in 1998, was
halted three years early, in 2002, when it showed that the combination of synthetic estrogen and progesterone (progestin) increased a
woman's risk of heart disease, breast cancer, and strokes.* Unfortunately, despite this evidence, prescribing practices for synthetic
hormones in the U.S. have not changed, and physicians continue
to prescribe them at staggering rates. Traditional physicians also
discourage women from using natural hormones as they lack the
understanding of the difference between natural and synthetic.

Natural hormone therapy

Over many years of helping thousands of women go through
menopause, I have had the opportunity to observe which treatments are most effective and which offer minimal to no benefit. *I
have observed that natural hormone balance in addition to a plant
based, anti-inflammatory diet, with regular exercise, provides the best
therapeutic response for the majority of menopausal symptoms.*

Using a common sense approach for treatment and balance is
the best way to navigate through menopause. If women can view
their symptoms from the context of estrogen dominance and make
choices that decrease it, they can greatly improve their health.

As shown by The Women's Health Initiative study, synthetic
progesterone (progestin) does not carry the safety we have been
told that it does. Synthetic hormones have significantly different
effects on the body than natural hormones. Even a small difference
in molecular structure can cause a big difference in efficacy, risk
and side effects. As shown, synthetic progesterone has a different

molecular structure than natural progesterone (Figure 2). Since natural progesterone has a molecular structure that is identical to a woman's body, it is safer to take. Our bodies would not produce a hormone that was unsafe and did not support our health.

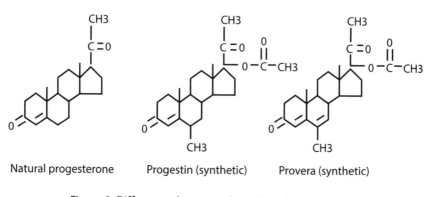

Figure 2: Differences between the molecular structures
of natural and synthetic progesterone

Compounding pharmacy

A *compounding pharmacy* is a pharmacy where natural (plant based) and compounded bio-identical hormones are available with a prescription. Bio-identical is identical to what the body produces (Figure 2). Natural, or bio-identical hormones are made from diosgenin, a substance extracted from wild yams and soybeans. Diosgenin is synthesized into a substance with the same molecular structure (bio-identical) as hormones produced by human endocrine glands. Bio-identical or natural estrogen, progesterone, and testosterone are all available from a compounding pharmacy.

Synthetic versus natural hormones

As synthetic hormones do not share the molecular structure of natural hormones they can be patented and sold by the pharmaceutical industry. Natural substances cannot be patented. Synthetic hormones are recognized and processed by the body differently than natural hormones. This is what causes their side effects and risks. They create toxicity rather than balance. Since the liver is not equipped to process synthetic chemicals, it cannot adequately break them down and eliminate them. Traces are stored in fat cells that result in health problems. Additionally, synthetic hormones suppress the secretion of natural hormones produced by the ovaries.

Synthetic progesterone is termed *Progestin*. This should not be confused with progesterone. Unopposed synthetic estrogen (estrogen without *progesterone*) prescribed by the health care system is dangerous and a contributing factor to the peri- and postmenopausal symptoms in the U.S. This is prescribed primarily in women who have had a total hysterectomy where both the uterus and ovaries are surgically removed.

A woman on five or more years of synthetic hormone replacement therapy has a *66% increased risk of breast cancer and a 22% increased risk of death*. Numerous studies performed since 1989 and published in traditional medical journals in the U.S. have consistently shown significant health risks in women who use synthetic hormones *for up to 10 years after their discontinuation*. The risk of breast, uterine, and ovarian cancers, as well as strokes and heart attacks, increases and must be considered before taking any form of synthetic hormone replacement therapy.

Natural progesterone

The hormone that women need most during the perimenopausal years is natural or bio-identical progesterone. Women continue to produce estrogen during this time, but as the progesterone level declines from the inconsistent and decreasing frequency of ovulation with age, symptoms of estrogen dominance are more prevalent, particularly during the *luteal phase* of the menstrual cycle. It is critical to measure hormone levels in the *blood* periodically and regulate the dosage of natural progesterone to maintain estrogen and progesterone balance and ensure safety. High doses of even natural hormones may carry health risks. *Balance* is the goal of natural hormone therapy. It can be achieved with the lowest doses of natural hormones that improve symptoms. Menstrual or *replacement* doses of hormones administered during perimenopause and menopause may carry potential danger of side effects and health risks. It is not natural for women going through menopause to take doses of hormones that result in menstrual levels of estrogen and progesterone.

For most women, the initial effects of natural progesterone can be felt *as early as two days after starting it.* A woman will find that her sleep cycle becomes more regular, and she experiences a deeper and more restful night's sleep. She awakens less often and, when she does, she is able to fall back to sleep again. With the sleep cycle restored, her stress hormones decrease, and she feels more rested and less fatigued.

Women also begin to feel more grounded and emotionally balanced within a few days of taking natural progesterone. After taking it for a few months, symptoms of estrogen dominance are significantly reduced. Women find it easier to lose weight once hormone balance is attained and sleep is restored, as the thyroid also works more efficiently when estrogen dominance is corrected. *Estrogen dominance causes mild suppression of thyroid function that decreases metabolism and increases weight.* In addition, estrogen increases the accumulation of body fat by decreasing its breakdown and increasing its production. Progesterone counterbalances the fat stimulating effects of estrogen and also restores the thyroid back into balance.

Natural progesterone:

- acts as a mild diuretic decreasing water retention
- relaxes the intestines decreasing bloating and constipation
- improves the integrity of hair, skin, and muscles

- regulates the sleep cycle
- reduces anxiety and depression
- decreases heavy menstrual flow
- regulates the insulin receptor increasing the efficiency of sugar metabolism
- clears foggy thinking
- improves memory
- relaxes blood vessels lowering blood pressure
- reduces fatigue
- promotes weight loss
- improves thyroid function
- decreases muscle aches and pains
- restores menstrual balance

Dosing of progesterone

Many brands of natural progesterone, available over the counter and by mail order, may contain a very low dose of progesterone that *may not provide adequate balance* during perimenopause. Sometimes over-the-counter brands have not been compounded as absorbable progesterone, preventing their therapeutic efficacy.

The dosage of natural progesterone required for balance should be determined by your physician, based on your blood levels and clinical response, such as a restoration of feelings of well-being and a reduction in the symptoms of estrogen dominance. The usual prescribed dose of natural progesterone ranges from 12.5mg to 200mg per day, with the need for higher doses during perimenopause due to a greater E/P ratio. Postmenopausal women do not require a high dose of progesterone as their estrogen levels are low requiring a lower dose for balance. Natural progesterone is available as a cream, gel, capsule, or as sublingual drops. Your physician can help determine the form that works best for you. Natural hormones are cycled in conjunction with the menstrual cycle, with progesterone being administered during the luteal phase. If you are postmenopausal, the dosage regimen of progesterone can be administered for either six out seven days per week, or up to 26 out of 30 days per month. If either or both natural testosterone and estrogen are prescribed, they are usually administered as a daily dose rather than cyclically.

Women who are overweight have higher levels of estrogen in their bodies, as fat cells produce estrone (E1) that converts into estradiol (E2). Sometimes women who have excess body fat initially need higher doses of progesterone in order to achieve balance, and their levels should be closely monitored to make sure that they are *not converting progesterone to estrogen.*

Some symptoms of too high of a progesterone dose may include increased sedation, bloating, weight gain, headaches, fatigue, and breast tenderness.

As women become familiar with the process involved in restoring hormone balance and notice improvements in their symptoms, they can tell if they need additional blood levels checked between testing intervals as they may feel symptoms of imbalance if their hormone levels are too high or too low. They may experience headaches, bloating, and fatigue if progesterone levels are too high; or symptoms of estrogen dominance if levels are too low relative to estrogen, elevating the E/P ratio. This would indicate the need for a dose adjustment.

My patients often inform me if they feel the need for a dose adjustment sooner than the regular testing interval of three to four months. In the majority of cases, they are correct. If they feel balanced, they only require their levels checked at the regular testing intervals.

Natural estrogen

Most women produce small amounts of estrogen throughout their lives. As mentioned above, estrogen levels are higher in women who are moderately obese compared to thinner women.

Estrogen *replacement* is rarely needed in peri- and postmenopausal women. The most common situation requiring estrogen *replacement* is in a woman who has had a complete hysterectomy (uterus and ovarian removal) before menopause. It is a shock for the body to go through surgical menopause, and hormone receptors often experience moderate to severe hormone withdrawal. Women in this situation need natural estrogen *replacement* for severe hot flashes, night sweats, and extreme insomnia. The replacement doses of estrogen can be gradually weaned over time. It is important to always *combine natural estrogen with natural progesterone and testosterone* even after a hysterectomy, as the ovaries are no longer present to secrete hormones. With their sudden absence, replacement is needed to prevent symptoms of hormone withdrawal. An additional reason for using natural estrogen is to replace synthetic estrogen as described previously, before weaning off estrogen altogether.

Women who suffer from severe hot flashes and night sweats are often helped with low doses of natural estrogen. Again, using the lowest dose of natural estrogen to decrease or eliminate symptoms is much safer than replacing it with high doses. This must always be done under the guidance of a physician who monitors blood levels to ensure the estradiol to progesterone ratio is therapeutic and safe.

Hormone imbalance and withdrawal can cause adrenal stress aggravating the symptoms of fatigue and exhaustion. If present over a long period of time, this can lead to adrenal fatigue where the adrenal glands are unable to produce adequate amounts of the hormones needed for health and well-being. In this case, a low dose of natural estrogen for symptomatic relief can decrease adrenal stress.

Estriol cream

As mentioned earlier, estriol (E3) is a form of estrogen that is produced almost exclusively during pregnancy by the developing fetus when it crosses the placental barrier and enters the mother's body. It has been found to be safer than estradiol (E2), in women who are not pregnant, as it carries a much lower risk of uterine and breast cancers than estradiol. Estriol provides benefits to the vagina, cervix, and vulva. Vaginal atrophy resulting from the absence of estrogen can cause symptoms of vaginal pain, bleeding, cystitis, and painful intercourse. *Vaginal insertion of estriol in the form of a cream is helpful in restoring moisture and reducing the occurrence of urethral and bladder inflammation.* Synthetic estradiol inserted intra-vaginally, can increase the blood estrogen level, causing an increased risk of breast and uterine cancers and additional health risks previously mentioned. In contrast, vaginal insertion of Estriol cream does not carry these risks. Estriol undergoes only minimal conversion into estradiol in the body, presenting few if any health risks, and greatly increases vaginal moisture, virtually eliminating vaginal dryness.

DHEA

DHEA is a vital adrenal hormone, which is a *precursor* of estrogen, progesterone, and testosterone. A precursor is a chemical or molecule that gives rise to another chemical or molecule. Under conditions of chronic stress and adrenal fatigue, DHEA levels can fall. A blood test can measure its level and multiple DHEA levels measured during the day give the most accurate reading. The morning level can provide adequate information to determine whether adrenal stress is present and whether DHEA supplementation is needed.

Short-term supplementation to restore the DHEA level can be extremely helpful in *decreasing fatigue and restoring vitality.* DHEA is available as an over-the-counter supplement, but should *only be used for short periods of time at low doses and under the guidance of a physician.* It should be weaned once its levels rise and its blood levels should be carefully monitored. When DHEA is taken without supervision, it can increase the risk of hormone-sensitive cancers.

Any level of chronic stress can lead to adrenal fatigue. Once the stress is managed or passes, the adrenals are able to recover and restore the DHEA level. The body is extremely resilient when cared for with an understanding of how to support its process of restoring balance. Once balance is restored, the adrenals can recover completely without the need for external support.

The thyroid during menopause

The thyroid gland regulates our metabolism and feeling of well-being. T4 or thyroxine and T3 or triiodothyronine is produced by the thyroid gland. T4 and T3 exist in a protein bound and "free" or unbound state. Free hormones regulate cellular function. TSH, or Thyroid Stimulating Hormone, is a hormone produced by the pituitary gland that stimulates the thyroid gland to produce T4 and T3. When free hormone levels decrease, the TSH level increases; when they increase, TSH decreases, due to a reduced need for thyroid stimulation. The optimal range for TSH is between 1 and 2.

It is worth noting that estrogen dominance can affect thyroid function, particularly the level of free T3 (fT3), rarely tested by primary care physicians or endocrinologists. The mechanism of fT3 reduction by estrogen dominance is unrecognized and therefore unknown, but has a profound impact on a woman's well-being in midlife. Replacing it to a normal level quickly restores a woman's feeling of well-being and eases her ability to lose weight and recover from the chronic fatigue that accompanies a low fT3 level. Free T4 (fT4) also affects vitality and weight and is the one more commonly tested and replaced.

My hope is that as we observe and experience the protective effects of natural or bio-identical hormones over time, their use will become standard therapy. Until clinical research in the U.S. is funded to study their effects, many traditional physicians will continue to resist prescribing them. When using natural hormones, we must always rely on scientific method and the clinical experience of physicians who have prescribed them for decades to thousands of patients. The data from Europe offers clinical guidance for prescribing natural hormones and has demonstrated their safety for the past three decades.

All hormone usage carries a certain level of risk. The field of natural hormone therapy is one that continues to evolve and grow. We must remain informed and stay open minded, always using science as our guide. Even though natural hormones have been shown to carry less risk than synthetic ones, they should be used only under the guidance of a physician who practices with rigorous scientific method, a high standard-of-care, and is skilled in both the art and science of hormone balancing.

4

Food as Medicine

Let food be your medicine and medicine be your food.
~Hippocrates, 390 B.C.

Our cultural relationship with food has a profound affect on our personal relationship with it. In many parts of the world, sharing a meal is central to the physical and emotional nourishment of family and community. It is at the heart of the dinner table and the focal point of social gatherings. It is a catalyst for connection. It is even seen as a form of living art and is the basis for health in most of the world. Viewed from this context, food is the foundation of health and well-being. Cultures that value food through this context are healthy and happy.

American's have a dysfunctional relationship with food. It is not considered integral to health. The health care system does not acknowledge its role in health or illness. It is not seen as a form of art or nourishment. It is not central to our time together at the dinner table. We are the country that created "fast food." In addition, eating is a highly charged emotional issue for us. Our focus is on dieting, not nourishment, on weight loss, not health. Food is associated with feelings of failure and shame, and the relationship that many American women have with it is far from sacred. Physicians receive little or no training in nutrition. Hospital dieticians are not ecologically focused and follow health guidelines dictated by corporate health care and "agribusiness" which lack an ecological and sustainable perspective. They do not educate their patients to view food as central to health. On the contrary, they focus on its calorie content rather than nutritional value.

They lay emphasis on quantity over quality, which triggers fear and scarcity. Our relationship with food needs to be reframed and healed for society to be truly healthy. We need to understand the intrinsic relationship between food and health.

Europeans have a better relationship with food than we do. Food is central to their culture. Europeans began the "slow food" movement. They drew this from their experience of generations that considered food to be the foundation of health. Seen as integral to health, Europeans have a positive and healing relationship with food. It is the same for people in other parts of the world. Other cultures understand the importance of a healthy diet and lifestyle in the promotion of health and well-being.

Food consumed in the U.S. is largely synthetic, processed, and genetically modified. It takes effort and expense to eat whole foods that are unprocessed and organically grown. Preparing and eating meals is seen as a chore. Preparing meals takes time so people seek to maximize their time on more "productive" pursuits than cooking. Our relationship with food lacks heart and understanding. It lacks consciousness. We need the awareness to understand that when we eat unnatural, processed, and genetically modified foods we do not feel full or satisfied. Because we lack a positive association between food and health, our relationship with food is dysfunctional. This relationship does not nourish or sustain us at any level. Because processed food does not satsify hunger, people eat larger amounts of it, increasing their caloric intake. Foods labeled as "low fat" substitute carbohydrates for fat. Sugar and starches that are heavily processed and added to enhance flavor comprise the bulk of calories in "low fat" foods. People become addicted to foods that are high in sugar, altering their physiology and their mood. This pattern of overconsumption has caused obesity and chronic inflammatory diseases currently epidemic in our country. Our health care system views going on a diet as a solution to this problem.

The "diet and weight loss" industry is a multibillion-dollar industry with a failure rate of 97%. It's focus is to control the volume of food with little to no emphasis on the quality necessary to support nourishment and health. This does not heal our unhealthy relationship with food; rather, it polarizes it. Food becomes the enemy that we work hard to resist.

Midlife is a time when a woman's relationship with food takes center stage. During midlife, a woman's body begins to change. As muscle is replaced with fat, her caloric needs decrease. In addition, she may become less active due to fatigue and perimenopausal symptoms. When hormones become imbalanced creating a state of chronic stress, women can lose their vitality and vigor when they eat foods high in carbohydrates and sugar. Hormone imbalance can cause lethargy and fatigue which decreases the will power needed to stay healthy. Many midlife women eat comfort foods to restore energy and medicate feelings. It is the only way they know how to comfort themselves, as society does not offer them a healthy framework for emotional support. They confuse emotional for physical hunger. The act of eating does not heal emotions. It is a mere substitute. When midlife women eat for emotional comfort, they do not provide their bodies with needed nourishment. It leaves them malnourished, craving needed nutrients. Their lack of awareness of how to nourish their bodies is a result of learned behavior. Over time, this becomes a pattern which results in illness and obesity.

This problem is epidemic among midlife women. Physicians do not address these issues central to women's health, and many suffer in silence. They are unable to access the self-care needed to engage self-control while under stress. Since they don't have a safe place to heal their relationship with food, many find their way to traditional diet and weight-loss programs where they feel pressure to succeed at losing weight and shame when they don't. Hospital dieticians offer dietary protocols that are difficult to follow, many of which promote chronic inflammation. Women are too ashamed to disclose their struggle to follow them. Unless we explore this dilemma, we will not be able to find lasting solutions to our health. This topic is of great importance for midlife women. My goal is to explore some of these issues to release the distortions currently present in our relationship with food, and restore it to one that is healthy and whole. To accomplish this, we need to first understand how food can help or harm us; which foods promote health, and how our emotional well-being impacts our relationship with food.

The effect of food on the midlife body

In order for us to support our bodies with healthy food, it is important to understand our changing body's needs. This understanding is of prime importance for us to make healthy choices. Midlife marks a time when the switch to natural, organic, and earth-based foods becomes critical for restoring health. Because cells are more vulnerable under the influence of changing hormones, the chemical makeup, energy, and vitality of the foods we eat has a greater positive impact on them. Similarly, if unhealthy foods are eaten, they can rapidly influence our body's cell structure *toward* disease and increase our vulnerability to it. Our cells are constantly engaged in repairing cell damage. Due to the increased biological sensitivity present in the midlife body, when whole foods are added to the diet, they can even repair cell damage that resulted from unhealthy foods consumed in the past.

The sensitive midlife body

The sensitivity of receptors on the cell surface increases in midlife and women become more sensitive to foods that they could previously tolerate, such as: *gluten, dairy, sugar, and alcohol.* Many midlife women gain weight, have joint inflammation, muscle pain and foggy thinking due to the side effects of these foods. I advise them to try a diet free of gluten, alcohol, and processed foods for three months, while also reducing their intake of dairy and processed sugar. Moderately reducing or eliminating these foods restores *clarity and vitality* and significantly improves inflammatory symptoms. A majority of women who eliminate these foods also lose a significant amount of weight. Their hot flashes and night sweats improve, and their skin becomes supple and vibrant. As they introduce root vegetables, greens, brown rice, and quinoa into their diet, they experience increased energy and resilience. Many of these foods have been shown in clinical studies to have a cholesterol-lowering effect. Cholesterol levels can drop as much as 100 points in a few months without medications when these dietary changes are made in conjunction with moderate exercise. In addition, they significantly reduce the incidence of heart disease, diabetes, and cancer.

Dietary influences on estrogen dominance

Estrogen dominance is aggravated by the pesticide-laden processed foods we eat, as pesticide residues on plants have estrogenic effects in our body. These are the xenoestrogens (synthetic estrogens) mentioned in chapter 3. Meat and dairy are laden with hormone residues that accumulate in the human body and increase the estrogen to progesterone ratio. The epidemic use of synthetic hormones in agribusiness, as well as their rising concentrations in the groundwater from animal runoff and the urine of women taking synthetic hormones and oral contraceptives, creates an unhealthy environment that puts everybody at risk for estrogen dominance. It makes us vulnerable to breast and uterine cancers, fibroid tumors, endometriosis, hypothyroidism, insulin resistance, hypertension, weight gain, heart disease, and the myriad of symptoms caused by estrogen dominance. *Estrogen dominance opposes thyroid function* and decreases metabolic drive, creating a losing battle for women trying to lose weight with calorie control and exercise. Physicians rarely, if ever, address these factors that also contribute to menopausal symptoms. In addition, using synthetic hormone replacement for perimenopausal symptom management can increase a woman's risk of estrogen dominance and its associated symptoms and risks.

Heart disease in women

Heart disease is the leading cause of death among American women. Despite growing advances in technological medicine, a quarter of all deaths before the age of 65 are from heart attacks. *Inflammatory foods are the leading cause of coronary artery disease.* When we eat foods high in sugar or simple carbohydrates (which break down to sugar in the body), our arteries become inflamed. Most of these foods are high in saturated fat and partially hydrogenated oils and accelerate the formation of coronary plaque. This also increases blood cholesterol levels for which cholesterol lowering medications are prescribed. *High cholesterol is NOT a risk factor in over half of the heart attacks in our country.* Despite this fact, cholesterol-lowering medications are some of the most frequently prescribed medications in midlife. In the health care system, nutrition and lifestyle are not emphasized as treatments for preventing and reversing heart disease (or any disease). Physicians who do not inform their patients about the importance of lifestyle modification for the prevention and treatment of illness cannot make an impact on preventing future occurrences of cardiac events.

Sadly, physicians who focus on prevention in their medical practice are not adequately compensated for time spent educating their patients. The majority of patients are left to educate themselves about these issues. It is vitally important that patients educate and empower themselves with the information available on the significant impact that lifestyle can have on health.

It was believed for decades that a *fall* in estrogen levels after menopause was the cause for an increased incidence of heart attacks. Premenopausal women have fewer heart attack deaths than postmenopausal women. The more likely hormonal culprit is not the lack of estrogen, but the lack of *progesterone*. This has been shown in numerous studies from Europe. My own clinical observation is that women become more sensitive to cellular wear and tear from stress hormones due to *falling progesterone levels and estrogen dominance*. Their bodies manifest illness with greater intensity after menopause, especially when inflammatory foods are consumed. When women are stressed, adrenalin and cortisol, the main stress hormones, increase in the bloodstream. Often, these cause small tears in the coronary arteries that become foci for plaque formation. Stress hormones also cause coronary artery spasm. *Under their influence, a 20 to 30% occlusion in an artery can clamp down to a 100% closure causing a heart attack or coronary event.* Natural progesterone relaxes the coronary arteries and reduces arterial spasm that can lead to heart attacks. *It also increases the beneficial cholesterol, HDL,* which when present at high levels, is able to clear harmful cholesterol from the body.

Multiple studies have shown that *synthetic* estrogen and *synthetic* progesterone (progestin) *increase* the risk of coronary artery spasm. Many physicians do not differentiate between synthetic and natural progesterone and do not prescribe the latter, leading to a perpetuation of estrogen dominance from synthetic hormone replacement and its associated symptoms and risks. In fact, many discourage patients from using natural hormones without a scientific understanding of their benefits.

With the burgeoning amount of information available about food and nutrition, women are confused about what diets to follow, what supplements to take, and how to weave lifestyle changes that incorporate whole foods into their pantries, refrigerators, and bodies. For some, this is the first time they are learning about healthy eating. Many of my midlife patients have spent most of their lives eating prepared and processed foods purchased from the freezer section of the grocery store. Eating these aggravates inflammation, estrogen dominance and its associated symptoms. Many women have never cooked whole foods and become used to eating packaged foods that are processed. Now they must learn the association between food and health, the importance of true nourishment and the healing power of whole foods.

Easy food rules

The educational framework that is most successful in my medical practice is simple: eating should be easy, simple, and fun. The following points can be helpful in creating a nutritional plan that is fast, easy, and provides maximal health benefits:

1. Half of your plate should have color, the color of organic vegetables—green, orange, red, purple, or yellow.

2. A quarter of your plate should contain an organic protein-rich food, preferably fish (not farmed), or *hormone and antibiotic-free* free-range organic chicken, beans, lentils, or tofu, and minimal to no red meat.

3. A quarter of your plate should have an organic complex carbohydrate such as brown rice, quinoa, or wild rice. Any white-colored processed foods made with white flour or white rice should be minimized (Figure 3). Many pastas are made from genetically modified wheat and are high in gluten. Many organic gluten-free pastas are available at your local grocery store which can be a healthy substitute for genetically-modified gluten rich pastas.

4. Eat nuts and seeds between meals and small amounts of dark chocolate if sugar cravings are intense.

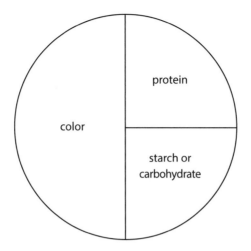

Figure 3: The optimum plate

5. Drink no more than *one cup* of organic coffee per day; drink 6 to 8 glasses of filtered water per day (preferably not from a plastic bottle) and 1 to 2 cups of green tea.

6. Eat a handful of organic berries. Blueberries and strawberries are the most nutrient dense.

7. *The darker and deeper the color food is in its natural form, the richer it is in antioxidants.*

8. Eat plenty of organic root vegetables. Always choose organic because root vegetables are scavengers that keep the soil clean by absorbing pesticides more than other vegetables do.

9. Eat a moderate amount of *organic* soy. A recent study from China performed with 5000 women ages 25–75 with estrogen positive and negative breast cancers divided the women into two groups. One group ate 5g or less of fermented soy per day, and the other group ate 12g or more of soy per day. The results showed *a 30% reduction in mortality in the group that ate 12g or more of soy per day as part of their diet.* Soy is a *phytoestrogen* or a plant-based estrogen. Phytoestrogens are effective in reducing menopausal

symptoms and decreasing a woman's risk of breast cancer. Natto, tempeh, miso, and tamari are several forms of fermented soy. However, it is necessary to consume *only organic soy*, as nonorganic soy is heavily sprayed with pesticides, and the majority of it is genetically modified.

The optimum plate

Diets often fail because they are complicated and have too many rules. It is important to keep our relationship with food simple. Living in harmony with nature and consuming mostly earth-based foods is a good way to support this relationship.

My patients have greatly benefited from simplifying their diets with the understanding of how to divide their plate. An easy way to make sure you are getting a balanced diet, as mentioned before is to divide your plate into three sections. *First divide it in half and then divide one half into two quarters. Half of your plate should consist of dark-colored vegetables; a quarter should consist of a protein, and a quarter should consist of a complex carbohydrate* (Figure 3). If two meals a day are eaten according to this formula, you will get *80% more nutrition than you are currently receiving from your diet.*

Good rules of thumb:

• Dark-colored vegetables and fruits have plenty of cancer fighting properties. Eat a variety of them daily.

• Dark leafy greens such as kale, collards, Swiss chard, romaine lettuce, and spinach are nutrient rich. *Kale is the most nutrient dense green you can eat*, packing beta carotene, vitamin K and C, lutein, calcium, and sulforaphane (a chemical with potent anti-cancer properties).

• Minimize your intake of *acidic foods* such as dairy and red meat. All *animal protein, including dairy creates an acidic environment* in the body. To neutralize this acidity, the body draws calcium from the bones, increasing bone loss. Over time, this causes a reduction in bone density that leads to osteopenia and osteoporosis, currently epidemic in the U.S.

• Refined sugar is toxic to the body.

• Obtain information on nutrition and health from reputable nutrition books or practitioners, not television advertisements.

• Eat foods from the *produce section* in the far end of the grocery store, not from a box. The majority of boxed/packaged foods and foods located in the middle aisles of a grocery store are processed.

• Eat as much *local organic* produce as possible. It has less chance of being nutrient poor. Produce shipped from long distances loses its nutritional content over the time spent in transport. In addition, supporting local organic farmers and sustainable farming practices supports your community.

• Minimize salt intake.

• Replace butter and margarine for cooking with monounsaturated and polyunsaturated oils such as olive oil and canola oil. Although it is saturated fat, coconut oil has been shown to help dementia, skin conditions, and remains stable when heated.

• Eat whole grains and a variety of nuts and seeds.

• Minimize the intake of gluten rich foods such as wheat and white bread, cookies and crackers, and white flour-based pasta.

• Replace foods containing processed flour with organic and non-hybridized or sprouted substitutes.

• Keep portion sizes small and eat until you are no longer hungry. This will require you to remain conscious while eating.

• Avoid foods that are high in pesticide residues. The best way to avoid eating these is to eat organic fruits and vegetables. The following fruits and vegetables, called "the dirty dozen," are classified as containing the highest concentrations of pesticide residues:

1. Celery
2. Peaches
3. Strawberries
4. Apples
5. Blueberries
6. Nectarines
7. Bell peppers
8. Spinach
9. Kale
10. Cherries
11. Potatoes
12. Grapes

Insulin resistance

The body produces a hormone called *insulin* in response to a sugar load from a meal. The main sources of sugar consumed in the U.S. are refined sugars and simple carbohydrates in the form of bread, pasta, snacks and desserts. Carbohydrates break down to sugar in the body. Insulin is required to mobilize sugar into cells where it is used for energy. If a person eats a large amount of sugar or carbohydrate containing foods, the body does not need to use up its fat stores for energy, especially when not exercising. It further adds to them, as excess sugar is also converted into fat and not into energy. This is how a high carbohydrate intake can cause obesity.

When sugar or glucose enters the body, it signals the pancreas to produce *insulin*. Insulin levels increase with elevations in blood sugar. Insulin's role is to keep the blood sugar within a narrow range (between 80 and 120). A blood sugar level above this range can be toxic to cells. Insulin converts excess blood sugar into a sugar storage compound called glycogen, stored in the liver and muscles. If the blood sugar is too high, it is converted to fat rather than glycogen, and stored in fatty tissues.

When large quantities of sugar or glucose enter the cells, the body secretes a large amount of insulin. Over time, this causes a now common condition called *insulin resistance.* Glucose levels rise in the blood, signaling the need for more insulin. This creates a vicious cycle resulting in high levels of *both glucose and insulin* causing an increase in cholesterol, blood pressure, belly fat, and arterial plaque. This condition is called *metabolic syndrome.* It is believed that 60% of heart disease in women is caused by insulin resistance.

The high levels of insulin and sugar in the blood also increases the production of androgens or male hormones in the female body. This accelerates their conversion into estrogen, further aggravating estrogen dominance. This can cause a condition called Polycystic Ovarian Syndrome (PCOS). Women with PCOS have painful and irregular menstrual cycles, and a higher incidence of obesity, hypertension, insulin resistance, and infertility.

Insulin resistance is a precursor to:
- diabetes
- heart disease
- high cholesterol
- abdominal obesity
- estrogen dominance
- fatigue
- hypothyroidism
- water retention
- hypertension
- irregular menses
- polycystic ovarian syndrome

To counteract this cycle and decrease insulin resistance, a healthy diet consisting of ample vegetables, fiber, protein, and complex carbohydrates is necessary in addition to regular aerobic exercise. We need to eat more whole foods and minimize sugar to maintain health and prevent the development of metabolic syndrome and PCOS.

Gluten sensitivity

Gluten sensitivity has become a rising health condition and concern in midlife in the U.S. Gluten is a protein contained in flour that creates the elasticity present in dough. Unlike decades ago, our wheat is now a hybrid crop, unnatural for our body to process. The majority of the wheat in the U.S. is genetically modified and does not resemble natural wheat. In addition, the original wheat grinding process preserved the oil in the wheat berry. Since wheat was coarse, when eaten, gluten was not released in high concentrations into the blood stream. In contrast, today's wheat processing methods pulverize the wheat berry destroying its integrity and releasing high concentrations of gluten into flour. When we eat foods containing hybridized wheat flour processed in this manner, the gluten contained in it is easily released into our bloodstream. Bread, processed crackers, cookies, and baked goods contain high concentrations of gluten. Oats, barley, and rye may contain small amounts of gluten. If you are sensitive to gluten, you can tell by the way you feel after eating a meal that is high in gluten.

Gluten can cause irritable bowel symptoms such as intestinal spasms and irregular bowel movements. In addition to abdominal bloating, gluten sensitivity can also cause depression and anxiety, as well as neurological symptoms such as numbness, tingling, mental fog, joint pain, headaches, skin rashes, and an increase in belly fat. Some cases of mental illness have shown profound improvement when gluten is eliminated from the diet.

There is a large amount of surface area present in the small intestines due to the folds that form their inner lining called "villi." Their function is to aid in the absorption of nutrients from food. When a person is gluten sensitive, villi become flattened due to inflammation that causes their eventual breakdown. This decreases the surface area of the small intestines, decreasing the absorption of nutrients, particularly iron and vitamin D.

Blood levels of iron and vitamin D can be measured by laboratory testing. If they are both low, despite the consumption of a balanced diet and supplementation, this can indicate gluten intolerance. When gluten is eliminated from the diet of gluten sensitive individuals, the villi grow back within several months, and the surface area of the intestines is restored. This leads to a dramatic improvement in iron and vitamin D levels and a decrease in symptoms. If gluten is reintroduced after eliminating it for a few months, an exaggeration of symptoms, especially abdominal bloating and mental fog, may occur. In my medical practice, patients can quickly tell if they are gluten sensitive after eliminating gluten from their diet. They begin to think more clearly, lose weight, and feel more energized.

The most conclusive test to determine gluten sensitivity is a small intestinal biopsy. Since this is costly and invasive, it is not recommended unless one's symptoms are severe. Discontinuing gluten for a period of one to two months and then reintroducing it with resulting symptom recurrence is a reliable indicator for gluten sensitivity or intolerance.

Celiac disease is a condition where gluten is considered a foreign substance by the body. With this disease, the body exhibits an exaggerated and sometimes dangerous inflammatory response upon ingesting gluten. This can present with symptoms such as severe rashes, diarrhea, irritable bowel symptoms, depression, anxiety, chronic fatigue, malabsorption, and sometimes even mild symptoms of mental illness. A blood test can demonstrate if a person has celiac disease, although it may not be 100% definitive.

A very disturbing problem in our food supply at this time is the high prevalence of *genetically modified* grains such as wheat, corn, and soy. The DNA of genetically modified foods (GMO) has been chemically altered to make them resistant to insect and pest attacks. Since they are no longer natural, when ingested, these grains appear as foreign to the body, causing a severe inflammatory reactions within tissues. Inflammatory diseases have been more prevalent in the U.S. since the introduction of genetically modified foods.

Prostaglandins

Prostaglandins are hormone-like substances derived from fats such as Omega-3 and Omega-6. Good fats create prostaglandins that are good for the body. These are called *series 1-prostaglandins*. They reduce the stickiness of blood, control cholesterol levels, improve immune function, maintain fluid balance, and reduce inflammation. Series 1-prostaglandins are derived through Omega-3 from fish, nuts, and seeds. The highest concentrations of Omega-3 can be found in mackerel and cold water fish like trout and salmon.

Pro-inflammatory prostaglandins which synthesize *series 2-prostaglandins* are found in animal fats, particularly red meat, dairy, corn oil, high-fructose corn syrup, or any processed corn products, hydrogenated or trans-fats such as margarine, shortening, or lard. These are directly linked to coronary plaque and arthritic conditions. They are associated with inflammation and coronary thrombosis (*blood clots in the coronary arteries*). These are the prostaglandins that cause premenstrual syndrome (PMS) and uterine cramps. An effective way to heal symptoms of menstrual cramping and PMS is to increase the intake of anti-inflammatory foods such as fresh vegetables and fruits, flax oil, nuts, seeds, legumes, whole grains, extra virgin olive oil, Omega-3, and reduce the intake of animal and synthetically hydrogenated fats. High fructose corn syrup is *highly inflammatory* to cells and should be completely eliminated from the diet. Flax oil, fish, vegetables, nuts, seeds, organic eggs, whole grains, and legumes should be increased. These modifications in food choices alone can significantly improve PMS and menstrual cramps as well as the common perimenopausal symptoms experienced by so many women in the U.S. today.

Supplements for the midlife woman

Some basic supplements to consider in midlife peri- and postmenopausal years are:

1. A multivitamin: A food-based organic multivitamin available at the health food store can deliver essential trace minerals and is easy to digest. It is important that it not contain additives or chemical preservatives. It should be taken daily.

2. Vitamin D is a necessary vitamin shown in clinical studies to decrease the recurrence of breast cancer. It increases the body's core strength, builds bone density, and improves exercise tolerance. It is necessary to check blood levels if supplementing with this vitamin, as it is fat soluble and can become toxic if too much is taken and exceeds safe blood levels. In the Pacific Northwest and the Midwest, women have a need for greater doses of vitamin D in the winter months due to the prolonged lack of sun, since vitamin D is produced in the skin during sun exposure. Caucasians and African-Americans do not produce as much vitamin D as people with olive skin tones. The best food sources of vitamin D are herring, mackerel, salmon, oysters, and eggs. The best vitamin D supplement is cholecalciferol or vitamin D3 of animal origin. Some physicians prescribe vitamin D in doses as high as 50,000 IU (international units) per month as a single dose. It is better to divide it into smaller daily doses taken over time and to monitor blood levels. The usual daily dose of vitamin D should be around 1000 to 2000 IUs per day or more as directed by your physician. People who suffer from colitis or bowel diseases, including gluten intolerance, risk vitamin D deficiency due to malabsorption by the intestines. It is important to supplement with adequate doses of vitamin D3 to maintain a blood level around 50 to 60. In women at risk for or a history of breast cancer, maintaining this level is important in decreasing the incidence of recurrence.

3. Vitamin E: Most food-based multivitamins contain an adequate daily supply of vitamin E (400 IUs per day). If you suffer from symptoms of breast tenderness and hot flashes, the addition of a vitamin E supplement can help ease these symptoms.

4. Omega-3 fish oil: *Omega-3 is one of the most important supplements one can take.* It is actually a supplement that everyone should take from cradle to grave. Our body does not produce DHA (docosahexaenoic acid), the active component of Omega-3, so we are dependent on food sources to obtain it. The richest food source for DHA is cold water fish. Our ancestors consumed a 1:1 ratio of Omega-3 to Omega-6 fatty acids. Omega-6 fatty acids are present in vegetable oils in addition to red meat and processed foods that compete with Omega-3 for space in the brain. Today Americans consume an approximate ratio of 1:25 of Omega-3 to Omega-6, due to their heavy consumption of animal products and processed foods (made with Omega-6 rich fats and oils), and their low consumption of fish like salmon and sardines that are rich in Omega-3. Krill oil is also high in Omega-3. Omega-3 has been *shown to reduce the symptoms of PMS, particularly menstrual cramps and mild depression.* Mood, emotions and mental concentration are adversely affected by low levels of Omega-3 in the diet. Omega-3 fats maintain the suppleness of the membranes surrounding the brain. They also *increase the levels of dopamine and serotonin*, two neurotransmitters when low are linked with depression, anxiety, and addictive behavior. High levels of DHA present in fish oil are critical to the promotion of healthy brain function and development, and can have a *significant impact on improving depression, anxiety, ADHD, and ADD.* DHA can also decrease joint inflammation, muscle pain, and reduce the incidence of muscle and ligament injury. EPA (eicosapentaenoic acid) is a fatty acid also present in fish oil that has a *significantly positive impact on cardiovascular health.* It has been shown to decrease total cholesterol, increase HDL, decrease inflammation in blood vessels (thereby *decreasing cholesterol*

plaque formation), and decrease the risk of blood clots in addition to several kinds of kidney disease.

An effective Omega-3 supplement should be pharmaceutically graded and micro-distilled to remove potential traces of mercury, and should contain at least 300 mg of DHA per 1000 mg of Omega-3 and 300 mg of EPA per capsule. I recommend a daily maintenance dose of 2000 mg of Omega-3, (600 mg of DHA and 600 mg of EPA). Therapeutic doses are between 4000 to 8000 mg per day. Omega-3 has a blood-thinning effect, so it is important to talk with your physician about its safety while taking blood thinners, or if bleeding tendencies are present. Wild-caught salmon has approximately 1000 mg of Omega-3 per 3 oz. serving. Farmed salmon *does not* contain high concentrations of Omega-3 and, in addition, is high in pesticide residues as most of the farmed salmon feed is heavily treated with pesticides. Atlantic salmon has higher concentrations of mercury than Pacific, Norwegian or Alaskan salmon. Flax oil, a vegetarian form of Omega-3 *does not* contain DHA or EPA but ALA (alpha linoleic acid) which has anti-inflammatory properties different than DHA and EPA present in fish oil. It has *not* been shown to have the same therapeutic benefits as EPA and DHA.

5. Magnesium is a beneficial supplement for women who suffer from leg cramps during perimenopause and menopause. Estrogen dominance can cause magnesium depletion resulting in these symptoms. Estrogen dominance increases the influx of water into the cells and causes the loss of potassium and magnesium from cells. This can lead to fatigue and muscle cramping. Moreover, the influx of water into cells can cause (water) weight gain, hypertension, and headaches. When natural progesterone is used in therapeutic doses, these symptoms dissipate and the addition of magnesium can ease the cramps and relax muscles. It is not wise to add potassium to the supplement regimen unless the measured blood potassium is low and it is

prescribed and monitored with blood levels. Too high or low blood levels of potassium can result in fatal heart arrhythmias.

6. Calcium is used to build bones and to promote heart health. It is necessary for healthy cell membranes and muscle function. It is best to consume calcium from *food sources such as greens rather than as a vitamin supplement.* Calcium supplements have been linked with the formation of calcifications in the coronary arteries and breast tissue. The form of supplemental calcium best absorbed is calcium citrate combined with magnesium and boron. If you have osteopenia (moderate loss of bone density) or osteoporosis (significant loss of bone density), it is important to consult with your physician before starting a calcium supplement.

Caffeine, alcohol, and acidifying foods such as meat and dairy, in addition to causing estrogen dominance, can cause a loss of calcium in bones. The best sources of calcium are almonds, brewer's yeast, parsley, corn, artichokes, cooked dried beans, dark leafy greens, and broccoli. Problems arising from excess calcium, such as kidney stones, can occur while taking *excessive* doses of calcium and vitamin D. *Plants are a healthier source of calcium than dairy.*

7. Vitamin C strengthens the immune system and fights infections. It is a potent antioxidant that can protect the body from cancer. The best food sources of vitamin C are peppers, broccoli, kiwi fruit, cabbage, watercress, strawberries, lemons, oranges, and citrus fruits in general. Cigarette smoking, alcohol, fried foods, and stress rob the body of vitamin C. The daily recommended dose for Vitamin C is 1000 to 2000 mg.

Dietary influences of yin and yang balance

It is important to understand that all food contains energy. Traditional medicine divides food into three categories—fat, protein, and carbohydrates. It does not take into account the intrinsic energy

FOOD AS MEDICINE

contained in food and how this energy affects our bodies. If we acknowledged the importance of this in our culture, we would stop eating processed foods and only eat whole foods.

In Eastern traditions, the prevailing perspective is that the forces of Yin and Yang effect and shape the energies in the world. *Yin* energy has cool, damp, and dark qualities. It is the dark portion of the Yin and Yang symbol. *Yang* is warm, dry, and light. It is the white part of the Yin and Yang symbol. Night is Yin; day is Yang; winter is Yin; summer is Yang. Cool is Yin; hot is Yang. Yin is the coolant for the Yang engine of the body.

All foods contain these energetic qualities. Yin and Yang energies need to be balanced in order for us to be healthy and feel well. During perimenopause, Yin energy begins to recede resulting in the prominence of Yang. When Yin energy recedes and Yang predominates, we experience the common symptoms of perimenopause and menopause such as:

- hot flashes
- anxiety
- acid reflux
- dry hair
- night sweats
- hypertension
- dry skin
- skin rashes

Yin deficiency also causes fatigue that causes us to crave sugar. Our bodies attempt to compensate for the lack of energy caused by Yin deficiecy by increasing our cravings for sources of quick energy such as sugar and carbohydrates. Yin deficiency and Yang excess is common in the U.S. because the processed American diet is high in Yang energy. Processed foods, alcohol, and meat are high in Yang energy, hence they tend to be warming to the body, exaggerating Yin and Yang imbalance and aggravating menopausal symptoms.

If we consider which foods contain higher amounts of Yin or Yang energies, we can choose foods according to the nature of our symptoms. If we suffer from symptoms of Yang excess such as hot flashes or night sweats, we can decrease these symptoms

YIN FOODS: calming, nourishing, cooling
Cucumber, daikon radish, eggplant, dandelion greens, romaine lettuce, endive, spinach, millet, celery, cauliflower, bok choy, apples, apricots, asparagus, carrots, Chinese cabbage, zucchini, turnips, rutabaga, squash, watercress, cantaloupe, green tea, seaweed

YANG FOODS: stimulating, energetic, warming
Meat, lamb, beef, chicken, cheese, salt, bell peppers, shrimp, mustard greens, onions, scallions, chives, garlic, egg yolks, leeks, kale

NEUTRAL FOODS:
Beets, brown rice, buckwheat, chard, corn, fish, lettuce, peas, string beans, sweet potatoes, taro root, turkey, yams

by increasing our intake of Yin foods. If we feel slow, sluggish and stagnant, we can eat more warming foods like spices, chicken, eggs, and kale. It is recommended to eat more Yin (cooling) foods during midday and more Yang (warming) foods in the morning and evening. This is because the morning and evening are cooler and midday is warmer. Eating in this manner results in balancing the body's energy. More Yin foods should be eaten during the hot season and more Yang foods during the cool season. This is a helpful way to balance our body's energy.

Most perimenopausal women in midlife, suffer from Yin deficiency. The foods they eat should be higher in Yin energy to compensate for this loss. A practitioner trained in Traditional Chinese Medicine can help balance the Yin and Yang energies in midlife with acupuncture, Chinese herbs, and nutritional guidance.

Neutral foods are not high in either Yin or Yang energies. They are balanced and hence termed *neutral*.

Many women have strong reactions to *alcohol* and *dairy* during midlife. Their hot flashes and night sweats improve significantly when they minimize or eliminate their intake of these foods. There is an overwhelming amount of evidence to suggest that an earth-based, vegetarian diet is best for preventing cancer and heart disease. It also contains more balance in Yin/Yang energies. As we choose our foods consciously with a basic understanding of how to keep our energy balanced, we can promote health and vitality and prevent many of the illnesses caused by our unhealthy lifestyles by reducing inflammation and improving the integrity of our immune system.

Exercise

There is no substitute for regular aerobic exercise. It is a necessary part of self-care. My recommendation is to do *30 minutes of aerobic exercise at least five to six times per week.*

It is valuable to keep the exercise routine varied and interesting so we sustain it. It is one of the best therapies for stress reduction and weight loss, cholesterol and blood sugar reduction, for improving cardiac capacity, and decreasing depression and anxiety.

Special food considerations for Women's Health:

Foods that heal Premenstrual Syndrome (PMS)

An estimated 97% of American women have PMS at some time in their life. Dietary changes can have a significant effect on these symptoms. PMS is often triggered by estrogen dominance. Restoring hormone balance is influenced by the types of food we eat in addition to hormone balance with natural hormones. Foods high in animal or saturated fat are converted into reproductive hormones in the body. These can contribute to an imbalance in the estrogen to progesterone ratio, aggravating the symptoms of estrogen dominance.

Some simple food facts can help us make healthier food choices to support our body during perimenopause:

- Cholesterol is a precursor for reproductive hormones. It is present in animal fats and can increase hormone levels leading to hormonal imbalance.

- Many symptoms of PMS are similar to symptoms of estrogen dominance.

- The liver needs B complex to break down excess estrogen. If the diet is lacking B vitamins (green vegetables), excess estrogen will accumulate in the body.

- If one does not eat enough fiber, the intestines slow down, absorbing more estrogen into the blood stream. This increases blood levels and the likelihood for estrogen dominance.

- Xenoestrogens from nonorganic or pesticide-sprayed foods can accumulate in the body mimicking the effects of estrogen.

- Consuming nonorganic meat and dairy increases estrogen levels due to the high concentration of synthetic hormones present.

- A diet high in sugar, and low in whole foods, results in elevations of estrogen, insulin, and blood sugar levels creating mood disturbances and aggravating symptoms of estrogen dominance. This can result in PCOS, metabolic syndrome, diabetes, elevated cholesterol, inflammatory conditions, weight gain, feelings of sluggishness, and mental fog.

The *luteal phase* of the menstrual cycle (approximately two weeks before and until the onset of menses) is when sugar cravings are most prominent. This is due, in part, to Yin deficiency during this phase of the cycle (in addition to estrogen dominance). A woman under chronic stress, who consumes a diet high in synthetic estrogens, sugar and carbohydrates, will experience an exaggeration of PMS symptoms such as pelvic cramps, weight gain, fluid retention, breast tenderness, depression, and anxiety.

Progesterone has *Yin properties*. It is responsible for women's menstrual cycles and it is produced cyclically every month in menstruating women. Adequate levels of progesterone can help women feel grounded. Women feel "ungrounded" when its levels fall. Estrogen has *Yang properties*. It is produced steadily and linearly in women's bodies, consequently, hot flashes and night sweats, common Yang symptoms, result from a drop in its levels during perimenopause.

Foods for menstrual symptoms

Cramps, low back pain, headaches, heavy menstrual flow, fatigue, anxiety, and depression are common before and during menses in American women. Many of these symptoms are related to their diets which stimulate the production of series 2-prostaglandin. Arachidonic acid, present in red meat and dairy, is converted into series 2-prostaglandin. Red meat contains the *highest* level of arachidonic acid followed by lamb, pork, chicken, and turkey. It is wise to eat more vegetarian foods during the *luteal phase* of the menstrual cycle to prevent an increase in series-2 prostaglandin levels. An organic diet high in B vitamins and fiber and low in carbohydrates, sugar, and alcohol decreases the incidence of estrogen dominance and minimizes premenstrual symptoms.

If your periods are heavy, you are most likely estrogen dominant. A small amount of natural progesterone under the guidance of a physician, in combination with an organic, plant based diet, can be very therapeutic.

Foods for perimenopause and menopause

Women in Asian countries who eat a diet high in vegetables and soy with an abundance of Yin foods have fewer symptoms during the peri- and postmenopausal years. One can create Yin energy stores by eating a diet high in Yin foods during the ages of twenty to forty. This is likened to a Yin savings account that we can use during perimenopause when Yin energy recedes. These are called the "Yin years," when Yin energy is utilized for creative pursuits such as building careers, having babies, and creating families. Most of us in the U.S. eat quick energy foods (such as processed foods high in Yang energy) during Yin years and do not create the Yin energy stores needed to support our bodies during midlife. If we lack these stores in our Yin savings account, we are more likely to experience the symptoms of Yin deficiency or Yang excess as described above.

Phytoestrogens

Phytoestrogens are plant-based estrogens. Their molecular formula is similar to estrogen and they have mild estrogenic effects on the body. They decrease the stimulation of estrogen receptors on cells. Contrary to the popular belief that phytoestrogens increase cellular estrogen and aggravate estrogen dominance, *they do the opposite*; they balance estrogen and reduce the damaging effects of synthetic estrogens on cells and tissues.

Phytoestrogens:

- mimic the beneficial effects of estrogen
- block the harmful effects of high estrogen levels
- protect the body against the harmful effects of xenoestrogens
- are high in antioxidants that protect against cancer
- reduce the incidence of breast, prostate, skin and bowel cancer
- reduce cholesterol levels
- reduce the incidence of heart disease and diabetes
- help symptoms of menopause such as hot flashes, night sweats, and breast tenderness
- improve symptoms of estrogen dominance
- help maintain healthy skin
- decrease bone loss

Phytoestrogens also have an impact on *decreasing* mortality in women who have previously had breast cancer. Soybeans are high in phytoestrogens; however, it is important to *eat only organic soy,* as mentioned before, as soy is heavily sprayed with pesticides, many of which breakdown to form estrogenic fragments. Many legumes, fruits, vegetables, and whole grains also exhibit phytoestrogenic effects. Tofu, tempeh, miso, natto, tamari, and organic soybeans are also rich in phytoestrogens. When phytoestrogens are taken in pill form, such as soy-isoflavone supplements, they may be *harmful* to the body as they can adversely stimulate the estrogen receptors. Soy bars should also be avoided for the same reason. It is important to remember to consume soy in its natural, organic form as a whole food.

FOODS RICH IN PHYTOESTROGENS:

Broccoli, cauliflower, fennel, carrots, radishes, parsley, beets, apples, pomegranates, cherries, citrus fruits, soy beans, split peas, red beans, garbanzo beans, barley, oats, rice, wheat, rye, corn, garlic, sesame seeds, flax oil, extra-virgin olive oil

---

Food as medicine for symptoms of perimenopause and menopause

Food plays an important role in both aggravating and alleviating the many symptoms of menopause. When we understnd the relationship between the food we eat and the symptoms we experience, we can make healthier food choices to promote our well-being in midlife.

Foods to avoid:

- alcohol
- dairy
- excess coffee and tea
- white flour
- red meat
- refined sugar
- excess milk chocolate
- spicy foods
- white rice

Foods to include:

- soy
- legumes
- green leafy vegetables
- tofu
- nuts
- brown rice
- melons
- seafood
- sardines
- flax
- berries
- root vegetables
- miso
- green tea
- water
- seeds
- cucumbers
- apples
- salmon
- eggs
- oats

The divided plate technique can help simplify your food choices to include wholesome, phyto-nutrient, and antioxidant rich foods in your diet. You may find that many of your symptoms will heal, and your health and vitality will be restored..

The inner relationship with food

Despite the information available for making healthy food choices, a crucial question still remains in every woman's life. Why do women continue to make unhealthy food choices despite what they know about their ill effects? Why does going on a diet feel stressful? Why do diets fail 97% of the time?

In the U.S., obesity is at an all-time high. Nutritionally vacant and toxic foods are widely available. They make up the common food choices in women's lives. They are the easiest to find, with "fast food" being the least healthy and least expensive. We have normalized these familiar choices that are responsible for most of our diseases. When "low fat" foods became popular in the 1980s, carbohydrates replaced fats resulting in the epidemic of obesity. Often emotional, not physical hunger commonly influences our food choices, causing our poor health. Emotional hunger drives us to eat comfort foods high in fat and sugar. It causes a loss of satiety and we find ourselves eating even after we have had enough to physically satisfy us. For example, we often eat foods high in fat and sugar when we are under stress. They offer only a temporary feeling of comfort.

Our wounded feeling function cannot be soothed in extrinsic ways. Food does not heal our emotional pain.

Patty

Patty is a 38-year-old woman who came to me for weight loss. She had hypertension and wanted to reduce, and possibly eliminate, the blood pressure medications she was taking. Her blood pressure was only partially controlled by medication and she weighed a hundred pounds more than her ideal body weight. She needed guidance to lose weight and lower blood pressure. She followed my dietary advice for three months. *She did not lose a single pound.*

At her three-month follow-up, she confessed that she had been eating a pint of ice cream five nights a week before bed. After her family went to bed, she went to the freezer, took out the ice cream, sat at the dining room table and devoured it. It was her little secret and she felt "high" during and after this ritual. The morning after, she was always consumed by shame. Her mind was controlled by a shaming script that told her she was "no good," "worthless," and a "failure." During the day, she successfully followed my prescribed food plan. But by night, she felt the tension between her unaddressed emotional needs and what she knew was healthy for her. She was addicted to the "high" she felt when she was alone with the ice cream. She had been living this way for years. She believed she had no control over her behavior and even felt shame while describing it.

My intervention for Patty was to ask her to follow through on her ritual that evening but this time, with her *full awareness*. I asked her to stand in front of the freezer, take a deep breath, and bring her awareness to the familiar "high," and the feelings inside she was medicating. If she also brought awareness to the trance that was typical during this ritual, maybe she could break this emotionally driven pattern that was adversely impacting her health.

When she tried this exercise, she was *unable* to eat the ice cream! She told me she stood in front of the freezer and sobbed for an hour. She went to bed without her usual dose. In a moment of focused awareness, she had connected with her emotional pain that needed acknowledgement, release, and healing. It had begun to awaken during midlife and the nightly ritual with ice cream was her way of medicating it through the "high" she experienced. It put her in a trance, suppressing her feelings. In addition, it added weight, elevated her blood pressure, and triggered her shame. She needed to bring consciousness to the emotional pain that was driving her ritual. She also needed a safe space where she was validated and empowered. Only then, was she able to make a more conscious choice to not allow her emotional pain to direct her behavior and take the steps needed to heal it. This was the beginning of her healing journey. She was able to address her pain in therapy and stop the drive to medicate with food. Over the next year, she lost 50 pounds, which significantly lowered her blood pressure. By bringing consciousness to her negative script and the emotional issues driving her unhealthy behavior, she was able to heal them and reclaim her self-worth and intrinsic power. By engaging her consciousness, she not only regained her emotional, but physical health as well.

My journey

As someone who suffered from bulimia in my late teens and early twenties, I know only too well how Patty felt. For me, the bulimic ritual symbolized the binging and purging of academic material necessary to get through medical school. It was also a time where I could experience the "high" that connected me to a feeling of "control" in my life when I felt overwhelmed. It was my way of medicating this feeling. It was also a symbolic way that my psyche represented a disconnected me from my authentic self, feelings, and instinct. This disconnection did not allow others to access me. It also kept me from accessing myself.

My healing came eight years after my eating disorder began. By then, I was worn out from it. My pleas for help and my attempts for being understood and comforted were not met by the people around me. Their denial about my condition prevented me from healing. This was also a time when eating disorders were just beginning to be acknowledged by the medical system. The medical culture that I was a part of was not able to accept this kind of issue affecting one of "their own." They were unable to help me. I was left to my own resources to heal myself.

I took my intention of healing to the mirror. One afternoon, I stood in front of it and brought consciousness to what I saw in my reflection. I wanted to become conscious of my self-talk, my script. This would uncover the nature of my relationship with myself. I discovered that my self-talk was anything but positive. I felt that in order to heal, I needed to find a way to change this negative self-talk into a positive one. I uncovered a deep level of self-loathing, the result of my script. When I could not find anything positive to say about myself, I heard a voice from deep inside that instructed me to stay in front of the mirror until I found something positive to say. Not only was this unfamiliar, it was terrifying. The process took over an hour. I said something like, "I have beautiful eyes." I was determined to take this compliment to heart, and to actually feel it. It took me an additional hour to align the thought of my eyes being beautiful with my feeling function. This was only momentary and I had to work hard to actually *feel* it. This part of my process took months to accomplish. Before this, I had been unable to access any positive feelings towards who I felt I was, or how I thought I looked.

Until then, my worth was dependent only upon how well I *performed*. Only while performing *perfectly* did I feel worthy of love and acceptance. My self-identity was one of a "perfection addict." By the age of 20, I had won numerous awards, earned all A's and was a successful medical student. On the inside, I had little contact with my real self. It had been replaced by self-doubt and a self that had adapted to what I thought was expected of me. My conditioning deeply wounded my self-worth. It was only based on performance.

I awakened to this at 25 when I began to become conscious of the connection between my body and food. Simply bringing a positive thought towards myself was a new and healing experience. I became aware of how the many self-critical and fear-based thoughts affected my relationship with food. This was the gateway through which I began to heal my eating disorder. I had identified the thought patterns that led me to behave in unconscious ways that were harmful to my health. With this awareness, I could no longer identify with the neurosis that caused me to binge and purge for the illusory feeling of "control" in my life. When it became integrated, kindness and self-compassion permeated my relationship with myself. At last, I began to heal.

The journey for me, like for many others, is the journey back to our real selves. As we engage our wills and evoke our consciousness to mitigate our unhealthy rituals with food, something deeper and more heartfelt awakens. This place of self-compassion and kindness can feel unfamiliar at first. We may not trust it due to the familiar voice of the self-critic, the voice of shame within us that evokes fear. After many years of practice, it gains enough momentum to sabotage a heart-centered relationship with ourselves. It is important for us to be aware of these feelings if we are to heal our relationship with food. If we don't, our attempts at losing weight will fail 97% of the time.

Fear and food

We need to stop obeying the self-critic. We do this because society reinforces its script. Injunctions from society have wounded the individual and collective female psyche. Society bases our worth on our looks and our performance. Over time, we normalize this. This form of externalization disconnects us from our real self. Often, our family's definitions of our performance-based worth become imprinted within us, and reinforce our inner critic. Society normalizes this. Our self-evaluation is then dictated by society. It is *extrinsically* based. If we do not perform in accordance with society's expectations, we often feel shame, like we have somehow failed. This is how we define our worth. We become vulnerable to abuse when we live with the shame evoked by the inner-critic. Many women have such a loud critic in their heads (like I did) that it disassociates them from their bodies.

Many of my obese patients tell me they do not look at themselves in the mirror. They lose contact with their feeling function. Consequently, they feel emotionally regressed and vulnerable. Parts of their psyches feel infantile and they feel unsafe in their bodies. As infants, we craved oral contact for connection to feel safe.

As adults our *vulnerability* drives our need for connection to feel safe. In this state, our behavior is driven by our basic instincts. As infants, when we expressed our stress, we were fed. As adults, when we feel stressed we feed ourselves. We regress into an infantile state. We associate stress with eating. We lose our limits and boundaries. We overeat.

My work with women to help them heal their relationship with food also helps them heal their relationship with themselves. Often the emotional pressure they feel when they think about losing weight evokes their fear of failure. It is not possible to fully engage in healthy behaviors when there is fear lurking in the psyche. We need to support each other into loving ourselves enough to heal our fear and low self-worth that we have erroneously identified with our performance. We need to dismantle these conditioned feelings and reclaim our intrinsic worth.

Women doubt their ability to heal and reclaim their health. They doubt their ability to reframe their definitions of success and self-worth. None of us can do this alone. We need others who have successfully gone before us to support us and hold space for our process. Without this, it is difficult to build the endurance and momentum needed to cultivate self-love.

Midlife consciousness and our relationship to food

As we explore the midlife journey and its powerful and terrifying process of connecting with our truth and intrinsic power, we will no doubt be transformed for the better. Over time, our voices of shame will weaken. They will be replaced with our voices of self-compassion and love. As we heal our relationship with food, we can even heal our core wounds and reconnect with our real selves.

Our healing can only begin when we bring consciousness to our rituals of eating and repattern our relationship with food into a healthy one. If we eat to medicate our shame, or our fear of failure, we risk sabotaging our goals. We can only heal by engaging patience and self-compassion. The shaming critic in our heads does not allow for self-care. Loving behavior is in contrast to the inner-critic's shaming directive. If we are unaware, the critic can control our relationship with ourselves. It can dominate our inner world. The inner-critic periodically goes dormant, then rises up only to sabotage successful attempts at self-empowerment and self-love. Despite temporary setbacks, we must keep moving forward and inward toward our real selves to build new momentum. Every failure is a lesson learned that can serve to deepen our consciousness. It is important for us to remind each other of this during moments of struggle on this difficult yet healing path that can lead to the reclaimation of our emotional and physical health.

Society normalizes our critical and self-sabotaging behaviors. Society itself is in a paradox. On one hand, obesity is epidemic in the U.S., and on the other, clothing companies have expanded their sizes to accommodate bigger bodies. This is a subtle yet illusory way of hiding reality from consumers. A size 10 today is larger than it was five years ago. The clothing industry attempts to give women the *illusion* of being smaller than they really are. This perpetuates the illusions and untruths we have about our bodies that we need to uncover and dismantle.

The following steps can help in maintaining your commitment to a healther relationship with food:

- Bring consciousness to your feelings of fullness while eating. Stop eating when you begin to feel full. Eat *slowly*.

- Learn the language of the inner-critic and behave in ways that are contrary to its directives for self-shaming and self-abuse. These contrary, self-nurturing behaviors will lessen its control over your psyche and create healthy patterns over time.

- Make a commitment to yourself witnessed by a trusted friend who can remind you of your progress when the momentum of the inner-critic's script takes over, attempting to sabotage your forward movement.

- Invest in your personal growth with a trusted psychotherapist to transform your relationship to yourself into one that supports self-care and authenticity.

There are many ways to reclaim our health through our relationship with food. We each need to find our own unique path and practice it. Despite setbacks along the way, we need to stay on this path with consciousness, remaining open to learning and seeking. Staying on the path is more important than failing a hundred times. It builds the endurance contained in the archetype of the Warrior within us and brings us into contact with our real self and intrinsic worth. Unless we become conscious of our inner dialogue, it will continue to unconsciously direct our behavior, keeping us entranced and disconnected from our body.

This process requires great courage. It may be difficult at first, but I promise you, it will be worth the effort invested when you can finally view yourself through more positive lens of self-worth aligned with your feeling function. Living from self-compassion is a spiritual path. Developing a healthy relationship with food can heal many levels of wounding. It can also heal our wounded relationship with nature and bring joy and vitality to time spent with our families and communities. We can, once again, make food a form of living art and "medicine." Healing our relationship with food can ultimately restore the health of our society.

5

The Four Body System™

Using complementary with traditional medicine to promote health is colloquially defined as Integrative Medicine. However, creating a system of health care that is truly integrative requires more than just placing multidisciplinary modalities together under one roof. It requires medical practitioners to work from "open system" principles, where causes are explored at levels deeper than just physical, to achieve wholeness. This increases the likelihood for illness to be cured rather than merely managed. This is in contrast to the current "closed system" of traditional medicine that focuses exclusively on the diagnosis and management of symptoms only at the physical level. Shifting our thinking from the principles of a closed to an open system is the leap we need in order to shift our context from a superficial to a more expanded one. Ancient healing modalities, which comprise complementary medicine, have had greater success in healing illnesses than traditional medicine alone. Combining both with the correct framework carries the potential to cure illness.

The current framework of what many term Integrative Medicine is also limited. From the current perspective, "mind-body" medicine is a more complete approach to health and illness. However, the "mind-body" connection alone is limited for healing the causal roots of illness. The mind is fickle and changeable. It adapts to survive. Its focus is narrow and mental. However, in recent years, breakthroughs in research show that thinking can impact biology. The mind-body approach is deeper than the physical level alone, but is still too superficial for real healing.

New Age teachers have instructed us to replace our negative with positive thinking to manipulate our physiology into reducing our symptoms.

Science has demonstrated that the "mind" is indeed within the body. The neurotransmitters that respond to our thoughts affect every cell. They impact our physical and mental health. We have been informed that positive thinking produces "good" chemicals in the brain and body that facilitate healing. However, the manipulation of the body with the mind does not heal illnesses at their root levels. It does not restore intrinsic balance. Originally, mind-body medicine was the field from which Integrative Medicine emerged. Early in my career I utilized this framework, but found it limited in many ways:

1. We cannot fool ourselves into thinking what we don't feel.

If we feel sad due to an experience that triggers our grief or anger, positive thinking cannot change how we feel. We still have to process our feelings to return to a state of balance. Our feelings will override any attempts to think them away. We can try to think positively, and this may work for a while, but our feelings will eventually surface, sometimes as emotional or physical symptoms. One can surmise that this occurs due to the "emotional pressure" that builds within us when we invalidate our feeling function in favor of thinking, resulting in their suppression. For example, studies have shown that heart attacks are more common on Monday mornings at 9 a.m. when people begin their work week. This is thought to be a result of an increase in stress hormones (because of how the Emotional body processes work stress) that activates coronary spasm. It has also been shown, that when feelings are processed, stress hormones fall, reducing the incidence of heart attacks. Validating and processing feelings (not thinking) affects this risk. In addition, positive thinking can fool us into denying and suppressing how we really *feel*, creating a greater health risk.

2. Mind-body medicine suggests that we can think ourselves out of fear.

This approach invalidates how we feel. Fear is the body's attempt to protect us from harm, but when fear becomes chronic, it can damage our health. In circumstances where fear is chronic, as in toxic working conditions or relationships, it can manifest as anxiety or depression. If our attempts to heal this with positive thinking fail, we risk engaging the inner-critic who will no doubt shame us at failing, perpetuating fear and anxiety. The conditions that cause chronic fear cannot be "thought" or wished away. They must be uncovered and processed.

3. Mind-body solutions do not work for people who have a sensitive feeling function.

Sensitive people (sensitives) relate to life kinesthetically. They process information and life experiences through feelings, not thinking. One way to tell if you are a sensitive is if you feel overwhelmed in a crowd or overcome by a deeper feeling state relative to others. This is because sensitives feel so deeply that their feeling function gets "flooded." Their senses become overwhelmed around people. In contrast, they feel rejuvenated in nature. They are deeply empathic to the point of feeling another's pain as their own. Sensitives engage their feeling more than their thinking function. Since our culture values thinking over feeling, sensitives have difficulty feeling that they "belong." They feel lonely and invalidated in a world that is thinking rather than feeling focused. They often mistake their intense feelings for mental illness.

Women become more sensitive in midlife. Feeling function becomes more pronounced as hormones begin to change. A woman is no longer as easily able to manipulate her body with her mind, or replace negative feelings with positive thinking, like she may have been able to when younger. This sets her up to feel shame and self-criticism around her feelings in a society that does not understand or validate their intensity.

4. We all carry the energy and memories of our life experiences in our "energy field."

For the past 100 years, our culture has not had a framework to include, acknowledge, or understand the energetic aspects of our bodies. These neglected aspects are often where the causes of emotional, mental, and physical illnesses originate. We ignore these aspects due to this lack of framework, which is reinforced by health care's limited approach to health and illness, and often miss the opportunity to heal imbalances that occur at these levels. Our Energy body operates from a much deeper and subtle level than the mind or body can access, and has a direct effect on our Emotional, Mental, and Physical bodies. Our current cultural framework excludes this level. Our ancestors had an understanding of this. Traditional medicine deems this unnecessary, unimportant, and scientifically invalid. For Integrative Medicine to be effective, practitioners must understand and address the workings of the Energy body to facilitate healing.

The only two "bodies" our current medical model addresses are the Physical and Mental bodies. Even the Mental body is placed in the physical category and seen as a physical network of neurotransmitters. The Emotional and Energy bodies are not addressed. These are the levels at which both illness and healing occur.

The *Four Body System*™ is a framework I have developed to diagnose and treat illness and restore health at all levels of the Physical, Mental, Emotional, and Energy bodies. It is a more complete framework for Integrative Medicine than the fragmented, potpourri approach that currently exists. Examining and balancing these levels makes healing and even curing possible. It uses traditional and complementary methods more effectively.

In contrast, the mind-body approach alone is not deep enough to cure or heal. This framework is limited, as feeling function and emotional process are not addressed.

When the "mind-body" framework is utilized within the closed system of medicine, we endanger the use of our tendency to dominate and control the body with the mind. Since our culture already engages the concept of mind *over* matter, the concept of "mind over body" reinforces our pathological approach of "war on illness" rather than its healing. This does not promote true healing or evoke intrinsic health. Instead, it reinforces our feelings of powerlessness and shame when we do not heal.

Cartesian theory

The focus of traditional medicine is the Physical body. Its clinical analysis is based on the principles of reductionism. The body is reduced into its component parts in search for the physical causes for symptoms—also known as the Cartesian model. This narrows its focus to fix only the physical without accounting for emotional or energetic levels. Although the emotional and energetic levels of the body are not physically visible, they have powerful effects on the Physical body. They cannot be seen, but are felt. In working from a merely physically focused Cartesian approach, the connection to the emotional and energetic aspects of patients is deeply compromised. Due to these limitations in the current paradigm, physicians lose sight of wholeness and process, both important aspects of the Feminine Principle. They also lose sight of the impact of the Emotional and Energy bodies on mental and physical health. We can actually apply the Cartesian approach to explore the deeper levels from which illness may emerge. We can analyze the Emotional and Energy bodies in the same manner as the Physical, but from this deeper context. Without this level of inquiry, medical analysis remains superficial and incomplete, limiting the patient's ability to truly heal.

The art of healing

The relationship between the physician and patient also has a profound effect on the patient's healing process. When engaged from the heart, physicians can access their intuitive nature more deeply, enhancing their ability to diagnose with greater accuracy. Today's health care approach discounts the importance of this relationship in healing. It only values expertise and mastery to manage and fix illness. This limits a physician's accuracy to diagnose and treat. For a patient, a relationship that lacks connection feels sterile.

Patients may value their physicians' hearts even more than their expertise. The heart is not limited like the mind. It is open to the potential for healing and able to hold space for process. It can bear witness. It can validate and love. Love can often heal more deeply than expertise and mastery. Even scientific research has proven this. Patients arrive fearful in their physician's office even when they are well. They worry that their physician's expertise may uncover problems within their body. A patient's fear can even elevate their blood pressure. This is called "white-coat hypertension."

Physicians must be sensitive to the impact that fear can have on health. Awareness of this can help them to hold space for their patients with understanding and empathy. They must be able to help their patients replace their fear with empowerment. Without this, healing cannot be sustained. "Fixing" alone does not support healing.

The female patient

For the midlife woman, her physician's capacity to facilitate healing is critical for her transformation. She can intuitively sense if her physician connects from her heart and feeling function. She can also sense if her physician has empathy. If she does, a women will feel safe in her presence while expressing her feelings. She will be able to trust her physician's recommendations. Women need to know that feeling fearful and disconnected from their physicians is a sign that they are not connected with them. Unfortunately many women second-guess their need for connection. They arrive in the medical system, fearful, seeking relief for their symptoms. When they settle for expertise at the cost of connection, they risk invalidating their real needs as well as the healing that could be possible. In addition, their adaptations normalize the current health care system's absence of heart-centered focus.

This is the dilemma many midlife women face after encounters with physicians who analyze their symptoms and reduce them to mere hormone deficiency or lack of anti-depressants.

The normalized traditional medical solution is synthetic hormone replacement and antidepressant therapy. Process is largely dismissed. Women are seeking a framework that helps them understand and validate their process. While seeing the expertise oriented physician, who does not hold space for their process, they are unable to experience true healing.

The cost of emotional neglect

We have compromised our feeling function to be accepted by a society that is afraid of feelings. The Emotional body is where our feeling function resides. Our emotions are the closest connection we have to our souls. As a culture, we have been raised to undermine this aspect of ourselves. This comes with a heavy price. Our repressed feelings, gather "pressure" in the Emotional body, over time, and often manifest in symptoms or "dis-ease." Any feelings that are repressed for too long will need to be released. It is our sacred work to listen to and validate our feelings to help us connect with our souls. In midlife, we must release the "pressure" built in the Emotional Body from denying our feelings for over half a lifetime.

Our adaptations to society reinforce this repression. Fortunately, hormonal shifts catalyze a release of our patterns of self-compromise. In our late thirties, when these shifts begin, repressed feelings rise up causing us to question our mental health. Denial and repression create the intensity contained in the Emotional body. After years of valuing thinking over feeling, we require support when we reframe to valuing feelings over thinking. Since our society lacks a healthy framework to view the midlife process as transformative, it is no surprise we feel lost and afraid. We must not pathologize our deep feelings that arise during this powerful gateway.

This process is very difficult for many women entering peri-menopause. They may experience feelings of unexplained rage directed towards people they are closest to. Their conditioning reinforced the denial of their needs in favor of caring for others. Decades of self-denial emerges as rage from the Emotional body. This can be profoundly frightening. Women often feel ashamed at feeling the way they do and reach out to the medical system to help them. Too often they are medicated to suppress their symptoms, further adding to the pressure inside their Emotional Bodies. Due to the medical system's lack understanding of what women experience during the midlife process, they are unable to help them, making this gateway unduly stressful.

Mary

Mary is a 39-year-old woman who came to see me for symptoms of fatigue and heavy menstrual bleeding. She felt intense stress after taking on an in-home babysitting position in addition to caring for three children of her own. She was trying to help her family's finances after her husband lost his job. Within a month, she began to feel enraged towards the children she was caring for. She was ashamed of how she felt and became somewhat depressed. She said she felt like a "bad mother and wife," unable to help her family in a time of need.

It was clear from her heavy periods that her progesterone level was dropping. Heavy menstrual flow is a sure sign, as are anxiety, emotional agitation, anger, and depression. Serotonin levels drop alongside progesterone and a woman's emotions rise in intensity with these predictable changes. Mary did not understand the cause for the intensity of her feelings. Once she understood how hormone shifts evoked this in her Emotional Body, she uncovered a pattern within her feeling function. She found that she only felt rage in areas of her life where she compromised her needs in favor of others. She had reached her limit to continue this pattern.

As I listened to her story, I asked her who she felt was responsible for her compromises and for overriding her limits and boundaries. She acknowledged that *she* was. She also realized that she had expected her husband and children to be aware of her needs and advocate for her. She wanted *them* to be the ones to help her set her limits. She wanted to be able to rely on them for what only she was responsible for.

Her husband had recently found new employment and was stressed himself. Mary felt ashamed for admitting that the child care responsibilities overwhelmed her. She felt that she had failed her family.

As she uncovered her pattern of self-sacrifice at the cost of her sovereignty and gained awareness of her long standing tendency to ignore her limits and boundaries for the sake of "duty," she understood that her Emotional body was responding appropriately. She had been conditioned to not speak her truth in favor of what she felt was expected of her. She had been conditioned to override her limits for the sake of others.

She quickly realized that overriding her instinctive cues on behalf of cultural expectations was toxic to her. Her emotions expressed rage toward this. She realized that practicing self-care and self-advocacy were two of the most powerful gifts she could give herself and all the people she cared for. She quit her job as an in-home daycare provider when she understood the wisdom behind her rage.

She connected more deeply with her needs. Since then, she is much happier, and so is her family.

The importance of aligning with feeling function

Aligning with our feelings is critical, not only personally but collectively. No other time is more important than midlife to reframe and elevate our personal paradigm. Our sacred task during this time is to heal the deep wounds of self-neglect that become symptomatic when our feeling function uncovers them. We need to dispel the idea of "getting over" feelings (of grief, rage, and sadness) and learn how to understand and validate them. Without this, we can never fully heal. A collective symptom of this is our current epidemic of infertility and impotence. Infertility is symbolic of our wounded and impotent feeling function.

Deep feeling is a prerequisite for erotic and vivacious creativity. Without it, the soul's energy is dimmed rendering us infertile. Despite medical breakthroughs in overriding infertility, traditional medicine is unable to heal at deeper levels. Infertility is a sign of our disconnection from erotic feeling function. Neither pharmaceuticals nor mind-body medicine can restore this.

"Getting over" feelings or managing symptoms cannot heal this. In fact, this perpetuates emotional impotence. We risk remaining personally and collectively wounded underneath the superficial absence of physical symptoms, that we confuse with healing. Unhealed wounds at deeper levels eventually manifest as disease.

Jungian author and analyst, Robert Johnson, states that the cultural masculine and feminine kill the natural masculine and feminine. Nature responds by making the cultural man and woman impotent. I believe he means that the cultural definitions of masculine and feminine have replaced what we intuitively know as the healthy masculine and feminine. In order for our fertile nature to flow, we must behave in ways that engage our healthy masculine and feminine energies without compromising them for distorted cultural definitions. Only when we begin to live from this healthy inner place, can we heal our epidemic of infertility and impotence.

The relationship of the Four Bodies

For more than two decades, I have worked with thousands of patients and have gained an awareness of the trauma stress causes. Usually, trauma shocks us and places us in survival. Stress can be seen as an experience of trauma. This has a profound impact on our health at levels of the Mental, Emotional, and Energy bodies that reside within the Physical body. Since we live in a physically oriented society, we seldom realize that the stressors we experience can get "stuck" in the deeper bodies and need to be released for healing. We are taught to deal with the symptoms of stress by merely medicating our Physical or Mental bodies. As a result, we rarely heal as the Emotional and Energy Bodies carry the memory of stress and trauma,which causes imbalances within them. Addressing these deeper levels has a profound impact on true healing.

For example, when someone is in a car accident, the shock and trauma that accompany it gets stuck at multiple levels of the body. As people heal the physical injury caused by the accident, they often begin to experience feelings of anxiety. Anxiety is the manner in which the shock and trauma likely present at deeper levels makes itself known.

People are perplexed by these feelings of anxiety, especially when their physical symptoms are healed. They may describe it as a sensation of tightness or agitation or feelings that are overwhelming. When they experience these symptoms, they do not feel safe in their skin. Anxiety usually takes on a life of its own. The memory of the accident may replay itself. They may develop insomnia as a result of this repetitive recapitulation. They may experience palpitations, feel emotionally numb or paralyzed.

They may attempt to medicate their anxiety with prescription drugs or alcohol.

They often visit the emergency room or their doctor's office because of their anxiety which can often become chronic. Their doctors commonly label this as an "anxiety disorder" requiring medication. This adds to their lack of well-being. What they really need is a framework that helps them release the trauma and shock of the accident that is trapped in their deeper bodies. When this is provided, their anxiety heals.

When we expand the medical framework to include the Energy and Emotional bodies, we are able to understand the deeper levels impacted by trauma that manifest as symptoms of both physical pain and emotional anxiety. We can also understand how people may want to medicate their symptoms in order to function when a larger framework is absent. The cause of these symptoms lies deep in the Energy body, where memories of trauma and shock (resulting from the accident) commonly reside. Unless trauma is released from this level, it will manifest in anxiety, insomnia, or post-traumatic stress. The patient in this instance would be incorrectly labeled with an anxiety disorder. What she needs is an understanding of its cause. Medicating her will only cover her symptoms and not heal the trauma trapped underneath. It will not heal her.

A view of the Four Body System™

1. The Physical body is the densest of the four bodies. This is where physical symptoms manifest and the level that traditional medicine diagnoses and treats.

2. The Mental body is less dense than the Physical body. It is a combination of the Physical and Emotional bodies. It is made up of neurotransmitters that are affected by and also affect emotions. In our society, the fields of psychiatry and psychology address this body when imbalances manifest as symptoms.

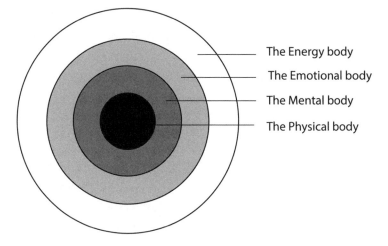

The Energy body

The Emotional body

The Mental body

The Physical body

Figure 4: The Four Body System™

3. The Emotional body, the area of feeling function, is even less dense than the Mental body. This is where "gut" or intuitive feelings are felt. Grief, sadness, rage, and joy reside here. If not addressed or released from this body, feelings can get stuck and manifest as anxiety or depression in the Mental body. They can also manifest as symptoms or diseases in the Physical body. We are conditioned to deny and suppress the Emotional body by our cultural and medical framework. This has a significant impact on the Physical and Mental bodies. Traditional medicine medicates stuck emotions. This pushes them further into the Emotional body where they are unable to heal (Figure 4).

Integrative Medicine offers a more effective framework for healing the Emotional body. Common therapies for healing it are psychotherapy and energy work. These not only address stuck feelings, but help release the energy built within. A safe space with tools to process are required to heal the Emotional body.

We can liken the framework of the Four Body System™ to different expressions of the molecular structure of water, H_2O. It is present in different densities as steam, water, or ice. Even at different densities, its molecular structure remains H_2O. Steam can be likened to the Energy body, water to the Emotional and Mental bodies and ice to the Physical body. Any contaminant in the steam will manifest in water and ice. In the same way, we are a continuum of energy that expresses itself at different densities. An imbalance or "dis-ease" in the Energy body will eventually express itself at the level of the Physical body.

We are keenly aware of the manner in which our Physical and Mental bodies express disease. This is the popular framework accepted by the traditional medical system. Understanding the manner in which the Energy and Emotional bodies contribute to illness and health is crucial for therapeutic efficacy. A logical yet broader approach to the Emotional and Energy bodies is needed for a more complete perspective for understanding the causes of disease and the restoration of true health versus mere symptom management offered by the traditional medical approach. It is important for us to expand our definition of health and medicine to include the Four Body System™ in the diagnosis and treatment of illness to support true healing.

The Energy body

The Energy body is the largest and most subtle body that surrounds and contains the Physical, Mental, and Emotional bodies. The Energy body has four main components:

1. the *electrical* system
2. the *constitutional* system
3. the *meridians* or energy lines
4. the *subtle* body

The electrical system
The electrical system is the part of the Energy body that regulates and affects the heart rhythm (the cardiovascular system), the

muscular, and nervous systems. We can measure the electrical activity of these systems with diagnostic medical tools. For example, we can measure heart rhythms with an electrocardiogram (EKG), the electrical activity of muscles with an electromyogram (EMG), and nerve impulses with an electroencephalogram (EEG). The electrical system is both electrical and magnetic. Although this part of the body is invisible, it has a profound impact on the electrical activity of the heart, the proper functioning of the muscles and the sensitivity and conductivity of the nerves and brain. They all conduct electricity and are negatively impacted by aberrations in the electrical system. The electrical system generates the electromagnetic field surrounding the Physical body. This field can be measured up to eight feet in diameter with a galvanometer, a device used to measure electrical currents. The electrical activity of the body is affected by the experience of trauma and shock (caused by stressors) as well as feelings of happiness, joy, and love.

The Institute of HeartMath in California has shown when one is in a state of stress, the electrical activity of the heart changes to an out-of-sync rhythm. This rhythm can be measured through a technique called heart rate variability analysis. Ordinarily there is a variability in the time and space gap between each heartbeat. The more variable this is between heart beats, the higher the heart rate variablity. The more uniform or similar (less variable) the time and space gap is between heart beats, the lower the heart rate variability (Figure 5). The Institute of HeartMath has found that a higher heart rate variablity correlates with a more resilient heart. This is important for maintaining a normal heart rhythm while under stress. In other words, an increase in heart rate variability gives the heart more resilience under stress, lowering cardiac risk. We can compare this to a loose rubber band versus a tightly stretched one. The loose one has a greater degree of elasticity and resilience (a higher variability), than tighter one that can more easily snap when stretched or stressed (low variability). A heart rhythm that indicates low variability appears tight and jagged (upper graph, Figure 5). A rhythm with high variablity appears smooth and regular (lower graph, Figure 5). In the upper graph in Figure 5, under the influence of frustration and anger, the beat to beat variability becomes tight or low, showing a jagged appearance. In the second graph, under the influence of sincere appreciation, the graph shows a smoother and more regular or cyclic rhythm called a sine wave. Anger causes the heart to have a low heart rate variability (jagged) and appreciation causes its rhythm to become more synchronized—a high heart rate variabilty. This clearly demonstrates that emotions affect the electrical activity of the heart.

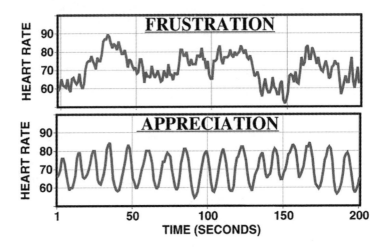

Figure 5: Heart rate variability graphs
(Reprinted with written permission—Institute of HeartMath ©1998, 2011)

This is one example of the impact that the Energy and Emotional bodies have on the Physical body. The energetic properties of feelings and emotions can have a direct effect on health in both positive and negative ways. Our electrical system responds to feelings. As we can see, their impact on the Physical body influences cardiac risk and can be measured by heart rate variability analysis. When we understand the connection between feelings and health, we can restore our health in more powerful ways than what only prescription drugs offer. When we respond with balance and equanimity, rather than reacting from anger or fear, we can improve the health of our electrical system.

Energy memory

The Energy body has the capacity to remember every experience ever encountered. Traumatic memories trapped in it can impact the electrical activity of the heart. The Energy body "remembers" experiences even without a conscious memory of them. It does not filter out negative ones. There are times it even remembers what we consciously don't, and we may wonder why we feel what we do. It is not uncommon for us to be emotionally agitated during the anniversary of a death, divorce, accident, or significant event from the past. This is due to the memory stored in the Energy body that reminds us of the event due to its ability to recall a specific time in our biography. When our memories are activated, we need to treat ourselves with compassion and offer ourselves much needed self-care and support. As we can see, the nature of the event and the way it was experienced in the past, effects our emotions in the present. These memories are all held in the Energy body. They are called *energy* or *body memories*.

Flower-essence therapy

There is a discipline unfamiliar to traditional medicine which many alternative healers utilize due to its profound impact on the electrical system. It involves a pharmacy of remedies called "flower essences." Flower essence therapy was established by Dr. Edward Bach. His healing framework described illness as "a force with the potential to facilitate the process required in dealing with the spiritual and psychological issues neglected before the illness manifested." He believed that illness was a way that destiny tried to help us deepen and evolve. He noticed the relationship between different personality types and the illnesses they manifested. He also found that certain flowers and plants could support and nurture the Energy body in ways that could balance and stabilize the Energy body of the person experiencing the illness.

Dr. Bach saw flowers as "receptors for the soul gestures of the cosmos." When a flower is placed in water in sunlight, he found the water incorporated the energetic essence of the flower. When ingested, it could shift the emotional and energetic patterns of the person drinking it and make their patterns more flexible. This would sometimes lead to emotional healing and also impact physical illness in positive ways. The essence could in fact, assist the person to *fortify their system against trauma,* (which made them vulnerable), and also strengthen their ability to release the trauma held in the Energy body.

We can apply this framework to the case of the patient in the accident described previously that resulted in anxiety, insomnia, and repetitive thoughts. These are all manifestations of shock and trauma resulting from the accident. These symptoms can be released to a large degree by taking a flower essence called Star of Bethlehem, specifically prescribed for trauma or fright. The body is able to heal more quickly at all levels, when the associated mental and emotional symptoms due to trauma are released. Dr. Bach observed that the Star of Bethlehem plant grew in moderately harsh environments. Its flowers contained properties of hardiness and when their essence was given to patients in states of vulnerability, they felt grounded and less vulnerable. They were able to heal the anxiety associated with the traumatic memories trapped in their Energy body. This is one example of how flower essence therapy works.

Dr. Bach created a pharmacy of essences by correlating the healing characteristics of trees, plants, and flowers with symptom relief in humans and animals. This pharmacy has the ability to heal many imbalances in the Energy body that also manifest as symptoms in the Mental and Physical bodies. Since these essences work at subtle levels, they must be taken regularly over time to be most effective, ideally under the guidance of a flower-essence therapist. Rescue Remedy is one of the more popular flower essences available in most health food stores. It minimizes feelings of anxiety associated with stress.

When we expand our framework of health to include an understanding of the impact of the Energy body on our state of wellbeing, we can understand how the limited framework of traditional medicine results in the overuse of pharmaceuticals for symptomatic relief and doesn't heal the underlying causes present in the Energy body. When issues at energetic levels are not addressed, they manifest as symptoms in the Emotional, Mental, and Physical bodies. Energy cannot be created or destroyed. It simply changes form. An imbalanced Energy body directly impacts the Mental and Physical bodies. If trauma floods the Energy body, it manifests in symptoms in denser bodies when it is not released or healed. It triggers a surge of stress hormones. We often see this in people with Post-Traumatic-Stress-Disorder (PTSD). The toxic effects of stress hormones can cause physical conditions such as ulcers, gastric reflux, headaches, colitis, muscle pain, fibromyalgia, chronic fatigue, insomnia, dizziness, and vertigo to name only a few. Obesity can be an eventual manifestation of trauma if the person overeats to medicate the anxiety caused by the trauma trapped in the Energy body. Obesity, alone, can lead to a myriad of diseases such as diabetes, heart disease, strokes, and hypertension. Here we can see how the root causes of symptoms, when tracked back to the Energy body, provide a greater chance for healing than merely managing them at the level of the Physical body.

The impact of the electrical system's state of balance plays a significant role in the health of our Energy, Emotional, and Mental bodies. Flower essence therapy, can sometimes alleviate subtle imbalances that manifest as anxiety in the Mental body, but have their roots in the electrical system.

The example of the car accident demonstrates the power that

flower-essence therapy can have in realigning the electrical system when symptoms of anxiety are a result of trauma. Combinations of flower essences can heal many kinds of imbalances in the electrical system and are safe to take at any age with few to no side effects. If the wrong essence is taken, it will be ineffective yet do no harm. Practitioners who are skilled in flower-essence therapy can help heal imbalances in the electrical system which may be the cause of mental and physical symptoms.

The constitutional system

Classical homeopathy is a discipline that restores constitutional balance to the Energy body by correcting chronic and sometimes acute aggravations of symptoms that occur when the system becomes imbalanced from stress. The constitutional system is the part of the Energy body responsible for feelings of "intrinsic stability" or groundedness within the organism.

We all adapt to stress on a daily basis. The purpose of our adaptations is to support our survival. Survival is a basic instinct that keeps us alive under threat. Even when a threat is minor, our brain is programmed to activate the fight-or-flight response to help us survive.

Fear activates the stress response. It can exaggerate our reactions to stressors by distorting our perceptions and exaggerating the reactions we have learned through our imprinting. If our parents were fearful or anxious, we were imprinted with the perception that we are not safe in our relationship to the world. The imbalances in our constitution that result from adaptations like these run deep, and are expressed with biological precision. In this manner, our biography has a profound impact on how we adapt to stress. These adaptations can cause constitutional imbalances that manifest as chronic mental and physical symptoms. In our traditional medical system, this perspective is not included when arriving at a differential diagnosis or treatment plan.

These are powerful and important aspects of health that have a significant impact on how we feel and whether we heal. Over time, many of our adaptations can become dysfunctional. We may adapt to alcoholism and become an enabler. This is an example of how an adaptation to survive can become dysfunctional. Many of us also compensate for what we feel we lack as a mechanism for survival. For example, we may compensate for our fear of failure by over-working or become a perfectionist, compromising our boundaries and limits. Eventually we feel depleted. Any behavior that is driven by our need to compensate is dysfunctional. We can try to heal this through psychotherapy and behavior modification, but unless the underlying condition causing it—our fear of failure—is addressed, it will always drive us to compensate. Over time, this causes adrenal stress and chronic symptoms manifest due to an imbalance in our constitutional makeup, the fabric of our being. Our constitution is deeply impacted by the way we adapt or compensate under the influence of stress. When it becomes imbalanced and manifests symptoms in the Emotional, Mental, and Physical bodies, classical homeopathy can heal this by restoring balance in the Energy body.

Homeopathy is a 200-year-old system of healing. Its underlying philosophy is intended to restore energetic balance to a person's constitution. *Homeo* means "same or similar" and *pathy* means "disease." Derived from the plant, mineral, and animal kingdoms, homeopathic remedies are capable of producing mild symptoms in healthy people, yet also help to resolve those same symptoms in people who are sick.

The homeopathic approach begins with an understanding that a person is an integrated whole and in response to the challenges of life, is engaged in an ongoing dynamic effort to maintain balance. Under normal circumstances one responds to and "rebounds" from various stresses, hopefully a stronger and wiser person. However, when challenges are too strong or too prolonged, one can become stuck in a dysfunctional stress response. The manifested symptoms are defined by our society as disease. Rather than suppressing the symptoms created by the stress response, like traditional medicine promotes, the homeopathic remedy works to *cue the person's system as to how one's adaptation are unhealthy*, or how the manner in which a person adapts to stress imbalances their constitution. This, in turn, provokes a healing reaction in the Energy body that restores its balance and alleviates the symptoms resulting from its imbalanced state.

Based on the patient's history (which is taken during a two-hour interview), the certified classical homeopath is able to understand the unique individuality and the state of imbalance present in the constitution. A very specific remedy is then chosen that amplifies the internal awareness or the body's "inner wisdom." According to homeopathy, the body's inner wisdom will recognize the state that resulted in "dis-ease" when the correct remedy is introduced into the body. This in turn, provokes a deep and integrated self-healing reaction on physical, mental, and emotional levels. By using this precise approach, homeopathy supports the person's own innate healing potential, resulting in a safe and natural return to health.

Arlene

Arlene is a 55-year-old woman who came to me with complaints of severe and chronic asthma and recurrent panic attacks for 10 years. These symptoms began soon after she divorced her abusive husband of twenty years. During her marriage, she lived almost daily from a fight-or-flight response pattern, adapting to the abuse with the behaviors she was raised with from her family of origin (an adaptation response). After she left her husband and felt physically safe, she began to have panic attacks. These were treated with three different medications prescribed by her traditional doctors. In addition, she was taking four prescription drugs to prevent asthma attacks that sent her to the emergency room at least a few times a year. She had been on multiple prescriptions for years. She came to me seeking a "cure" for her symptoms, as they were taking a toll on her quality of life and her finances.

After interviewing her about the nature of her attacks and the feelings surrounding her panic, it was clear to me that her adaptations to abuse had caused her constitution to become imbalanced. This was the reason that, even though she did not have to adapt to survive around the abuse any longer, her asthma and panic persisted.

I referred Arlene to a certified classical homeopath. After an extensive interview, the remedy that the homeopath selected was one derived from the willow tree. Arlene had survived abuse over a prolonged period of time by creating an "energetic wall" that offered her the feeling of "safety." It had resulted in characteristics of inflexibility in her nature developed as a reaction to abuse. She had unconsciously created this wall to keep her safe. Her inflexibility presented itself in other relationships as well. For example, if someone offered her constructive criticism, her "energetic wall" would go up and as a result, she would get defensive. Sometimes when people tried to connect with her, if she was stressed, she would push them away with this wall, as she feared she would be mistreated. After her divorce, she no longer needed this "energetic wall" to feel safe. But after years of exercising this, it had become her adapted pattern of survival. It caused her to continue to react to even minor stressors from the exaggerated patterns of inflexibility conditioned by years of abuse.

Her constitution had become imbalanced through this form of chronic adaptation and had manifested in symptoms of severe anxiety and asthma. The remedy which contained the energy of the willow tree was more like her innate balanced constitution—flexible, like the branches of the willow tree. This remedy resonated with her unadapted state of flexibility and reawakened it in her Energy body, restoring her to a state of intrinsic balance. It cued her constitution back to a state of health and balance. Within six weeks of taking the willow remedy, Arlene's asthma completely healed and her panic improved so dramatically she was weaned off her medications within a relatively short period of time.

She no longer visited the emergency room for asthma or panic attacks. In addition, Arlene had been medicating her stress by eating foods that were highly inflammatory. I guided her to change her diet to a plant-based, gluten-free, and anti-inflammatory one, high in Omega-3, to heal the physical causes of asthma. In six months, her asthma completely healed without recurrence using classical homeopathy and dietary changes. After eight years since treatment, I am happy to report she has not had a single panic or asthma attack!

Arlene was able to shift out of her inflexible state of survival into a flexible state of constitutional balance offered by the remedy from the willow tree. In addition, providing the constitutional history also made her aware of how she had adapted to survive. With this new found awareness, she was able to manage her anxiety in healthier ways when it became activated under stress. Now when her survival patterns arise and her anxiety surfaces, her awareness reminds her to treat herself with compassion. She is now able to behave in ways that maintain resilience and help her symptoms recover more rapidly.

As I broadened my perceptual framework for evaluating chronic symptoms that my traditional tool box only palliated, I gained a deeper and wider perspective of how the constitutional level of the Energy body affected health and illness. I was never exposed to this this level in my medical training, which only taught me to manage symptoms, *after* they manifested, with prescription drugs that had harmful side effects and did little to heal my patients. As I explored the underlying causes for my patients' chronic conditions, and referred them for classical homeopathy, they healed.

When physicians begin to include this perspective in their framework for diagnosis and treatment, it can have a profound effect on their patient's ability to heal. It can even improve their response to traditional medical treatments.

It is important that only a credentialed homeopath be consulted, one with thousands of hours of clinical training and experience, certified through the Medical Society of Homeopathy. Not all homeopaths are trained in classical homeopathy, which addresses and heals constitutional imbalances. Very few are trained and experienced enough to be effective in helping chronic symptoms. Discernment is needed to differentiate credible homeopaths from "pop" healers who practice homeopathy without extensive training. A homeopath who is not skilled and credentialed can actually harm a chronically ill patient if homeopathy is not practiced with high standard-of-care. Many claim credentialing, but receive it through internet courses, and do not have the clinical experience needed. They may use homeopathic remedies to merely palliate symptoms, but this does not heal at the constitutional level. The art of practice is as important as the science.

We need to establish a high standard-of-care for nontraditional (complementary) practitioners. We need to apply instinct and experience, for safe and effective healing, until high standards are established. Too often, people gravitate towards less than adequately trained complementary practitioners due to their disappointment with the traditional medical system, and they do not discern for quality of care or expertise. It is important to stay aware of this when engaging any traditional or complementary practitioner for healing.

The subtle body

The subtle body exists within the Energy body and consists of two main components:
1. The breath
2. The chakra system

The breath

Throughout history we have known that breathing has a pro-found influence on health. Breathing is integral to the practice of yoga, where breath is used to oxygenate muscles and connect to consciousness. Through yogic breathing, we can connect our mental, physical and subtle bodies. It is cyclic and, like nature, it ebbs and flows. When we inhale, we oxygenate the body; when we exhale, we detoxify it. This cycle of inhalation and exhalation sustains life. When interrupted for too long, life is threatened. Life itself depends on breath.

When we are stressed, our breathing becomes shallow. With shallow breathing, we are unable to oxygenate and detoxify our cells and tissues effectively. This reduces both physical and energetic vitality, causing malaise which furthers shallow breathing. Fatigue, lethargy, foggy thinking and mood disturbances may also result. These symptoms are epidemic in our country. Many people consume caffeine and sugar, hoping to restore their energy. These can become addictive, resulting in unhealthy patterns that promote illness.

A decrease in vitality also compromises the integrity of the immune system, increasing the body's vulnerability to illness. Shallow breathing stresses the cardiovascular system, increasing the heart's work load. The heart rate increases to provide oxygen to tissues deprived of it.

This can cause palpitations and high blood pressure. When the brain is not adequately oxygenated, mood is adversely affected increasing the likelihood of depression and anxiety. Being aware of the negative effects that shallow breathing has on our health is an important step in restoring it.

Just by breathing deeply and consciously, we can detoxify our body and keep the flow of vital energy from stagnating. In this way, the breath, a key component of our subtle body impacts our emotional, mental, and physical health.

The chakra system
In the East, the anatomy of the body is viewed at both physical and energetic levels. One form of medicine that defines the anatomy of the Energy body is Chakra Medicine. This is a healing discipline that

links seven concentrated wheels of energy in the Energy body to nerve and endocrine plexuses in the Physical body (Figure 6). These concentrated energy wheels are called "chakras." They are defined as *wheels of energy in motion* that receive, assimilate, and express "life force." They are said to contain "bio-energetic" energy, that is, energy that affects the body and is affected by the body. When they are spinning or in motion, the chakras are moving bioenergetic energy. When they are stagnant, this energy is blocked and affects the coexisting level at the Physical body causing symptoms. A sensation of bioenergetic movement would be the feeling of "butterflies in the stomach." This corresponds to the 3rd or the solar plexus chakra in rapid motion. An orgasm is a feeling of the bioenergetic life force flowing through the chakras. The chakras, like the breath, are also aspects of the subtle body. Consciousness flows through the chakras, and their movement, in turn, affects consciousness. Becoming stressed or carrying stuck emotions affects the movement of the specific chakras that correspond to the emotions we feel (Table 1). When energy stagnates in a chakra, it adversely affects the organs that correspond to its location. This can manifest as disease at any level of the Four Body System™. Specific emotional characteristics that correspond to the chakras are shown in Table 1.

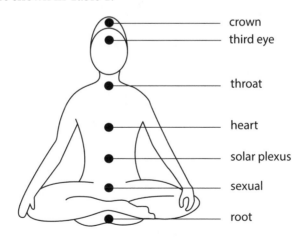

Figure 6: The chakra system

Table 1: The chakras and their corresponding emotions and organs

CHAKRA	LOCATION	EMOTION	ORGAN
1	Base of spine	Feelings of safety, security	Hips, vulva, rectum, sciatic
2	Between pubic bone and belly	Relationship with money, sexual potency, ability to relate to others	Lower back, pelvis, uterus, ovaries, bladder, large intestine, cervix, vagina
3	Solar plexus	Issues of power, fear, self-esteem, trust, self-confidence, self-worth	Abdomen, liver, gall bladder, adrenals, kidneys, pancreas, upper intestine, mid-spine
4	Mid chest	Love, intimacy, judgment, anger, grief	Heart, lungs, breasts, shoulders, esophagus
5	Throat	Self-expression	Throat, thyroid, neck, mouth, teeth, gums, jaw
6	Between the eyebrows	Insight, intuition, knowledge	Brain, pineal gland, eyes, ears, nose
7	Crown of the head	Relationships with spirituality, divinity, humanitarianism, larger perspective	Muscles, skin, nerves, skeleton

As we bring awareness to energy and emotions that correspond to specific chakras, we can heal at deeper levels of cause than merely managing symptoms at the physical level. We can also grow in consciousness and become self-aware when we include this context for health and illness to our definition of Integrative Medicine.

Joan

Joan is a 43-year-old woman who came to see me due to an unexplained increase in body weight and the sudden onset of diabetes. She had been healthy for most of her life, exercised regularly, and enjoyed a diet abundant in whole foods. She did not understand the causes for her conditions and was discouraged because nothing she tried altered her blood sugar or weight. She followed a diabetic diet without much success. She felt "stuck" and mildly depressed. She felt hopeless and disempowered.

The pancreas, the organ that regulates blood sugar is situated to the left of the solar plexus (the 3rd chakra). When I asked her questions pertaining to emotions related to her 3rd chakra such as power, fear, and self-esteem (Table 1), she could see that her issues with blood sugar ran deeper than just the physical level. She realized that her pancreas may not have been functioning properly due to unresolved emotional issues that caused stagnation of the 3rd chakra.

Although Joan was living a healthy lifestyle, she had not yet resolved her struggle with a low self-esteem that plagued her throughout her life. She was more vulnerable to disease in midlife due to the changes underway in her body. She had been abused as a child and had lived in fear for many years. She was constantly afraid of making mistakes and suffering the consequences. Her sense of self relied on how she was treated by others, and she lived with the fear of being punished for not being "good enough." This fear was the primary emotion that held her hostage, eroded her self-esteem, and blocked her third chakra. The stagnation she experienced at this level affected her adrenal glands. Her chronic, low grade, fight-or-flight response due to fear caused her adrenals to chronically produce stress hormones which caused an increase in blood sugar. It impaired the energy flow to her pancreas and reduced its vitality. In our work together, I helped her become aware of her constant fear and recommended a Reiki therapist to identify where in her body she felt the fear so she could release its energy.

Reiki is a form of energy work that can help restore energy flow within stagnant chakras. When energy begins to flow, the emotional issues blocking the chakras sometimes require psychotherapy for safe healing.

The intention, expertise, and understanding of the Reiki therapist is critical for providing a safe space for patients to release issues in the Emotional body.

Joan needed psychotherapy to work through her issues of fear and self-esteem that surfaced in her Reiki sessions.

Through this work, she was able to identify where she was disempowered and was able to reclaim herself. Approaching diabetes from an integrative context helped her heal faster than she would have with symptom management alone. In three months, her blood sugars normalized and she began to lose weight. Within six months, she was twenty pounds lighter.

Joan's healing was deeper than just the physical reversal of diabetes. She reclaimed herself from chronic fear through a combination of Reiki and psychotherapy. As her 3rd chakra healed, her fear was released and self-esteem restored. Through this process, she learned tools and strategies that raised her awareness and helped her dismantle her fear. Her life energy began to flow more freely and she felt more confident and empowered.

Diabetes had been the *catalyst* that brought her awareness to the issues stuck in her 3rd chakra. As she worked through these, fear no longer contaminated her relationship to her real self. She healed her diabetes as a "side effect" of healing her 3rd chakra and the stuck emotions within it. Her empowered presence could now help others in ways she had never imagined before. Becoming aware of her subtle body and its need for balance was critical for her healing.

Working from this framework for the past two decades has broadened my perspective of health and illness beyond just the Physical body. It has provided me with the insight to ask questions that identify causal levels of imbalance that manifest in illness and disease. This has assisted me in referring patients to appropriate practitioners who can help to restore balance at deeper levels. When combined with traditional medical methods, this approach brings the Four Body System™ into alignment. When alignment and balance are achieved, true healing can be experienced. In addition, this facilitates a level of self-awareness that assists patients to make conscious and healthy choices and deepens their wisdom about how to stay healthy.

Clearly, there is no single solution to health or illness. We are multi-layered organisms who live in energy fields that are constantly changing. We are influenced by the food we eat, the traumas we bear, the support we receive, and the choices we make. Our choices greatly influence our health. If we seek and choose from a place of consciousness, we are less likely to get sick. If we choose out of complacency or familiarity we are more likely to get sick. It is important for us to stay aware of the connections between our biology, biography, emotions, and energy and the powerful affects they have on health and illness.

The meridian system

Eastern philosophy is based on the premise that all life occurs within the cycle of nature. Things within nature are connected and mutually dependent on each other. Nature is one unified system, the Tao with polar and complementary aspects: Yin and Yang. Nature is in constant motion, following cyclic patterns that describe the process of transformation. When the elements of nature are in balance, life is harmonic and flourishes. When the balance of the polar forces is upset, disaster looms.

~Harriet Beinfield and Efrem Korngold

The Chinese coined the term *Qi* (pronounced, "chee") to mean basic stuff, or the "stuff that makes things happen," or "stuff in which things happen." It is the life force or life energy that flows through *energy channels* or *meridians* in the body in precise patterns that effect health and well-being. Precise meridians correspond to precise organs in the body. If the flow of *Qi* is blocked in the meridians, life flow stagnates and illness results by compromising the health of the corresponding organs. In order to restore a state of health, the restoration of the flow of *Qi* within the meridians is required.

The Chinese believe that for us to be healthy, we must be able to adapt to our environment in a way that keeps our "nature" balanced. When this balance is disrupted, our resources are exhausted and we become sick. They say, "The man is not sick because he has an illness, he has an illness because he is sick."

Just as imbalance in a garden caused by too much heat, water, dryness, or lack of sunlight effects the growth of the plants; excess heat or dampness, inadequate nutrition, excess or inadequate *Qi*, or its poor circulation, weakens our health. The doctor is likened to a gardener whose role is to restore the soil to health to make the garden healthy. In the same manner, the doctor's role is to help bring balance to excess heat, moisture, or dampness in the body for the *Qi* to flow smoothly. This is done through acupuncture, herbs, nutritional and lifestyle changes. In order to sustain balance, *Qi* needs to flow. Additional recommendations for restoring flow create additional impact. Acupuncture treatments that insert very thin needles at specific points along meridians can restore the flow of *Qi* bringing well-being to the system.

Yin and Yang:
As mentioned earlier, two main aspects of our nature are Yin and Yang energies. The Yin and Yang aspects are integral to maintaining balance in the Energy body. The Yang aspect is fast, erratic, light, and hot. The Yin aspect is slow, deliberate, cool, dense, and persevering.

With too much Yang, our body suffers from symptoms of excess heat such as hot flashes, night sweats, acid reflux, dry and cracked skin, insomnia, anxiety, hypertension, headaches, and a rapid heart rate. Too much Yin is associated with a slow pace, reduced metabolism, cool skin, fatigue, and the lack of resilience and vitality.

Internal organs correspond to Yin, and skin and muscles correspond to Yang energy. The upper body corresponds to Yang and the lower body (rooted in the earth) corresponds to Yin energy. Yin provides the substance required to sustain Yang. Without it, the Yang is weakened, and the body is unprotected. Yin and Yang mutually support each other. This is also necessary to sustain health and maintain the flow of *Qi*.

Yin energy commonly stagnates during midlife. As the body prepares to enter the second half of life and slow itself down from the high activity of youth, it becomes somewhat imbalanced with a tendency towards Yin stagnation and Yang increase. Restoring the flow of Yin and Yang channels, with acupuncture, herbs, and diet, is necessary to maintain health and vitality in midlife. When women consume Yang foods like alcohol and coffee (chapter 4) in excess, they are more likely to have the typical symptoms of menopause common in the West. A licensed acupuncturist or Doctor of Chinese Medicine can offer them nutritional and herbal guidance as well as acupuncture, which can balance their Yin and Yang energies and restore health and well-being. Chronic imbalance increases stress hormone levels and compromises the integrity of the immune system, increasing the risk for disease.

> Health as defined as the poised balance between Yin-Yang, and sickness is the result of a deficiency or excess, a Yin-Yang disharmony. Survival is based on an organism's capacity to adapt to changing conditions and maintain equilibrium. Yin-Yang harmony is a metaphor for sustaining adaptability and equilibrium.
> ~Harriet Beinfield and Efrem Korngold

Chris

Chris is a 48-year-old woman whose perimenopausal symptoms were not responding to natural hormones. Her blood levels of hormones showed balance, but she continued to suffer from hot flashes, night sweats, and insomnia. She had difficulty falling asleep and when she did, she awakened, anxious, at 3 a.m. She was perplexed with her symptoms and came to me for help.

Chris was working in a stressful job and felt tired and depleted at the end of the day. She regularly ate fast food, washed it down with soda, and drank multiple cups of coffee to maintain her energy. For dinner, she ate a high-fat meal followed by a nightcap to relax and medicate her anxiety. She craved sugar and frequently snacked on candy and chocolate.

From her symptoms, it was clear that Chris was 'overheated' due to Yang excess. She needed to reduce the heat generated by her diet high in Yang energy. She also needed acupuncture to restore flow to her stagnant and depleted Yin channels.

After eight sessions of weekly acupuncture and changes in her diet and lifestyle, her symptoms began to heal. She eliminated alcohol and coffee and began eating root vegetables and greens. She eliminated sugar and drank plenty of water and green tea. Within two months, her symptoms resolved. They returned if she drank alcohol or coffee in excess. She learned how to follow a lifestyle that balanced her Yin and Yang energies. Her sleep cycle was restored and she regained resilience and vitality.

The Emotional body

The Emotional body is one of the most neglected yet important bodies that needs understanding and attention. Since our society encourages the denial of feelings, our relationship with this body is compromised. We often view intense feelings as abnormal, pathological and a sign of weakness. We feel shame when we express them. We apologize when we do. When society views the expression of feelings as negative, our Emotional body risks imbalance.

Our feeling function is our connection to our heart and instinct. It connects us with our soul. It helps us discern right from wrong. The pharmaceutical industry makes billions of dollars on prescription drugs that suppress feeling function. The Emotional body is the body that connects us with what is real. If we deny or suppress the feelings that emerge from it, we lose our capacity to truly heal.

Our Emotional body informs us when our Energy body is traumatized, overloaded, or imbalanced. It warns us when we are not safe, or in harm's way. If we obey society's rules and deny or suppress our feeling function, we risk losing our health and sometimes even our life. Our soul can only be accessed through our feelings. An aligned and connected Emotional body expresses the wisdom of the Feminine Principle.

After spending half our lives denying our feelings for acceptance, the Emotional body becomes charged. The pressure that builds from self-denial and adaptation needs release. It can manifest in strong reactions or sometimes even as illness (Table 1). We begin to lose tolerance for "the small stuff" we adapted to before now. My patients call this "intolerance to bulls**t! In midlife, hormonal changes catalyze this process in women. This impacts the Four Body System™ in precise ways. When hormones shift, feeling function rises. The Emotional body becomes exquisitely sensitive during this time.

I have observed how a woman's sensations in her body and the sensitivity of her nervous system are profoundly impacted by a fall in progesterone. She can sense things in ways she may not have been able to since she was a child. Perimenopausal women tell me that they often feel like a "ball of nerves." Their feelings are deeper and more intense than ever before. They have difficulty understanding this new level of feeling. It frightens many who have been emotionally repressed or who have denied their feelings for half their lives. They now react and respond more frequently from a place of truth.

They suddenly have a harder time compromising themselves to adapt. Many women who held their truth inside before now while adapting to the expectations of others, experience a newfound sense of freedom and empowerment. Their feelings remind them of who they really are underneath familiar compensations. They are finally able to feel and experience the strength of their intrinsic power. They are now transforming into women who can no longer deny strong feelings. This is one of the most powerful ways in which women reclaim their emotional health in midlife.

The Mental body

The Mental body contains elements of the Emotional and Physical bodies. When feelings are suppressed, they build energetic pressure inside the Emotional body and alter the physiology of the Physical body. Serotonin levels are adversely affected and any system in the body that relies on serotonin for normal function is compromised. These imbalances also manifest in the Mental body especially in women who suppress or deny their feelings. They often see their physicians for symptoms of anxiety or depression, as they don't understand their causes. Traditional medical physicians commonly prescribe psychiatric medications for anxiety and depression to manage their symptoms but rarely empower women to understand or process their deep feelings.

When symptoms are managed without exploring their causes, patients remain unhealed. It is important to understand that in midlife, symptoms in the Mental body are often the result of the repressed feelings present in the Emotional body. Women in midlife need validation and a safe space to process these feelings and gain an awareness of the power that lies within them.

Many of my patients who have been on anti-depressants for years for situational depression or anxiety want to discontinue them in midlife. With gradual weaning, close follow up and psychotherapy, many are successful. They feel more connected to their real self and more whole without medication. In addition, they feel more empowered and unafraid to feel deeply.

Many women are appropriately put on anti-depressants during a stressful life event when they are not able to work through the anxiety or depression that may have arisen as a result. It is not uncommon for them to be continued on medications for years, even after the event passes. Continued use of anti-depressants in this unfortunate manner can numb a woman's feeling-function longer than is therapeutically necessary. They risk being erroneously labeled with a mental disorder and fear coming off medication. They need to be closely monitored as they wean off these medications. Many of my patients who have been on antidepressants for years for situational depression and anxiety want to discontinue their medications in midlife. With gradual weaning, close follow-up, and psychotherapy many are successful. They feel more connected to their real self and more "whole" without medication. In addition, they feel more empowered and less afraid to feel deeply.

The majority of symptoms in the Mental body have their roots in the Emotional body. One of the main dysfunctions in our society is the lack of validation and framework to understand and process our feelings. This places us at risk for imbalances in the Mental body in midlife. As long as we suppress our feeling function and believe that denying feelings is a sign of "strength," the Emotional body will remain imbalanced and unhealed. If we self-medicate for symptom relief, we can develop addictive patterns, creating additional imbalances in the three other bodies.

The field of psychiatry is very effective in the treatment of *true* mental illness. When I refer to the inadequacy of psychiatric medications in helping symptoms caused by hormonal imbalance, I am not speaking of true mental illness. I am referring specifically to the symptoms of anxiety and depression that frequently accompany perimenopause and menopause. These do not need to be medicated. A majority of them are not due to true mental illness.

The Physical body

$$E = mc^2$$
~Albert Einstein

Albert Einstein stated that energy and mass are equivalent. The Physical body is the densest of the Four Body System™. It holds the three other bodies within it (Figure 4). When they remain imbalanced, disease manifests with precision at the level of the Physical body.

The traditional medical model views illness only through the lens of the Physical body. Its focus is on the physical repair needed after a disease has manifested. Medical training teaches physicians to manage symptoms, rather than evaluate and heal the causes of illness and disease. The *cause* of disease is commonly confused with its *manifestation*. The deeper causes of physical manifestations are rarely explored. When viewed from the context of the Four Body System™, causes at the Energy and Emotional body levels manifest with precision at the Physical body level. From the traditional medical framework, disease is not viewed from the perspective of imbalance. It is only seen as a breakdown at the physical or biological level. The treatments offered merely manage symptoms or remove diseased parts. They do not offer true healing. Since we have normalized the traditional framework for the past 200 years, patients rely only on palliative treatments as they are conditioned to think that diseases cannot be cured. They remain dependent on prescription medications alone, abdicate their responsibility in healing and rely only on the physician's expertise to manage their symptoms.

This costs our country trillions in health care dollars and Americans remain chronically ill. This form of medicine is "sick care," not health care, as it does not restore health. It is only when patients explore the causes for their illness that they can reclaim their health.

When a critical mass of people begins to view health and illness from the perspective of the Four Body System™, our country's health care crises will end.

As we have seen, our lack of healing is often a result of the limited framework utilized in our medical system that is superficial and "sick care" oriented. We need to realize that we can never heal through physical means alone.

As we expand our perspective to include the body's emotional and energetic aspects, we will be able to restore health, healing, and harmony to our life at all levels. This larger context can evoke the seeker in both physicians and patients. Through this new and expanded lens, we can find areas of imbalance that run deeper than just mental or physical levels for *true* healing. This can also deepen our consciousness and restore meaning to our life's journey.

It is imperative that women in midlife advocate for the healing of their Four Body System™. It is important to be discerning in their search for practitioners, both traditional and complementary that engage a high standard-of-care. For our health care system to evolve, it is imperative that traditional physicians expand their diagnostic tool box to include ways of diagnosing and treating illness that heal all four bodies in addition to empowering their patients to become self-responsible. This framework is truly integrative and describes the practice of Integrative Medicine more completely and from a higher standard than what currently exists.

Additional medical training is not needed for physicians to effectively practice Integrative Medicine. What they need is a broader and more comprehensive framework through which to understand and treat patients. This would require them to be open to collaborating with complementary practitioners.

They must be able to expand their framework to include the restoration of balance at all levels. This would involve working within a context such as the one described above. Unfortunately today, physicians who claim expertise in Integrative Medicine learn an abbreviated skill set of complementary practices and compete with certified complementary practitioners with extensive training in these disciplines. Not only is this unsafe, it is misleading to the public who assumes that a traditional physician's knowledge of complementary medicine rivals a certified practitioner's expertise. Integrative Medicine views both traditional and complementary practitioners as equally valuable. It is their collaborative effort that can most effectively heal their patients.

As we have seen, the framework of the Four Body System™ has the potential to change the face of health care by increasing the likelihood of healing diseases at levels of cause rather than by just managing symptoms. This approach can deepen our consciousness and restore meaning to both physicians and patients as they collaborate to seek answers to the crucial questions that disease and illness evoke. Patients could actively participate in their healing without normalizing their fear-based relationship with the medical system. Instead, their relationship would transform into a partnership and serve medicine's original and sacred intention for wisdom and healing, currently missing in the health care system.

Additionally, in the system where physician burnout is at an all-time high, this expanded paradigm of diagnosis and treatment can restore meaning to the practice of medicine. Imagine the possibilities for growth and learning that this could bring to our society and engage us all as we reclaim our personal and collective health.

6

What Is Love?

Love

What do you call love?
It has a strange definition
infected by the unholy
surface of the mask.
That is not love.
That is—
living from the shell
without feeling
the animal that breathes beneath,
who crawls close to the earth,
in warmth and sand,
and dirt and mud.
Love is—
becoming that animal,
that breathes deeply
when broken open by
pain and grief
and carries scars that
reveal its soul.
Love is—
having communion
with the mess of it all.
It never closes.

It is felt in the cries of a mother
during birth
and the cries
of anguish from loss.
It carries joy -
a medicine
that feeds the hungry ghosts
and lays them to rest.
Love is not fillet sentimentality.
It brings out what is buried
and uncovers what is hidden—
dark secrets that betray life.
The love I feel is not a mask,
but a deep cauldron
though carrying pain,
offers beauty to life.
It is an opening to the sublime,
a portal to what is Holy.
It bears everything transforming
and never breaks or dies.

To love oneself is the beginning of a life-long romance.
~Oscar Wilde

As we approach midlife, many of us find ourselves responding in
ways that are unfamiliar and often startling. The deep transformation underway in our psyches attempts to connect us with our
authentic selves. Our old definitions for what we value and how we
relate are called into question to be reframed and purified. We realize that we need to dive underneath familiarity and connect with a
deeper level of meaning that resonates with authenticity and truth,
rather than the expectations of society. Sometimes our truth is

contrary to society's definitions. This can create a tension that feels difficult and disheartening. In midlife, it is no longer possible for us to obey society at the cost of who we really are.

Susan

Susan is a 45-year-old woman who came to see me after a year of worsening symptoms of perimenopause. She was frightened by the anger she now felt towards tasks she had happily performed for many years, such as picking up after her children and preparing dinner when her husband arrived home from work. She worked from nine to five in customer service at a department store. She felt depleted at the end of the day after dealing with customer complaints.

Her job was unfulfilling and lacked meaning. It was merely the means for making a living. Every day, she came home to a mess made by her children, and a husband who expected a cooked dinner and a clean house. She had tolerated this for sixteen years, but now felt agitated and angry. For the first time in her life, she felt what was expected of her as unfair and unjust. She had performed these tasks singlehandedly, her "duty" as a wife and mother. When she made her newly felt discontent known to her husband and children, they told her that she needed to see a therapist to "fix" her discontent. They felt she was acting "crazy" and with "too much" emotion. Her need for balance was unlike her previously adapted state. They wanted her to continue her adapted ways of being.

Love defined as self-sacrifice

Susan was beyond frustration. Like many of us who have been programmed to obey society's expectations for the sake of "duty," while sacrificing our own needs, we suddenly find ourselves angry at what is expected of us. We realize that for many years we undermined our needs in favor of others. We were conditioned to not question this. A "good girl" sacrificed herself without complaint. This was defined for us as "love." We were rewarded for this form of "loving." We were told we were virtuous. If this felt unhealthy, we second-guessed our feelings. We saw women behaving like this everywhere we looked. We were outnumbered. We learned to undermine our questioning. We lost trust in our deepest wisdom, our instinct and intuition.

As children, when we felt the dissonance between society's expectations and our inner wisdom and questioned society, we were told to adapt to what was expected. We learned to stop questioning. We adapted for acceptance. Over time, these became our patterns of behaving. We confused love with self-sacrifice. The care of others held more value than our own needs. We saw this as a virtue. We gave without receiving.

When we continue to give without receiving, the imbalance created in the Energy and Emotional bodies can manifest as anger. Since we were conditioned to believe in the virtue of self-sacrifice, we ignored our feelings in favor of obedience. In midlife, this catches up with us. Our anger is actually a *normal* response to this unhealthy pattern and rises up in our feeling function, but we are don't trust it as a sign of health. Instead, we feel there is something wrong with us for questioning what seems normal for others. Furthermore, society shames us for questioning. Suppressing our feelings made us vulnerable to adapting to society's rules. For the first half of of lives, we associated love with self-sacrifice. One defined the other. We disconnected from our feeling function. In midlife, the pressure created by this kind of emotional suppression, attempts release, heralding this medial time. We are no longer able to contain it. We call this rage.

The Emotional body would not suffer this way if we were taught that giving and receiving are both necessary for healthy love, and that anger can be a sign of health. Questioning society's definitions is also a sign of health, and trusting in the wisdom of our feeling function is required for self-respect. In midlife, the Emotional body can no longer hold the charge caused by the suppression of truth and wisdom. This charge is viewed by many as pathological. It is the fury resulting from neglect of our real self, in favor of society's rules that do not resonant with the truth of who we really are. This charge is what we are punished and shamed for, and what we need to validate and understand, for its release and for our healing. Contained within this charge is also the call from our "double" who reminds us to love ourselves and honor our needs. We must redefine the meaning of love. This takes courage. If we don't listen, imbalance will surface. It will seep into our Mental body as depression. Depression is the symptom that brings us to our physician within the medical system.

We normalized society's unhealthy definitions of love that we were imprinted with. These patterns became familiar. These distorted our definition of love.

The pattern of selflessness that contaminates healthy love is not even love. It is over-care. We have confused over-care with love. Over-care is a word that means "caring too much for the other." Over-care is disempowering. We over-care for others in relationships when we assume they are unable to care for themselves. Unknowingly we disempower them. This is the definition of rescue, not love. When we were being imprinted with this pattern, although it felt unhealthy, we still behaved from it. We ignored how we felt. We were socialized to rescue at the cost of our own needs. We dismissed any thought of self-care as selfish. Self-care is what our Emotional body craves. It is the only way it can stay balanced and support our health.

Alongside anger, a feeling of "loss of self" results from many years of self-sacrifice. This is a feeling that all women know but are not able to name. The ways in which we give ourselves over to others compromises our connection to our authentic self. When anger and irritation arise, we feel confused and ashamed. This new and frightening feeling resists our obedience to familiar rules. This is how our soul informs us that we can no longer pour ourselves forth "for the sake of love" and expect nothing in return.

We can no longer live this way and expect to feel whole. We can no longer compromise our integrity and expect our relationships to be healthy. We can no longer compromise our sovereignty in an attempt to normalize society's rules. Our "double" calls to us for a course correction back to living from our truth.

We are conditioned by society's standards

There is a term used in psychology called operant conditioning. It is a form of learning where a pleasing or noxious stimulus is delivered when a behavior is expressed, whose purpose is to either encourage or discourage the behavior. When a person in a position of authority punishes us with painful consequences for certain behaviors, we learn to not behave in those ways. When they reward us for certain behaviors, we learn to behave in those ways. Some rewards, such as praise and acceptance are pleasing enough to make us perform behaviors associated with reward. We quickly learn the behaviors that reward us and those that punish. We adapt to society's expectations in this way, through operant conditioning. When we were children, our family was our small universe that prepared us to function in the world from their patterns of behavior. These patterns were modeled to us by our parents, teachers, the media, and the society at large. They were reinforced through reward and punishment. Often, the reward was acceptance; the punishment was rejection. Physical and emotional violence are both forms of punishment whenare associated with specific behaviors. We quickly learned to avoid punishment. Since we all craved connection, we learned to define "right" and "wrong" behaviors this way. It was through operant conditioning that we were imprinted with our family's definitions.

Many of us watched our mothers sacrifice themselves when they over-cared for others. We watched them becoming depressed and anxious in midlife. We heard them rationalizing and normalizing over-care with other midlife women. They did not see their symptoms as a sign of a need for self-care. They did not have a relative position for health. Many of us dread ending up like our mothers. Our mothers did not understand the struggle between the needs of the real self and the demands of society. They did not have the framework that we do. In midlife, we need to redefine ourselves from this new and healthy place. We need to consider self-care a priority. We need to trust our feeling function and the wisdom it holds. We need to reframe our definition of health. A deeper challenge for many of us is the belief that *our needs do not matter*. We often confuse this with the belief that *we* do not matter. This injunction leads us to believe that our needs are secondary to the needs of others—that our purpose in life is to serve others. Nothing could be further from our soul's truth.

This is what awakens during midlife, marking the journey back to our authentic self. For many women, this journey is marked by breast cancer. Women who fail to nurture themselves are at risk for diseases of their breasts. Many of my patients with breast cancer feel their cancer is a symptom of depleted energy, and a message from their Emotional bodies that they need self-nourishment. They feel this deeper cause of cancer resulted from half a life of serving others at the cost of themselves. It is a wake up call for them to look at the imbalance due to the depletion present in their Energy bodies from the lack of self-care. Cancer of their breast is a symbolic yet precise message from their bodies to now reframe and redefine what love means. As they examine these levels, they are able to reclaim their worth and validate their needs. For some, it means reframing their illness as the catalyst to redefine and transform behaviors that no longer work. This helps them reconnect to themselves and return to a state of wholeness. In the U.S., one in seven women will be diagnosed with breast cancer every year. We must address its emotional and energetic causes by learning how to balance giving with receiving. This can be life-saving for all.

What does this have to do with love?

This has everything to do with love. The basic fabric of love is encoded in our hearts. We innately know this, but are conditioned to forget it. We have lived half our lives from the unhealthy definitions of love normalized by society. They have compromised our health. When we behave from society's unhealthy definitions of love we lose our personal boundaries. We lose contact with our limits— where we end and another begins. Our "double" demands that we end this cycle.

Women in our culture are not taught how to be feminine except in relationship to men. Women allow men to define them. This definition is an extension of society's distorted one, which is incorrect and superficial. These distortions are imprints that undermine the feminine. These attitudes pervade our world. The relationship women have with themselves is heavily influenced by the culture in which they live. This wounds women. When definitions of the self are extrinsic, women become vulnerable to abuse. Abdicating their power to others disconnects them from their intrinsic power. These patterns make it impossible for them to live from the truth of who they really are.

In extreme cases, women are even conditioned to stay in abusive marriages or dysfunctional jobs for the sake of "love" for their families.

As a woman who lived from these definitions, I realized in hindsight how I became vulnerable to abuse. My instinct for boundaries was wounded and I second-guessed my needs and placed the needs of others before mine. I unknowingly betrayed myself like many women do. The midlife gateway forced me to awaken to my unhealthy patterns and redefine who I needed to become.

Love is a feeling

In the English language, there is only one word for love. In Inuit, there are 23 words for love. In Eastern countries, there are close to 50 words for love. There, the description of the different kinds of love is qualified with sensory and poetic undertones. The many definitions have different meanings and inflections. The different ways the word "love" is used evokes different feelings. In the West, since feeling function is not valued, the definition of love is easy to distort. It is too general and lacks feeling. We are conditioned to understand this word as society defines it. The Western definition of love does not include qualities of truth and integrity. These are core qualities that reside in the heart alongside love. Love is the energy that emanates from the heart. Fierce love is fearless and resilient. It is active, not passive. It expects us to behave in ways that support health and healing.

Tough love, like fierce love, is a love that transcends fear of conflict. It is committed to doing what is best for others despite their displeasure when it is expressed. It is able to hold a standard of integrity. It asserts truth. It evokes patience and is able to endure rejection for the sake of health. This kind of love is no stranger to parents of teenagers. Our difficult journeys with them teach us how to express it. This is the kind of love we all deserve. It arises from a deep place of heart and does not settle for compromise. It is also the kind of love that awakens in midlife women in relationship to themselves. It is worth exploring and living from. It has within it the power to restore self-respect and self-esteem. It can teach us to honor our feelings and to not compromise our truth or integrity for anyone. It can even heal us from abuse.

What love is not

No person is your friend who demands your silence,
or denies your right to grow.

~Alice Walker

We need to question our integrity when we sacrifice ourselves to be accepted. When we follow societies expectations despite our resistance towards them, we run the risk of self-betrayal. Duty at the cost of self is not love. Distorted definitions of love are not synonymous with health. Our definitions of love must support our health.

In my marriage, when I spoke my truth strongly, I was asked if I would rather be "right or alone." Healthy love holds a space for truth to be received and heard. In contrast, I was threatened with rejection and abandonment if I spoke my truth. I was conditioned early on to suppress what was true for me, in the service of "duty." My adapted self did not question this. This was familiar.

Many women who are imprinted with distortions from society confuse love with compliance to the rules of the system within which they live or work. They are taught through conditioning to not question their unhealthy patterns. These are the rules of a closed system. In closed systems, its unhealthy members in positions of authority define love in unhealthy ways, distorting its healthy definitions. They demand secrecy as a sign of love, and expect others in the system to adapt to it's unhealthy rules. We confused compliance with love and were manipulated to adapt through operant conditioning. Until we can see this, we remain vulnerable to losing contact with our real self. In midlife, our "double" requires us to dismantle these distortions. Since our need for connection is like oxygen for our hearts, we may feel terrified at the thought of losing connection with people we love. We must remember the truth of who we are and have faith in our process. The pain of separating from others is worth the joy of reconnecting with our authentic self. If people leave us when we connect with what is real, we must question the health of these relationships. As we leave them behind, our commitment to our health will draw relationships to us that support our process. We have to remember this. When we enable relationships that normalize the rules of a closed system, we become a part of the problem, not the solution. Redefining ourselves requires that we dismantle our conditioned adaptations. If we do not do this consciously, the pressure within us, built from adapting for so long, is guaranteed to arise from the Energy and Emotional bodies in the form of a "crisis."

Often, this crisis marks our midlife gateway. Our Energy and Emotional bodies require us to balance them and dismantle our adaptations that are no longer working. Our soul calls us to live from our true purpose. Without this process of reframing and reclaiming, we are unable to live authentically. Indigenous people consider this a form of "soul retrieval." If we choose to not engage in retrieving the denied parts of our soul, we risk living the second half of our lives without real meaning, relying on others to fulfill our unmet needs.

Sentimentality confused as love

Carl Jung defined sentimentality as a "superstructure covering up brutality." I believe what he meant is that covering our authentic self with distorted definitions disconnects us from our feelings. This puts us at risk for "brutal" behavior. When we compromise our feeling function by adapting to society's rules, we are not able to truly love. Love is connected with feeling function. Sentimentality is not. Instead, it is the theoretical understanding of the word "love" without the depth of feelings described earlier. Sentimentality lacks connection with integrity and truth, which is integral to healthy love.

Sentimentality risks nothing. It does not arise from the heart like love does. Love in its purest form takes risks. Love makes us vulnerable. By nature, love is messy. We risk a broken heart when we love deeply. But in order for us to find meaning and fulfillment in relationships, we must take this risk. Sentimentality does not share this quality. Sentimentality does not risk true feeling.

Love is a verb. It is *behaved* in relationships with others. Sentimentality is a noun. It is not behaved or truly felt.

Some examples of sentimentality are a partner who verbalizes love without loving behavior; parents who verbalize love, or show it through financial support, without behaving in loving ways. Sentimentality is not connected to feeling function. It arises from the mind, not the heart. It lacks passion and emotion. It is not connected to the real self. It is an extension of the adapted self. In some families, *sentimentality is mistaken for love*. When people are imprinted with sentimentality rather than love, they are unable to be authentic in relationships. Their relationships remain superficial. Authentic love frightens them. It feels unfamiliar and risky. They avoid it and as a result they miss the experience of depth and meaning.

Many people who carry this pattern suffer from depression, as their hearts are not intimately engaged in their relationships. They substitute what is sentimental for what is real and feel emptiness. If they awaken to this later in life, their journey towards loving authentically can be difficult. They have to be willing to take risks in order to experience real love in relationships. If they have the courage to dismantle this imprinted pattern, they can finally experience depth and meaning. It is our task in midlife to replace what is sentimental with what is real. It is the only meaningful way in which we can spend the second half of our lives.

Agitation as a sign of health

All over the world, women in midlife are reconsidering the definitions of love and power. Like Susan, they feel agitated when they are manipulated into adapting to the rules of closed systems, where they are expected to serve everyone's needs but their own. Their agitation is a sign of health. It is a sign that these rules no longer work. They are not based in healthy exchange. They require self-sacrifice at the cost of health. Women need to pay close attention to their needs, dismantle their over-caring behaviors and hold a standard of self-care for themselves. They must first fill themselves up, before they overflow onto others.

Reclaiming our health

Many women feel that they are being selfish while transforming their unhealthy behaviors into healthy ones. They confuse self-care for being selfish. If long-term depletion can cause breast cancer, we must pay attention to the price we pay for self-neglect. We need to take responsibility for healing our energetic imbalances through self-care. We need to incorporate this into our society as a core value.

Our society has a responsibility to support us as we reclaim our health. It, however, expects us to maintain its status quo where we adapt to being dominated. Without our cooperation, society can actually transform into an open system. We must change our behaviors from conditioned ones that make us sick, to healthy ones that support health. When we adapt out of fear, we unknowingly betray ourselves.

A woman's voice and will are the strongest powers on the planet. We must find our voices and assert them. If we don't, we will lead the future generations like the Pied Piper into a river of dysfunction, where love is distorted as self-sacrifice and expresses itself in symptoms that risk our health. We must transform our unhealthy relationships into ones that support self-love and self-honor.

What is healthy love?

Love and health are interdependent. We must replace our distorted definitions of love with healthy ones and integrate these into our personal and collective psyches.

Renee

Renee is a 43-year-old woman who came to see me for symptoms of severe anxiety and insomnia that began when she discovered that her husband was having an affair. He told her that if she truly loved him she would be happy for him for finding someone better than her. This shocked her into examining his definition of love, which did not resonate with hers. She came to see me to discuss this inner struggle and to validate her definition of love that she felt her husband had violated. Her symptoms resulted from this struggle. She felt his version of love lacked integrity, and he expected her to compromise her version to normalize his betrayal of their marital commitment. She was outraged.

His family, whom she had considered as her own, turned a blind eye to his behavior and asked her to capitulate and to "get over" her anger towards him. They even asked her to forgive him. She was unable to forgive him despite what they expected of her. She felt he needed to *earn* her forgiveness by feeling how he had hurt her. If she forgave him without this, she would be colluding with them against herself. She felt she would be enabling his disrespect towards her. She would be normalizing his act of betrayal. She would be endangering her integrity by "forgiving" his disrespect of their marital commitment. Her feeling function was not in alignment with what his family expected. If she "forgave" him for their sake, she would be behaving from a place that was not real for her. She realized that his love towards her was sentimental, imprinted and reinforced by the closed system of his family. She was only willing to forgive him if he transformed his sentimentality into love through true remorse and changed his behavior towards her to one of respect and honor. He never did.

With her truth and feelings validated, Renee gained comfort in connecting with the integrity of her values. She resolved the struggle between what was true for her versus injunctions from others. She did not compromise her definition of healthy love. This healed her symptoms.

Inner resistance

The expectation to compromise our integrity for "love" will evoke feelings of resistance. If we override these feelings out of obedience to society, we risk second-guessing our inner wisdom, wounding our intuition and *betraying* ourselves. Self-betrayal commonly manifests as anxiety or depression in the Emotional and Mental bodies. The boundaries mentioned earlier that are needed for relationships to be healthy sometimes become known to us through the resistance we feel. These must be honored. Many women are unable to define these feelings of resistance as a sign of health. They have been taught to question their feelings. Instead, they need to learn to honor them.

Therapy can help women on the journey back to themselves. It can uncover the cause of depression or anxiety and trace it back to the flawed definitions they have been living from. They can learn to honor their inner resistance and finally reframe it as a sign of health. Resistance is a signal from inner our wisdom which warns us of danger.

Self-talk in most women takes the form of self-criticism or self-doubt. If women obey their wounded script, they risk compromising their self-worth. Our imprinted and wounded scripts are intimately connected with our feeling function. Many feelings that arise from our critical self-talk deprive us of joy. They cause depression and anxiety and drive us to self-medicate with behaviors that can become addictive. When these distractions do not work, we may take prescribtion medications to suppress our feelings. These further disconnect us from our feeling function. True healing requires us to uncover the roots of our unhappiness. It requires us to reconnect with ourselves and realign with our truth. In doing this, we can reclaim our happiness and joy.

Love is not rescue

Love does not shame others into obedience. This is the definition of manipulation, not love. When one attempts to manipulate and control others in the "name of love," they are operating from the patriarchal dynamic of domination. Domination is a rule present in closed systems. Since we often mistake rescue for love, we need to be aware of any hooks that engage our need to rescue. One of these hooks is *pity*. Women often confuse pity with empathy. They misunderstand pity to be a sign of love. If pity is being evoked within us, we are on treacherous ground. We are vulnerable to falling into the trap of rescue mistaken for love. We unknowingly dominate others by rescuing them. This act makes us feel powerful. We believe we can rescue them through this power. They become dependent on our efforts. This is codependency, not love. Pity hooks many women into codependent relationships.

When they begin their process of recovery, women awaken to this. They must reclaim themselves from the disempowerment they feel as a result of codependency. They mistook pity for empathy, and rescue for love. Pity evokes feelings of obligation. When we feel obligated to help others, our Energy body is in danger of giving without receiving. It is in danger of becoming depleted.

Many women who are imprinted with this definition and conditioned by it find themselves in relationships with deeply wounded people. They feel a sense of personal power and purpose as they set out to "heal" the other with their unconditional "love." Many abusive marriages operate from this dynamic. Rescue through over-care will often lead to feelings of entitlement from the other and resentment if the care is withdrawn. This can lead to emotional and physical abuse. Women who are in recovery from domestic violence often see how difficult it was for them to separate themselves from the dysfunctional definitions of "love" they behaved from in their unhealthy marriages. Their recovery often involves learning what healthy love is and behaving from its definition. When they stop rescuing, they can restore self-care. This connects them with their intrinsic power. It also encourages others in relationships with them to become self-responsible.

We need to understand that we are all responsible for our own journey towards wholeness and health. We must remember this as a basic truth. In contrast to what we have been conditioned to believe, our health depends on living from truth. Another person's happiness is not our responsibility. It is theirs. Our love can hold space for others to heal themselves. The best and the most honorable gift we can give to another is our belief in their ability to heal themselves. Their commitment to their journey towards health is honorable and worthy of our support. Their lack of willingness to grow and be self-responsible is a warning for us to not enable them. It will evoke resistance within us. We must behave in accordance with the wisdom in the resistance we feel, and honor our boundaries. This is love redefined from a place of health. Love that evokes empowerment is healthy. Love that evokes dependency is not.

Resistance to the closed system is a sign of self-love

The inner resistance we feel towards unhealthy behaviors is a gift of our midlife process. We need to discern our true needs from those we compromise for the sake of duty. Learning this is a spiritual practice that takes constant awareness. Our disconnected feeling function often begins to awaken when our hormones begin to fall, and the charge within us rises towards outside expectations that weigh us down. We need to learn the language of our feeling function. The rules of society have no regard for our *real* needs. To redefine ourselves, we must remember the wisdom contained in our feelings. Once a woman befriends her resistance toward unhealthy patterns, she can never fall asleep again. If she tries, she risks feeling the tension between her feeling function and the expectations of closed systems.

This tension can aggravate her menopausal symptoms and she may experience an increase in hot flashes, night sweats, insomnia, anxiety, and even fatigue. If she does not listen, her feelings will manifest in symbolic ways, sometimes even physically through her heart and her breasts. Breasts are symbolic of nurturing and nourishment. The heart where truth, love, and integrity reside cannot remain in balance without self-care. It will eventually manifest an illness. *Fifty percent of us will suffer heart attacks if we continue to favor society's definitions and neglect our needs.* Making healthy choices from a place of self-love is one of the ways we can reduce our risk of suffering a heart attack.

We need to work at the level of the Energy body to redefine ourselves with guidance from our feeling function and dismantle any fear that directs our behavior to adapt. It is imperative we do this as it is the only way to transform our society into one that is is heart-centered and honors the feminine. If we do not behave from self-love, we cannot change how others treat us. Their behavior towards us is a reflection of our relationship with ourselves.

The integrity of healthy love

True love takes courage. The root word for courage is *coer*, which in Latin means "the heart." Courage resides alongside love within the heart. It enables us to live from integrity despite our fear of rejection. Changing our pattern in relationships can evoke fear. This is normal during transformation. It is important for us to grow our courage greater than our fear and do whatever it takes to transform our lives to a state of health.

Once the fear passes, our connection to our authentic self can offer us comfort during times when we feel alone. This is a normal stage in the journey back to ourselves. Being alone for self-reflection is necessary. This is when our inner eye opens. When our instinct heals, we recover our ability to see reality underneath the illusions around us. We are able to sense what is healthy and what is not. We develop discernment. From this stage forward, we are less vulnerable to illusion and only settle for what feels real. This process helps us feel safe in our skin and heals our fear of being alone in the world. Through it, we can befriend our real self.

The danger of familiarity

Too often, we unconsciously recreate dynamics in our adult relationships that we learned from our families of origin. Since many of us do not have a relative position of health, we recreate these unhealthy dynamics out of familiarity. Many times the feelings of "comfort" in a relationship is a wound-based, familiar feeling. It feels like we and the other are "one." This feeling is often mistaken for resonance. Wound-based relationships are common in our society. They lead to dysfunctional dynamics and codependency. They often fail, as they do not serve the real self. If a relationship like this endures in a marriage, the children raised in this family will be imprinted with a distorted and codependent definition of love. They will choose partners from dynamics they were raised with. Wound-based relationships do not support wholeness or health. People in these relationships must become self-reliant to heal. They must undertake the hard work of recovery. We can never expect the other in a relationship to "complete us," as our society mistakenly tells us they can.

Adults who separate from familial imprinting are adults who have individuated. Seeking and living from one's individuality is a difficult yet necessary process. Individuation is always difficult because when one attempts to separate from imprinted behaviors, it may feel as though one is betraying one's family of origin. One may feel guilt and shame while doing this. Our soul requires us to individuate in midlife for us to authentically serve our life's purpose. People who find ways to relate to their families of origin from their individuated self can stand in their truth and are no longer vulnerable to being manipulated by shame or guilt. They learn to relate to their family from a place of sovereignty and truth. They are able to reclaim their health and have healthy relationships. Even their relationship with their family can deepen when they engage from their individuated self.

Love as self-care

Self-love needs to be behaved through acts of self-care. I have observed four ways in which women are able to do this:

1. make a commitment to speaking your truth

2. make daily exercise a priority

3. make a commitment to self-nourishment by eating organic and whole food

4. invest in a personal growth process that restores balance at all levels of the Four Body System™

Many women complain that they do not feel worthy to spend money on themselves. Some, who are financially dependent on their partners, feel they are undeserving of this expense. They do not want to "rock the boat" in their relationships by caring for themselves. They feel they will be perceived as selfish. Similar comments are not uncommon even from women who support their families! Ultimately, this is an issue of self-worth. Self-worth determines the extent to how we are able to love ourselves. A majority of women have been shamed into lowering their worth and view themselves through this lens. When they attempt to elevate it as part of their healing process, they may feel shame. They must transform this in order to truly heal. They will find this lens contaminated by the ways in which they were imprinted and conditioned. Sometimes acts of self-love can bring the critical messages embedded in our scripts into awareness. Women need to have the courage to do this difficult work. It takes endurance and patience to recalibrate our self-worth, but this is necessary for us to be able to love authentically, as well as reclaim our health.

Illness forces self-love

Sometimes when faced with a life-threatening illness, our priorities shift to the extreme towards self-care. A threat from the body often causes us to pay attention to our physical, emotional, and energetic needs. Many women find the courage to leave abusive marriages and dysfunctional jobs when diagnosed with a life threatening illness. They reframe their lives and redefine their relationships from a place of health. The possibility of death has the ability to bring unprocessed "baggage" to the surface for transformation. These women realize that in the end what matters most is how deeply they loved and were loved, and whether they lived from integrity and truth. They feel at peace if their love was healthy.

A life of distorted love is one disconnected from what is authentic and real. The greatest gift midlife women can offer themselves and others is healthy love that is real. It is fearless, courageous, and uncompromising. This kind of love is what one is remembered for. Being in the presence of a one who has mastered this can transform us into a higher version of ourselves. This kind of love is greatly needed to heal our hurting world.

This can only be experienced when we give ourselves permission to speak our truth. When we live with the misunderstanding that our truth must be accepted by others, we live from the fear of rejection. This is how we betray ourselves. We need to transform this in midlife. Healthy love always supports our authentic self. It is necessary for us to speak it, so we can know ourselves and be truly known by others.

Modeling healthy love

As we redefine love towards ourselves from a place of health, we can model this for others. We have become desensitized as a culture. We spend hours in front of the television living vicariously through definitions and distortions that are not real. We become desensitized to the violence we watch. It numbs us. It wounds our feeling function. Love is not possible without feeling. If we become desensitized to the world's tragedy and suffering, we risk becoming sentimental. This wounds our feeling function. It disconnects us and erodes our sense of meaning. We compensate for this wounding. Many compensate by over consuming. This is a disease in our society. These behaviors make us sick. We can only be fulfilled through self-love and self-care.

Many women define themselves through the eyes of others. We need to awaken our inner-eyes and redefine ourselves intrinsically. It was harder to do this when we were young, as our dynamics for relating were defined by our parents. If they modeled unhealthy pattens, we recreated them in relationships until this caused us enough pain to awaken our need for change. As we redefine ourselves in midlife we can, at last, relate more clearly from a place of health. From here we can individuate into our real selves.

Our sons and daughters are always watching. We are mentoring them even when we are unaware. If we raised them with our learned distortions and then transform into our real selves in midlife, we can find solace in knowing that we can now offer them a new relative position of health. This offers them a choice between the unhealthy, previously imprinted patterns, and healthy new ones that we now embody.

In my own recovery process, I was able to see how I was conditioned to doubt and second-guess myself. I was not able to connect with myself authentically, and I unknowingly enabled an environment at home where the Feminine Principle was violated and then betrayed. I was feared into adapting to unhealthy and distorted definitions of love. I adapted out of fear. Now, I have the capacity to heal myself and my children by reclaiming what is true for me and behaving from this truth. This is the power of self-love. When we behave from it, it is palpable in our presence. When others are in our presence, they receive permission to connect with themselves from a place of love as well.

When we are intrinsically connected to our real self, our self-worth and self-esteem rises and self-care becomes a priority. This is a process I have observed in my patients. The ones who have connected with their real selves do not hesitate to invest in self-care, as they feel worthy of the investment. Self-advocacy arises from self-love. Without self-love one is unable to make a true commitment to health or wholeness, as the needs of others are valued more than the needs of the self. If you find yourself making this sacrifice and neglecting self-care, you may need to evaluate your relationship with yourself and your definition of love.

In midlife when symptoms arise as a result of years of self-neglect, we must learn how to nourish and balance our Four Body System™. Ironically, our symptoms become the catalysts that force us to learn how to be true to ourselves and fulfill our needs.

As midlife women, we owe this to ourselves, each other and our children. When we redefine ourselves in these ways, our closed, corporate systems will be forced to value health and empowerment. Through our healing, our families and communities will also heal.

Love and soul

Midlife calls us to connect with our soul. It speaks through the voice of our "double," who asks us to reclaim health and meaning The soul is uncompromising in midlife and does not rest until we live from it. It becomes our constant guide and does not part ways with us until our death.

We need to understand the language of our soul. It asks us to restore the balance and harmony always present in nature, aligned with universal law.

To honor our soul, we must:

1. speak and behave from our truth
2. honor our feelings
3. live from integrity without compromise
4. live from truth and honesty in every moment
5. advocate for ourselves through *acts* of self-care
6. invest in methods that will support individuation
7. reframe and honor feelings of resistance as signals of health
8. redefine and behave out of healthy definitions of love without compromise
9. allow others to be self-responsible and not enable them through rescue
10. listen to our instinct when it warns us of danger to our Energy and Emotional bodies

When we feel the need to defend our truth, we are likely being asked to compromise it. It is important to trust that individuation will, no doubt, transform us. It takes courage to individuate. In midlife, we need to support each other's individuation so we can all access our intrinsic power.

Susan's progress revisited

In Susan's journey to self-love, she discovered she was betraying herself by compromising her truth. She realized how her adaptations to unhealthy definitions, where she confused "duty" for love, enabled her family's lack of self-responsibility. This depleted her, causing rage and resentment. As fearful as she was to assert her truth, she began to express it with the therapeutic strategies she had learned. At first her family resisted, but over time, they began to respect her and even become self-responsible. They began to share daily chores. As she consistently learned to care for herself, her need for balance was honored and she felt heard and nurtured. Her husband began to support her needs and their relationship began to heal.

Susan also became empowered enough to behave from these patterns at work. Her relationships with her coworkers became healthy. She began expecting health in all of her relationships and released the ones that did not support it. She used her symptoms of depression as a catalyst to dismantle patterns of self-betrayal and reclaim her self-worth. This restored balance in her Energy, Emotional, and Mental bodies. Her symptoms were replaced with joy. She began to see them as the gifts that they were. They helped her to grow in ways she never could have before. As an added benefit, she reduced her risk of breast cancer and heart disease.

Redefining love and living from healthy definition is a powerful way to heal ourselves and transform our closed systems. We need to remember that we have more intrinsic power than we think. As we make a commitment to becoming real, we can make a profound difference in restoring health and wholeness to ourselves and our wounded world.

7

What Is Power?

My Gift to You
(for my children)

I offer you a gift,
from one who was shaken by terrible suffering.
I am becoming whole.
I have walked on my knees
for a thousand miles through the desert, repenting.
I am done with that.
If I am not "good enough" then so be it.
I offer you my gift of humanness
and awakening to
not having lived from my Real self.
Now I stand in my Truth.
It is my shield.
Now it is healed.
I reclaim myself in shattered places
You help me with your
wild rebellion and rage—
Medicine for my alchemy.
Now my truth will carry you.
It will keep you safe.
It will heal your tears.
It will bring you home.

Change is frightening, but where there is fear, there is power.
If we learn to feel our fear without letting it stop us,
fear can become our ally, a sign to tell us that
something we have encountered can be transformed.

~Maureen Murdock

Menopause as an initiation into our intrinsic power

"What is power?" This is an important question in midlife. Most of us feel disempowered by the time we arrive at this gateway. Women come to see me, feeling battered by life. They feel as though they have no voice to express their needs. One woman told me she wanted to scream without stopping. She felt that even if she screamed for the rest of her life, it would not heal her. She had never connected with her intrinsic power until her hormones began to change. It was only then that she felt it. It was a pressure inside, a "charge" that had built up over the years from self-denial and adaptation. It felt raw and primal. It was her feminine power. She had never lived from it. It had never been given a voice. She had been too busy living a life that was not real for her by allowing others to define her. She had not awakened to this until her changing biology began to unleash the power trapped in her Emotional and Energy bodies.

Nan

Nan is a 42-year-old woman who was 100 pounds overweight and came to me in hopes of healing her depression and anxiety. She also suffered from chronic fatigue. She frequently medicated herself with wine and disassociated from her body. Drinking was her way of coping. She felt "empty" inside. To compensate, she overate. This was her daily pattern.

In addition, her periods were heavy and her libido was low. She began to weep in the exam room. "I don't know whose body this is," she said, "I have never weighed this much or felt this awful. It must be my hormones. I think I need a hysterectomy. I just want to stop bleeding and become my old self again. I want my old body back."

She is not unlike many women in their forties when hormonal shifts begin and their deeper bodies awaken the imbalance present within as mental and physical symptoms. Nan was also grieving as her last child was leaving home, and her sense of self as a mother was threatened. With her children gone, she didn't know who she was. She had been so busy mothering them that she had never stopped to serve her own needs. She did not know who she was apart from her given identity. She did not know how to explore these issues.

This is a common experience for many women in midlife. Not only do their Physical bodies change, the roles through which they defined themselves also change. They arrive at the "medial place" where, as Jungians say, "women can no longer live from the expectations of the world." Now they need to live from the expectations of the *soul*. Like Nan, many women are not aware of this medial territory and like her, many do not even know where to begin.

For Nan, the question itself will be a journey through the second half of her life; and no, she will *not* get her young body back. It was busy serving the world, and did a good job at that. In this medial gateway, the rules change. Even if she found another identity (defined for her by the world) it would not fulfill her. Now she needed to move her focus inward, through framework and strategy to make the journey back to herself through transformation and rebirth. She now needed to define herself from an authentic place.

Years ago, I gave a presentation to a group of midlife women executives. I asked them who they were without their families, their jobs, their status, and their homes. A majority of them could not answer my question. They had been defined by outer roles for so long, they had no connection to their real self. They were vulnerable to feeling the emptiness that often marks the midlife gateway. Sometimes it is marked by a crisis. Hidden within the "crisis" is its higher purpose—the possibility for uncovering our true self, waiting, beneath our assigned and conditioned roles. This can facilitate our connection with our intrinsic power.

Intrinsic power

Intrinsic power is the power of our truth, our innermost self and our soul. This is different than the power of domination by the "power principle." In most of our world, power and domination are synonymous. People in positions of authority often assert this form of power. Unlike intrinsic power, this power is extrinsic. Fear is always present around domination. This kind of power is present in closed systems.

Intrinsic power is supported in relationships that honor truth and sovereignty. It does not evoke fear. On the contrary, it empowers. Intrinsic power does not dominate. It arises from integrity and truth. Nelson Mandela lived from his intrinsic power. Although he spent most of his adult life in jail, dominated by the patriarchy, he never lost his connection to his intrinsic power. Mahatma Gandhi's acts of intrinsic power led India into freedom from being dominated by British rule.

Intrinsic power is the power felt within that is evoked through connecting with and behaving from our authentic self. It is not fear, but truth-based and transcends our fear of rejection. It evokes courage, commitment, endurance, and fearlessness. When we live from these qualities, we are fiercely connected to truth and our personal power can be felt in our presence by others around us. It evokes respect, not fear. Intrinsic power is always a threat to the "power principle" as it cannot be dominated. It's mere presence can expose the patriarchy's lack of integrity.

Women and power

Women are intrinsically powerful. Their monthly cycles make it possible for them to create life. Intrinsic power generates the endurance for giving birth, raising children, and facing hardship. There is no power on earth greater than a mother's love. All through history, women have midwifed birth and death. Despite what they have collectively endured, they continue to love, persevere, and believe in possibility.

We were imprinted to disconnect from our intrinsic power by closed systems when we were young. All parents imprint their children with their own patterns. As children, when our intrinsic power surfaced as truth telling, we were silenced. If our truth was accompanied by strong feelings, it was considered abnormal. They were seen as a threat to the closed systems we lived in. The medical system, being a closed system, often medicates strong feelings. When feelings are medicated, our Emotional body is numbed, disconnecting us from our real self, the inner place where our intrinsic power lies.

Since we are conditioned to disconnect from ourselves, we become frightened any time intense feelings surface, and view them as abnormal. When hormone levels drop, the intensity of feelings rises. This is our soul's attempt to express our repressed feelings. In midlife, it asks us to dismantle our adapted parts and bring forth the parts that resonate with our truth and our real self.

For as long as we remain disconnected from our real selves, we are unable to transform the state of our world. We remain helpless in this weakened state. Women arrive at physician's offices hoping to find answers to explain the depth of their feelings and to learn to relate to them in new ways. They hope to connect with their real selves that have suffered neglect and repression while dutifully serving the needs of the world. Their physicians are rarely able to help them.

In a culture where fairy tales portray the sleeping princess rescued by a knight in shining armor, we are programmed to live a life of expectancy, patiently waiting for a knight to awaken us and rescue us from our plight. We are conditioned to feel like *victims waiting to be rescued*. We integrate these fairy tales into our psyches. Unfortunately, society has taught us to externalize these characters rather than see them as parts of ourselves. They are meant to help us connect with the inner parts of our psyches symbolized by the characters portrayed, then integrated so we can feel whole. Fortunately, societal distortions lose their grip in midlife, as now, reality feels different than illusion. In midlife, a woman must realize that the "knight in shining armor" lives within her and *she* is responsible for her own happiness. She needs to awaken to her strong and healthy masculine energy and rely on it, not on that of an external man. When the Hero and Heroine awaken within her, she must heed their call. Her changing hormones catalyze this awakening and she must now individuate to reclaim herself and become whole. Now, she must begin to live from her integrated self and soul.

This framework is missing in our society and women everywhere long for a way to orient themselves through their midlife gateway to connect with what is real, true, and authentic for them. Women long to live from their intrinsic power. They must connect with it and empower each other to do the same. Now they must live creatively and release the fear based compromises they have made thus far.

The process of empowerment

Restoring a woman's intrinsic health requires her to awaken to the distortions she has been living from that abdicate her power and creativity. At first her awakening can cause deep sorrow and disillusionment. She may first feel anger, then grief. She may project this onto her loved ones. After blaming others for her feelings of disempowerment, she soon realizes that she is the one responsible for reclaiming her power. She was conditioned to rely on her partner's masculine energy rather than her own. This dependency disconnected her from her creativity and authenticity. Anger resulting from this loss of inner connection is what she projects outward. She must become aware of this as unhealthy and codependent and use her anger creatively to reconnect with her true self. This will awaken her inner "knight in shining armor," her untapped masculine energy, that evokes her ability to become self-reliant and productive. This also restores her self-worth.

This is difficult, but necessary work. The more a woman is aware of losing her creative energy through projected anger, the faster she awakens the dormant and sleeping parts in her psyche. These are the parts that were disempowered when she lived codependently. For as long she defines her worth and her value through others, she will not be able to connect to her intrinsic power.

When she first connects to her real self, it will feel unfamiliar, as her adapted self is still familiar. As she awakens to health, the discomfort she may feel within can be caused by the tension between her real and adapted selves. This tension is where her power lies. The more she behaves from a place that is authentic and true, the more she will gather momentum behind these new behaviors that intrinsically define her. Her real self will soon become the one she identifies with and models for others.

It takes great courage to connect with one's truth after having lived from the distortions that one is leaving behind. During midlife, many women feel rage when they realize that their lives have been lived for the most part in the service of others. When these "others" move on, they feel the loss of their identity and self-worth.

As we can see, conditioning by family and society disconnects us from our intrinsic power. Our resistance to perpetuating these behaviors is an inner signal that informs us that we are compromising ourselves through adaptating. Honoring this resistance can empower us to not adapt to the "power principle."

By the time we are in midlife, we have abdicated so much of our power to societal constructs that, like Nan, we may feel disconnected from our real self. We must remember the opportunity before us to reconnect with our truth through this powerful gateway.

Redefining intrinsic worth

When we are valued for our performance rather than for who we are, performance becomes an extrinsic measure of our worth. When we sacrifice ourselves in favor of others, we pay the price with our health. When midlife approaches, this pattern can express itself as an illness. It can also surface as anxiety or depression. After connecting with our intrinsic power, it is normal to grieve our feelings of loss as we redefine ourselves. This process is powerful, alchemical, and often painful. It forces us to lay a new foundation for our life, based on what is real versus adapted.

One of the greatest lessons midlife women need to learn is how to know their limits. While caring for others at the cost of themselves, they can easily lose sight of these. Knowing limits requires healthy boundaries. A foundation that has been defined only through relationship to others is not intrinsically grounded. Women must begin their journey of self-discovery and reclamation, where they are able to feel and discover what is healthy for them and what is not. This form of rebirth is necessary for them to restore and reclaim their health.

The signs of rebirth

Many women become extremely anxious and depressed during the midlife transition. As we have seen, the rules of the soul take center stage and a woman can often feel like she is on foreign ground. The tension created between the demands of the soul and the expectations of the world provokes anxiety. A woman at this juncture needs guidance and orientation as her identity shifts. Now she must learn to embody her wholeness. She needs to deconstruct her adapted self which carries momentum and familiarity, and replace it with an identity defined by her soul. She needs to learn to live from it and allow it to define her. She can no longer compromise herself. She now has to learn how to live authentically.

At this juncture she feels the chasm between what is intrinsically real and what she has been conditioned to believe. She may feel betrayed by her conditioning. Her changing hormones catalyze this powerful process of awakening.

Midlife women need the courage to help each other reframe this powerful time as a movement towards health. Those who have identified with their real selves must midwife those who are still in process. This is the work of community. We must mentor each other with framework and direction through midlife's treacherous terrain, where vulnerability and old momentum can easily pull us back into familiar patterns of self-denial. Our newfound power may not yet have gained traction, and we are very much like newborns in this rebirthing process. As we help each other understand and express the depth of our feelings and value their sacredness, we can heal our anxiety and replace it with curiosity and creativity.

The "power principle" in action

In the medical system, the "power principle" is prevalent in the physician-patient relationship. Physicians hold power over their patients through medical expertise. The patient relies on this to find answers to their problems. When their feelings and stories are dismissed or their symptoms are merely medicated, patients themselves risk dismissing and negating them. During my medical training, I often observed this in the physician-patient relationship, but did not have a framework to understand this as being unhealthy. No matter how much I was told to normalize this, I was unable to.

I felt out of place and disconnected from the system that I suppos-edly belonged to. The Indian culture that I was a part of taught me that sacrificing how I really felt was a virtue required for acceptance. Over time, I lost contact with my real self. Although I felt intrinsic resistance to my cultural framework, I was unable to see this as a sign of health. I felt that somehow I was wrong for feeling this. My worth became aligned with how well I performed and I lost contact with my limits. This pattern made me vulnerable to abuse by the "power principle." It also made me vulnerable to being dominated. Now my obedience to my conditioning defined my worth. The Indian culture still expects women to burn on funeral pyres in rural villages after their husbands die, as they are considered to have no identity apart from them. Women are expected to abdicate their lives in service to men. This expectation disempowers them.

When I fell in "love" with my former husband, it was through this unhealthy framework. Without a relative position for health, I tolerated disrespect from him and coped with it by working harder to hold my marriage together. I suffered deeply at the hands of the "power principle." I had no voice and no power. My conditioned self-doubt was constantly reinforced. My marriage was a closed sys-tem. During my recovery process, I had to reexamine all the ways that my fear had caused me to abdicate my power. I had modeled this adapted behavior to my children and was terrified that they would mimic these patterns in their relationships. Awakening to this was very painful. I lost nearly two decades of my life adapting through fear. I grieved deeply at my loss of self for all this time. I worked with my grief to understand how I had contributed to this and, after many years of process, came to understand it as a form of self-betrayal. I had unknowingly betrayed myself by adapting as I had been conditioned to and had allowed myself to be disrespected and abused for years.

During my recovery, I learned how to love myself and healed the disconnection I felt with my intrinsic power. I was guided by many women who had gone through similar losses before me and and trusted them to midwife my process. At first, my newfound sense of self felt vulnerable and fearful, but in time, it felt stronger and familiar. It began to define the new me.

I realized through this rebirth that I had created a relative position of health for my children. I had already imprinted them with my unhealthy conditioned self, now replaced with a new and healthy one. This could become their secondary imprint. They now had two imprints to choose from. The consistency of my commitment to my real self began to give them comfort and safety. They began to rely on it for strength and guidance.

Four ways in which women lose power

There are four ways in which women lose their power and connection to their real self:

1. The wounding of our instinct

When we were young, we were taught to ignore the voice of our instinct if it differed from the rules of the closed system. We were conditioned to obey these and compromised ourselves out of fear. We relied on our mentors for guidance. Many of them had also been conditioned. Over time, we lost contact with our inner cues, like feelings of resistance against what was not true for us. This was our inner wisdom, the feeling that told us that danger was near. We normalized this disconnection and our instinct became wounded. We second-guessed ourselves. We were programmed to rely on others and not think for ourselves. This was reinforced by the media and by society's injunctions. When we lost contact with our instincts, we also lost contact with what was real for us. We felt unsafe. We became disempowered. We learned to give others authority over ourselves and relied on their directives rather than our own. We felt powerless. We became vulnerable to abuse.

2. The wounding of our feeling function

Our feeling function is deeply wounded by society's injunctions towards it. Our strong feelings are considered pathological. In our society, passion is normalized only when it is associated with sex, but not when it is directed towards issues of truth and sovereignty. In this context, our passion is judged as abnormal and often medicated. As a result we feel unsafe with strong feelings. One of my patients described herself as having *too much* feeling. She criticized herself for this as partners in her previous relationships had left her because of *the intensity of her passion* for what mattered deeply to her.

This is a serious problem in our society. A society that is afraid of deep feelings will suffer from soul loss. Our feeling function is the expression of our soul, and its voice becomes louder in midlife when it demands to be heard through feelings. When we are able to have a healthy relationship with them, we become more creative and joyful. But, without a healthy framework, we risk compartmentalizing and suppressing our feelings and losing contact with our soul. This results in the loss of our intrinsic power. We often criticize ourselves when deep feelings emerge and apologize for them. We become vulnerable to being undermined. This leaves us feeling empty and disempowered. When we are disempowered, we are less able to experience joy.

3. Medicating our anxiety (during individuation)

Many women in midlife are in the process of individuating. They leave their old selves behind and in this gateway. They begin to live in alignment with their feelings. This "medial process," is accompanied by a new inner voice that keeps women up at night and speaks through their instincts and feeling function to help them discern what is authentic from adapted, and intrinsic from extrinsic. Since many women have wounded relationships with themselves, this causes anxiety. No one has prepared them for this.

When physicians medicate women during this process, it interrupts this alchemical process. A midlife woman's anxiety is often a signal that she is transforming. She must direct a great deal of her energy and attention towards rebirth. The medical experts she relies on often confuse her anxiety, a *normal* sign of transformation, with an anxiety *disorder*.

She must seek guidance to move through her sacred process with the help of a therapist or from those that have gone before her, and only use medications during this stage with awareness and caution.

4. Relationships based on the "power principle"

Many women also engage the "power principle" by trying to dominate and control others to feel a (false) sense of power and control. This is a passive-aggressive act from their shadow which is deeply disempowering for all. It creates distrust among women and deepens their wounding. This pattern is called "dark sisterhood," (I have described this in more detail later in this chapter). Some women may mistakenly think that a way to heal their powerlessness is to take power from other women overtly through domination or covertly through betrayal and competition. If normalized, these behaviors can become regular and unhealthy patterns in relationships. These can also deepen the wounds of powerlessness in the collective feminine psyche. One of my patients in her fifties, awakened to her dark sisterhood patterns and apologized to all the women she had previously hurt. She took responsibility for her malintentions towards them caused by jealousy and her own lack of self-worth. By owning this pattern, she healed her relationships with the women she had hurt and restored her intrinsic power and self-respect. She also served as a courageous mentor for others.

Anger as a sign of health

If a woman has to ask to have a need met, she is perceived as demanding, needy and dependent by others as well as herself. . . . When normal needs are denied, she begins to feel that she has no right to pursue activities that would fill her own needs and wants. Somehow she begins to expect that she has no rights at all.

~Maureen Murdock

In my own life, I was led to believe that expressing my needs was selfish and unreasonable. In my marriage, I lived in constant fear of having any needs at all. I felt ashamed when they surfaced and I tried talking myself out of them. My journals became the vehicle where I expressed my confusion about being punished for wanting to be loved and respected. I was frustrated for not understanding the causes for my confusion. I felt ashamed of how I felt. My shame disempowered me. I continued to adapt out of fear. I abdicated my power to survive. I felt trapped. When my husband betrayed me, I had no choice but to end my marriage. This was a level of disrespect that even my adapted self could not tolerate.

I felt lost when my marriage ended. For a long time after this I had difficulty connecting with my real self that was buried underneath the self that had spent half a lifetime adapting to domination by the "power principle." For many years in my marriage, I had been afraid to assert my real self for fear that I would lose everything that was sacred to me. I was convinced that one day my husband would emerge as my "knight in shining armor." I waited nearly two decades for this to happen. I had been conditioned to believe the fairy tales that externalized my inner knight. This came with a price. In my case, it was the sacrifice of my intrinsic power and my real self. I did not know of any fairy tales that spoke about my sovereignty, or my will. For years, I suffered in silence. I was imprinted to believe that for me, the virtuous path meant enduring this treatment as the mark of a "strong woman."

My journey through midlife forced me to deconstruct this painful and unhealthy dynamic. This is a common journey that many women take. The process of deconstruction and reconstruction, the death and life cycle needed for transformation, sometimes calls for a complete deconstruction of one's life that has been built around adaptations that resulted in the loss of intrinsic power. Some women go through this process consciously while others enter into it through a crisis which catalyzes their transformation.

As women move through the stages of death into life, they are able to feel safe again after they heal their wounded instincts and repair the boundaries that can shield and protect them from harm. This shield becomes a part of their presence and initiates them to mentor others.

Our life's themes

I believe that there is precision in what we need to learn in our lifetime. We come into this world to learn specific lessons and have specific experiences to grow in precise ways. Each of our lives has a theme. Becoming aware of this theme awakens us to living more consciously. The soul expects us to become aware of this and live from it. Staying unaware puts us at risk for feeling unfulfilled and depressed. Awareness helps us fulfill our sacred purpose. As we look for clues for healing our wounded parts, we often find that our life's theme has unfolded like a story and unraveling it helps us know more precisely what we need in order to reclaim ourselves and heal. This brings us closer to becoming whole.

It is impossible to feel like a victim while living from this framework. Identifying with the Victim is disempowering. When we can understand our purpose, we can piece together events in our biography to find the sacred thread running through it. Those who seek in this manner will attract others who are seeking in the same manner. Their resonance and shared intention will provide the help and support needed to remain on this sacred and conscious path.

Imagine the field of medicine practiced with an awareness of this transformational framework. This would make patients feel safe within the medical system. Authenticity and truth would be honored and patients would be encouraged to seek at the level of cause, thereby healing their symptoms rather than simply managing or numbing them.

Through this framework, the Feminine Principle would be present and honored in the physician-patient relationship. Integrating these elements would enable physicians to support and orient patients safely and authentically through their transformational gateways.

The midlife psyche

In midlife, the psyche becomes activated to live from a level of fierceness and authenticity that surprises many women. This is a necessary part of transformation. Currently, women all over the world are experiencing this at different levels. This awakening is bittersweet and challenges women's adapted and wounded identities. It also challenges the Victim within. Women must remember that this is a collective process and in order for them to heal their disempowered wills, they must engage the courage to live from their truth. *Every woman who dismantles her relationship to the closed system by becoming real takes a step towards health and wholeness that not only heals her, but the collective as well.*

Archetypes in the psyche

Carl Jung defined archetypes as thought patterns contained in universal forms in the psyche. These forms channel emotions according to the roles they embody. We relate towards each other through these archetypes that can be activated by life events and experiences. They exist in our psyches in both conscious and shadow forms, or high and low frequencies. The conscious forms operate from integrity in contrast to the shadow forms. For example, the conscious form of the Magician can operate as a strategist for resolving conflicts; as the shadow, it operates as the Sorcerer who manipulates and steals power to dominate and control others.

Other examples of archetypes are the Hero or Heroine, the Seductress, the Prostitute, the Victim, the Patriarch, the Matriarch, the Queen, the Warrior, the Lover, and the Crone. An example of the Prostitute would be working for financial security only, despite lack of respect, meaning, or purpose. The Patriarch would dominate and control others and disregard their sovereignty.

Living from the shadow is stressful. Fear is ever present in this state. To heal this, one must connect with the Warrior to access courage to correct compromises made by the Prostitute. The Heroine can activate courage and inspire the Warrior to look for a more fulfilling job, or access the Magician to find ways to reframe perspective from victimhood to one of meaning. It can also just simply disengage the Victim. The Prostitute and Victim operate from fear. The Warrior, Heroine, Magician, and Crone operate from truth, courage, and integrity. This is an example of how archetypes in the psyche affect our perspectives and, ultimately, our choices.

How the victim is born within us

A shadow archetype familiar to all of us is the Victim. When we live from the Victim we feel weak and helpless and lose contact with our intrinsic power. The "power principle" present in society, reinforces these feelings. Over time, the Victim can create a pattern of behavior that abdicates self-responsibility and disconnects us from our real self.

The Victim delivers the wound of disempowerment, yet our society normalizes and glorifies this. Our negative self-talk that shames and judges us, activates the Victim. Our inner critic drowns out the sound of our true voice. When we obey the inner-critic, our feeling of disempowerment deepens. Our relationship with the "power principle" often mimics our relationship with our inner critic. When women become aware of their inner dialogue and can name the archetype directing it, they can reclaim their power. Once they begin to heal, they are no longer able to tolerate abuse from the "power principle." Once they disconnect their identification with the Victim and begin to identify with the Warrior, Heroine, or Queen their intrinsic power activates the wisdom of the Crone, initiating them into becoming mentors for others.

The power of Venus' mirror

It is important for us to empower each other and to mirror back the power we see. When we lose contact with our intrinsic power, it helps to have it reflected back to us by another. The symbol for the female gender is Venus' mirror. This is the mirror we hold up to another and reflect their strength back to them. We owe each other this gift of mirroring. Mirroring the Queen buried beneath the Victim evokes empowerment. The Queen can dismantle the Victim. This is essential for reclaiming our intrinsic power.

The danger of a disempowered woman

Women compete with each other for power. Such women are not connected with their intrinsic power. They may covertly sabotage the efforts of other women, while presenting the *illusion* of support. They may also avoid being in relationships with empowered women, due to their fear of being exposed. While in their presence, we feel unsafe, a warning that we are in the presence of the "power principle." Since the intentions of disempowered women are not in the best interest of others, they cannot be trusted. Our feeling function will resist them. It must be trusted.

This shadow relationship between women is "the dark sisterhood" pattern described earlier. It is a relationship dynamic marked by behaviors that operate from jealousy, competition, and domination. Unfortunately, this is all too common in our society. Since many women feel disempowered, they behave from the dark sisterhood pattern and attempt to take power from others whom they feel pose a threat to them. Empowered women are a threat to disempowered women. Dark sisters compete with empowered women, to compensate for their lack of self-worth and intrinsic power. Since these patterns lack integrity, they damage their relationships with them and eventually feel shame and regret. They need to understand that relationships with empowered women can often be healing for their wounded self-worth. When an empowered woman has the courage to confront a dark sister about her behavior, it can help her heal the wounded relationship with herself and restore her integrity through this powerful act of mirroring.

Many women in midlife find that the women that they thought were their friends leave their lives when they connect with their intrinsic power. These "friends" no longer resonate with the woman transforming into her real self unless they are authentic themselves. The danger of staying in relationships like these is that they can sabotage connecting with healthy archetypes. Many women who are transforming struggle with the loss of these friendships when they lose resonance during the transformational process. They need to trust that as they are becoming healthy, relationships that support their growth will remain, but unhealthy ones will fall away. They must grieve their loss, release them and continue forward on the path towards becoming real.

The danger of self-doubt

Self-doubt is a hook that makes us vulnerable to the Victim. As victims, we are not connected to our power, but try to gain power through blaming others. The Victim weakens our Energy body. It causes a loss of vitality and creativity. It often sabotages our access to the Heroine and Warrior, who are needed to awaken the Magician and Queen, to access the wisdom of the Crone.

We must courageously awaken so as to not become vulnerable to the Victim through self-doubt, despite our grief from loss of unhealthy relationships. If we do, we risk sabotaging our forward movement that is necessary for true healing.

When our current paradigm eventually shifts from competition to collaboration, we will need to stay conscious of always engaging the principles of an open system. We must always support one another with qualities of the Feminine Principle.

Nan revisited

Nan was fully engaged with the Victim archetype. She wanted someone to rescue her so she didn't have to do the work of shifting out of familiar, yet unhealthy, patterns. She was looking for hormone replacement therapy or a hysterectomy to get rid of her symptoms. I could have easily taken the bait and capitulated as her Rescuer. I was trained to fix symptoms, but if I didn't engage her process I knew I she would miss the opportunity to connect with her intrinsic power.

In her current state, she felt like a victim of her changing body. She had lost contact with her feelings of satiety and avoided her reflection in the mirror. If she had seen herself becoming obese, she could have confronted and disengaged the Victim with the Warrior or Heroine early on. She had been conditioned to rely upon the expectations and solutions of others, not her inner wisdom or intuition. She expected me to act as her "knight in shining armor." If I had capitulated, she would have continued to be held hostage by the Victim and missed the opportunity to connect with her real self where her feminine power resided. It would have remained buried underneath many layers of adaptation and conditioning, building pressure in her Energy and Emotional bodies, waiting for a crisis to restore her wholeness.

Midlife as a transformative individuation process

Joseph Campbell stated in his book, *The Hero with a Thousand Faces*, that if one misses the opportunity to transform, life loses its meaning and will be experienced as a "wasteland." Here, one risks becoming a victim waiting to be rescued.

Many people in our society miss the opportunity to live an authentic life because of the limited framework present within the health care system. In order for us to truly heal, we must reframe how we define health and health care so we can restore our connection with the powerful archetypes within us. A prescription drug cannot provide this. Only a framework that empowers us to explore and live from the wisdom and precision of our deeper purpose can facilitate this sacred task.

For a woman, the halfway point is marked by physiological changes and the emergence of an intense feeling-function. Although hot flashes and night sweats are signals of hormonal changes, they also signal the resounding call from her soul that asks her to evaluate if she is empowered and authentic. If she is not, she must seek and journey to understand her needs and resist the temptation to feel like a Victim. She must find her voice, her truth, and her power, and she must gather the courage to stand at this gateway and reconstruct her life authentically. Menopausal symptoms mark the threshold where her feeling function is at last finding its voice. If she chooses to feel victimized by this, she subjects herself to great peril. The wasteland awaits her meaningless existence, where she remains occupied with symptom management alone while she behaves through her adapted and superficial roles to please the world. Her soul will inevitably speak to her through her fate in its ever loving faithfulness to offer her the opportunity to awaken and transform. This will be her "midlife crisis." She will be called here to arise out of her Victim. This initiation is necessary for her to reclaim her power and access meaning and wisdom.

If our society embodied this framework, it could transform into one that valued the midlife journey and encouraged us to live authentically. As we approach death, we would feel empowered and fearless, having lived the second half of our lives with meaning and purpose.

Our lives would be a testament to the mythic journey that regards initiation and individuation as sacred passages. Many cultures consider the start and cessation of menses as initiations into different phases of a woman's life. These rites of passage must be marked and honored as opportunities for a deeper awakening and empowerment, not as the "curses" they are currently considered.

Because my wake up call came as a deep betrayal of everything I held sacred, I realized this was precise "medicine" for my reclamation. To the degree that I had given my power over to another, was the degree that I could reclaim it. I sought strength and guidance from healers and therapists who mirrored my true self back to me. Their facilitation offered a safe space for my four bodies to realign as my real self emerged. This process was deeply terrifying, but also deeply empowering. As I began to hear my own voice underneath the injunctions of my conditioning, I began to feel more alive and found comfort in my intrinsic power. I channeled my energy into reconstructing my life from a place that was fearless and real. As I transformed, the space I held for my patients became even more powerful. I felt responsible to "pay forward" the gifts I received through my process. Those who transform through the midlife gateway have a responsibility to empower others in the same way they were by their mentors.

As for Nan, she learned how to feel safe with her process by understanding the territory of transformation. She slowly began to uncover the voice of her inner-critic who victimized her and she stopped obeying her negative self-talk. She began to make healthy choices, took walks, journaled, made art, and recorded her dreams. I helped balance her hormones and relieve her symptoms. She felt more whole. Over three months, she grieved the loss of herself when she recognized how she had betrayed herself by adapting. She was able to safely connect with her feeling function in therapy. Acupuncture restored her vitality, and body work released the stress her muscles carried. She paid attention to her breathing and exercised to strengthen her heart. She became conscious of the food she ate and how it made her feel. She also began to notice when she felt full and no longer overate. She reoriented and reframed her relationship to herself in a healthy way

She learned healthy boundaries. She stopped using alcohol to medicate. She found the courage to look at herself in the mirror and feel self-responsible, not helpless. She watched her body transform. In a year, she lost 65 pounds and was well on her way to a vital and more meaningful life that resonated with her soul. She felt called to become a massage therapist. It was her way to "pay forward" the wisdom and insight she received during her midlife transformation. She had a new lease on life, a renewed understanding of herself and a connection to her intrinsic power. Her inner dialogue now empowered her truth. She dismantled the inner critic and, with that, the Victim who had previously dominated her life. She connected with her Warrior and Heroine and awakened her Magician. The weepy, victimized woman I met a year ago morphed into a powerful and beautiful one who now understands the precision of life and trusts in her process. She has awakened her Queen and embodied her Crone. She is now able to mentor and empower others.

8

Reclaiming the Feminine

Flight

As I break open,
I uncover forbidden secrets.
They are set free,
flying out from dark places.
My soul heaves an exhale,
releasing years of oppression.
I transform.
Opening from bud to blossom,
I turn my face to the Sun.
I can now spread my wings
and take flight.

The most powerful word a woman can say is "NO."

~Rose Kumar, M.D.

What is the feminine? Society's projections distort her. It defines her by unnatural and unattainable standards we are conditioned to embody. These are imprinted in our psyches, and wound and contaminate our relationship with the Feminine Principle. They undermine feminine knowledge and wisdom. Our worth as women is associated with having large breasts and a sexual appetite. By these standards, we lose our worth as we age.

Feminine behavior is also defined by society. A woman is expected to say what is needed to keep the peace. She should be seen, yet not heard, and can feel only what is permitted. She cannot emote or "rock the boat." She learns to compromise who she is to adapt.

We all participate in defining the feminine through what we embody, how we behave, and what we enable. We model this distortion to our children. Over time, this becomes our collective impression of what being feminine means. This deeply wounds us.

One of my midlife patients, Anne, described her mother as a "saint." Her father was an abusive and dominating alcoholic and her mother said nothing. She simply bore his abuse. She thought that her mother's silence was noble, deserving of sainthood. Anne had a difficult time after leaving home and she struggled in unhealthy relationships. I asked her to consider what her life would have been like if her mother had spoken up against her father to protect their sovereignty. Maybe Anne would not have spent so much of her life recreating familiar patterns. In speaking up, her mother could have modeled a healthier position that would have given her children the opportunity to make healthier choices.

Anne realized that her definition of sainthood had been influenced by society's distortions where strength was confused with an ability to adapt. Through a healthier lens, she had a different definition of strength and was able to redefine sainthood.

Cathy

Cathy is a 49-year-old woman who came to see me with complaints of irritable bowel syndrome (IBS), which caused frequent abdominal cramping. In addition, she felt hot and cold throughout the day. She frequently felt agitated and angry while interacting with others. When she did, she felt shame. She isolated herself and stopped engaging activities that once brought her joy. She felt out of balance and afraid that she was gravely ill.

Her menses were heavy and she was unable to sleep through the night. She was always tired. She ate for comfort. She lost her vitality and zest for living. She felt no meaning or purpose. Cathy felt stuck, tired and hopeless.

She was a homemaker with two teenage children. Her husband, Bill, was a corporate executive. Economic pressures burdened him with stress and long hours at work. He was overweight, with health problems of his own.

Cathy looked forward to his arrival home to ease her loneliness. After work, Bill would de-stress by drinking. Bill was an angry drunk. He would yell at Cathy for not keeping a clean house. Her evenings were spent in "survival." In addition, she felt ashamed and inadequate.

She was overwhelmed by the expectations of her family, her shame, as well as her symptoms. She felt trapped and powerless.

Cathy and Bill had been married for seventeen years. When they first met they did not know what fulfilling the "American dream" would cost them. They sacrificed both their health and relationship for material possessions.

They were so preoccupied with achieving *society's* definition of success that neither one stopped to examine what was really important. Living by this definition came with a heavy price.

By 49, Cathy felt that her life was passing her by. In two years, she had gained fifty pounds. She did not feel well at any level. When she came to see me, she was on five medications: two for depression, one for abdominal pain, one for insomnia, and one for anxiety.

None were working. Her physician dismissed her, as he was unable to "fix" her. He had tripled her dose of prescriptions in the past six months. She lost touch with her feelings. She felt flat and numb. He called her a therapeutic failure.

At home, Cathy was caught in a pattern of fight-or-flight. In her forties, she became more sensitive to her husband's abuse. (This is not uncommon.) She grew agitated an hour before he got home, anticipating his drunken pattern. She felt demeaned and shamed. She remembered the magical time when they were first married and very much in love. Soon their desire for success took precedence over their marriage. Cathy had babies and stayed home to be a mother and wife.

Our culture associates success with performance and wealth. How much money we make begins to define us. Our big homes become symbols of success and expensive cars mark our status. We become consumers. We shop, drink, and eat rich food. We normalize this. The cultural motto we are serving is—the bigger the better, the more the better, the faster the better, the richer the better.

We lose sight of the fact that life is a journey, a process. We may lose meaning and feel empty, but continue these patterns ignoring our feelings and needs. We arrive in midlife, lost and imbalanced, seeking meaning and purpose, that we once thought we had.

Medications can't heal this empty state of being. It is a symptom of the life that we have missed. It will manifest as symptoms—anxiety, depression, IBS, hypertension, an addiction, or even a heart attack. We have sacrificed *process* for *product*. It is time to move inward and redefine who we are, so we can connect with what is real and reclaim our health.

The Masculine and Feminine Principles

The East offers a perspective that views wholeness as a complete circle. This circle consists of two halves, Yin and Yang. The energies of both are intrinsic in health. When Yin is balanced with Yang, we feel whole. When not balanced, we feel sick. Neither is associated with gender, and men and women embody both. Yin and Yang energies are always present in the natural world. The concept of "process versus product" can also be seen through this context. This perspective views our behaviors as related to the Feminine and Masculine Principles, or Yin and Yang energies. Emphasizing one more than the other creates imbalance. We must consider what health means from this context to be truly healthy and whole.

The Masculine Principle is defined by the following characteristics: linear, rational and analytical thinking, doing, action, product or outcome focused, external or outward focused, light, fast and quick, ego, mental focus, competitive, and "either/or" thinking. It is hot. It is Yang energy (Figure 7).

The Feminine Principle is defined by the following characteristics: cyclical, nonrational, strategic thinking, process oriented, inward or inner focused, dark, being, intuitive, creative, receptive, feeling, patient, heart and soul focused, collaborative, and "both and" thinking. It is cool. It is Yin energy (Figure 7).

Society glorifies elements of the Masculine Principle over the Feminine. We are valued and rewarded for Masculine behaviors. When we are product oriented, rational, and analytical we are considered a "team player" and an asset in our jobs. Our society does not value the elements of the Feminine Principle to the same degree. They have been dismantled from our political, legal, educational, and health care systems. We are expected to think "inside the box," defined by the Masculine Principle. Anything outside it is discarded. The Masculine Principle, at the cost of the Feminine, leaves us unbalanced and unhealthy (Figure 8).

Both men and women have associated success and worth with elements of the Masculine Principle. Cathy and Bill were so busy achieving (*doing*) the material dream (*product*) that they failed to spend time with their family (*being*). Process carried less value for

THE MASCULINE PRINCIPLE   THE FEMININE PRINCIPLE

THE MASCULINE PRINCIPLE	THE FEMININE PRINCIPLE
linear	cyclical
analytical	strategic
mental	feeling
fast/quick	slow
light	dark
active	receptive
either/or	both/and
doing	being
product/outcome oriented	process oriented
external focus	internal focus
competitive	collaborative
rational	non-rational/intuitive
hot	cool
Yang	Yin
fixing	healing
manifesting	incubating

Figure 7: Elements of the Masculine and Feminine Principles

them than product. This resulted in ill health. They arrived in their forties symptomatic and without any real meaning.

Another way our society values the Masculine over the Feminine Principle is with bonuses based on productivity. We strive to make money at all costs. Our media glorifies this. We value product over process. Analytical, not creative, thinking is rewarded. Qualities that are creative, kinesthetic, artistic, or sensitive are marginalized. We are expected to suppress these elements. When we do, we endanger compromising the Feminine Principle and perpetuating the imbalance normalized by society (Figure 8).

Our culture has become so obsessed with external definitions of worth that people go into debt to project the *illusion* of success. This

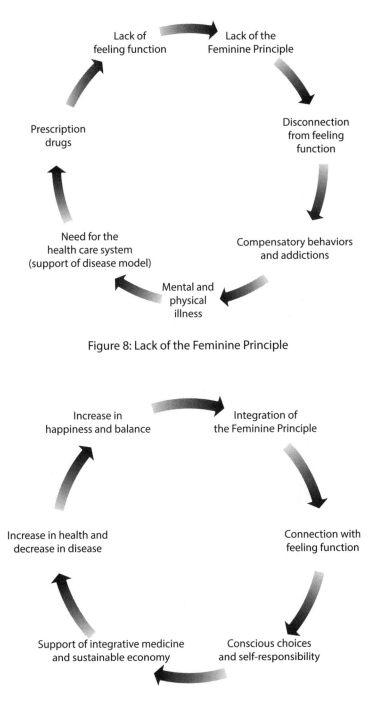

Figure 8: Lack of the Feminine Principle

Figure 9: Integration of the Feminine Principle

is not sustainable. It is not even honest. Eventually, we will have to confront the illusions we live from. The real place within, is always moving us towards wholeness. The Masculine and Feminine Principles are balanced here (Figure 9).

Our medical system is no different in its emphasis of the Masculine over the Feminine. It glorifies the Masculine elements of outcome, fixing, and analytical thinking over listening, intuiting, collaborating, feeling, and trusting in process. We use terms like "war on cancer" and "attack on heart disease." Keeping disease at bay is valued over *healing*. Within the medical system, patients are seen as "victims to be rescued." Instinct and intuition carry no worth and are ignored. If the expert cannot fix them, patients give up on themselves and sometimes even on life itself with no chance for healing or wholeness. They live out their predicted prognoses delivered by the experts. Illness is not seen as a process for seeking or learning.

Patients are not supported in their quest for answers. They are alone with their looming doubts and fearful of their process.

The price of the "quick fix"

In the sixties when symptom management became the focus of medicine, it deeply influenced our culture. The "quick-fix" mindset promoted a collective complacency. We normalized this, generalizing it to other areas of life. To this day we continue to be quick-fix oriented rather than self-responsible.

The pharmaceutical industry depends on this. The majority of pharmaceuticals numb our feeling function. Our "quick-fix" mentality has cost us dearly.

Unlike ours, other cultures value elements of the Feminine Principle. They value feelings. As a result, their state of health and well-being is far better than ours. Inner work is labor intensive. It takes effort. It is not a quick-fix. It requires strategy, insight, and commitment. It does not shirk from hardship. It trusts in process. It is enduring and tenacious. It is resilient and patient. It is transforming, transmuting, and regenerative. Unlike our quick-fix mentality, it exists in contrast to cultural traction. Without awareness, we unknowingly enable what is familiar. We must expect more than symptom management alone. We must normalize healing and expect nothing less.

Our quick-fix mentality has had a significant impact on our personal health, as well as the cost of health care in the U.S. Traditional medicine operates from only half of the circle of wholeness—the Yang or Masculine half. Without the Yin or Feminine half, it cannot truly heal. The linear approach of the Masculine Principle needs the intuitive approach of the Feminine to facilitate wholeness. The imbalance in our medical system leaves patients and physicians feeling empty and disillusioned.

Malpractice suits are a symptom of this. Many cases of medical malpractice result from neglecting to engage elements of the Feminine Principle during the patient encounter. Listening is critical for diagnosing accurately. Corporate health care values speed over time in a patient encounter. It values money over relationship. A physician cannot heal without listening. Mistakes are made while in a hurry, as clues to diagnosing and treating are missed. This causes suffering for both physicians and patients. Physician burnout and patient dissatisfaction occur due to the absent feminine. We all pay a price for this. Our medical system needs wholeness to preserve the health of its physicians and patients. This can only occur when the feminine is present in partnership with the masculine.

Like Cathy, many women become disconnected from the Feminine Principle at inner and outer levels. As children, we lived almost exclusively from the Feminine Principle. We lived in a world of imagination, beauty, and creativity. Over time, our conditioning associated our worth with elements of the Masculine Principle. We learned to override our instincts and feelings in favor of thinking. This disconnected us from our authentic selves.

Our instinct and strong feeling function are powerful intrinsic gifts. When we connect with these, we can heal many of the imbalances present in our Four Body System™.

Self-care is essential for healing. Women in midlife have to learn how to care for themselves at all levels. This is essential for connection with their real selves. Once they become self-aware, they are able to feel the imbalances caused by self-neglect. This is an important step in the journey towards reclaiming their health.

Patty

Patty is a 43-year-old woman who had a history of infertility. Between the ages of 38 and 40, she received four cycles of in vitro fertilization without success. She felt stress and shame for not being able to conceive and felt inadequate as a woman.

Six months after she stopped treatments, she became pregnant. After the birth of her baby, she began to experience anxiety. She had a recurring dream in which she was suffocating. In this dream she was surrounded by smoke and couldn't breathe. She was unable to see through the smoke into her future, and often awakened in a state of panic. She had no control over her fight-or-flight response. She was constantly agitated and overwhelmed.

Her feelings of inadequacy experienced during the fertility treatments suddenly returned. She felt the profound shame and anger that once accompanied them. She was desperate for healing.

As we worked together, she began to address the constitutional imbalances in her Energy body, caused by performance anxiety, now surfacing for release. She worked with a classical homeopath to restore balance. She needed to heal her feelings of shame and inadequacy she fell victim to. She was frightened of the unknown, unable to see herself in the future, hence the smoke in her dream. Financial pressures compounded this. Reiki helped release the pressure caused by the feelings of shame and stress she had carried.

Shame caused an imbalance in her Energy as well as in her

Emotional body. She processed her emotional pain in therapy to gain a deeper level of healing. She learned to treat herself with love and compassion, and to forgive herself for not "being perfect."

Over time, she felt safe in her skin. It was no longer the unsafe place of blame and shame. She learned about the parts of her that felt abused and victimized by critical self-talk. She released the sorrow that had built up inside her. She felt relief when she trusted in her process. After a month of therapeutic work, her anxiety lifted. Her recurring dream did not return. She slept more soundly. She felt lighter, no longer in fight-or-flight. Her desire to heal had uncovered a process that medications could not offer. Instead, they merely suppressed her symptoms.

Patty's confidence increased as she connected with her intrinsic power. She understood how she had devalued herself as a woman due to her conditioning. This surfaced during her fertility treatments. Although she became pregnant on her own, her inner critic dismissed this, attributing it only to chance. She worked hard to replace her self-criticism with self-acknowledgment. Patty was able to redefine herself and her worth from an intrinsic place. She began to trust the wisdom of her feeling function and its ability to connect her to a higher level of worth. This healed her anxiety.

Cathy's process was more complex. She needed to evaluate the neglected elements of the Feminine Principle in the way she related to herself and her family. This took over a year. Surprisingly, her husband, Bill, supported this. Through therapy, Cathy and Bill were able to identify the areas in their marriage they had sacrificed for material gain. They redefined their values. Cathy began to see how Bill's comments amplified her critical self talk that triggered her stress and shame. She had compromised her worth by suppressing her truth. This caused an increase in stress hormones that aggravated her symptoms.

When the possibility of a healthier future became evident, she began to make more empowered choices. She found the courage to engage in honest dialogue. She and Bill worked hard to change their patterns. I balanced her hormones and she changed her lifestyle into a healthier one.

Within a few months, Cathy weaned off prescription drugs and lost 20 pounds. Her IBS healed and she began volunteering at a local nursing home. This added meaning to her life. She and Bill spent more time together. After years, she was finally happy. She "filled herself up" and overflowed onto others. She restored her family's health by reclaiming her own.

After engaging elements of the Feminine Principle, Cathy was able to reclaim her health and experience joy.

The body's attempt to restore balance

The Feminine Principle is as necessary for process, as the Masculine Principle is for product. To be productive and healthy, we need to balance elements from both. Taking time for *being* is as important as taking time for *doing*. It helps us regenerate our body, mind, and spirit. Research in psychoneuroimmunology has shown that living from both principles is good for our immune system.

Both Patty and Cathy needed to balance their Energy and Emotional bodies. Their symptoms served as catalysts for awakening. This is common in midlife. Perimenopause and menopause will always bring our attention to the elements of the feminine we may have neglected. Our bodies call us inward for healing these neglected areas and recalibrating ourselves with a new language of self-care and self-respect. If we engage in this courageous work, we can heal; if we don't, we risk experiencing "dis-ease" when self-neglect expresses itself. Hidden in every disease lies the opportunity to uncover the imbalances that caused it.

The wounded masculine

Just as we are collectively living from the wounded feminine, we are also living from the wounded masculine. The wounded masculine identifies with the "power principle" and attempts to dominate others to compensate for its lack of power. This energy is neither intrinsically powerful or balanced. It is dominating and values competition over collaboration. In our culture, the wounded masculine is glorified. Our drive for material success at the cost of process, and fixing at the cost of healing causes great suffering. For us to be whole, we need to heal both the wounded masculine and feminine within. This is urgent and imperative. Just as women need to live from their sovereignty independent of men; men need to live from their sovereignty independent of women. Healthy relationships are independent, yet collaborative. We need to redefine ourselves through the balanced feminine and masculine and dismantle our patterns of adapting to and normalizing imbalance.

Feeling function

Our feeling function is the part of us closest to our soul. Our sentimental society is threatened by deep feelings. When hormones change and feelings intensify, women can become overwhelmed and frightened by the charge contained within. If their feelings are validated and supported, they are able to release this repressed energy. This can also be done creatively through art, music, or dance. Some women release through exercise, and some cry for months. Whichever way a woman chooses is the right way for her. She must cleanse her system to regain her balance. Through this process, she can connect with her Emotional body, often for the first time. "Good girls don't cry" is not a healthy injunction. Good girls express their feelings. These girls are healthy.

Our feelings are never wrong. They always have a good reason for being. Understanding this allows a woman to treat herself with love and compassion. This is one way she can accept and validate herself. We need to do this as often as we can. Trusting our feelings is the only way we can repair our wounded instincts and feel safe in our skins. Without this, we risk remaining vulnerable to being dominated. When we trust our feelings, they can direct us back onto our true path.

Midlife awakens us, facilitating our journey back to ourselves. Many women have expressed their anguish over awakening to the unfulfilling and superficial relationships present in their lives. Dismantling these relationships is painful, but they must reevaluate their values and dismantle everything that does not feel authentic. From this place, they can begin to trust what feels real and find their true voice. This deep level of transformation purifies them.

Some women reach their midlife gateway and choose to not walk through it. Familiarity holds momentum, and they are not able or willing to engage their Warrior. They risk slipping back into familiar patterns. They risk feeling like victims and relying on others to rescue them. These women are deeply wounded. They are difficult to be with in relationship because they expect others to compensate for their lack of intrinsic power. They substitute sentimentality for love. Sentimentality masquerades as true feeling, but it isn't. The real self cannot be fooled. Eventually, it will call to us. We must heed its call.

Discerning the difference between reality and illusion can be difficult when one compensates. Truth feels unfamiliar when living this way. We must be guided by our feelings and never choose familiarity over truth. As we practice living this way over time, our authentic self will gain momentum. This new and healthy self will become the one we are able to live from.

How to relate to one's inner critic

When we begin to transition through menopause and transform our relationships into more authentic ones, the inner critic may shame us. Many times this will manifest as feelings of guilt. The critic has gained traction over the years. If we heed its directive, we will feel depressed. We will also risk sabotaging our transformation.

Some women have difficulty hearing their truth as the inner critic's voice overshadows any other. They may even medicate themselves in an attempt to quiet it, to no avail. Attempting to silence the inner critic is usually futile. Its script is imprinted within and our obedience to it has given it power. When we allow the critic to victimize us, we lose our power.

An effective strategy for finding peace is through the practice of Mindfulness. Becoming mindful can disengage us from identifying with the inner critic's method of dialoguing. When we observe the mental chatter in our minds without engaging, the inner critic is disempowered. Being an observer removes us from critical self-talk. As small as this separation may initially be, it is an effective strategy for empowerment. In time, the separation between the self and the critic widens. This keeps the Victim at bay. In this way, we can disconnect the inner critic from our feeling function. It may continue to voice its familiar script, but is unable to impact our Emotional body. Women begin to feel a sense of freedom and regain their vitality through the regular practice of Mindfulness. Many no longer need to self-medicate. They are empowered when they create a more compassionate script to replace the critical one. They are able to treat themselves with respect. This brings them peace.

Mindfulness, when practiced as a strategic tool, can settle the mind and support the process of individuation.

Over time, as a woman engages with her real self and begins to resonate less with the adapted or compensated self, she begins to create a new and more real identity. Speaking her truth and being less concerned about how others react, decreases her risk for continuing to adapt. Her real self becomes her new normal and corrects her life's course towards her highest destiny. She enters yet another another level of individuation.

Liz

Liz is a 42-year-old woman with three children below the ages of twelve. She had been married for thirteen years and adapted to being emotionally abused by her husband. She remained silent to keep the peace. When she married him, she felt a disconnect that she blamed on herself. She believed that her love could heal this disconnected feeling and change his behavior towards her.

It didn't. When she turned forty, Liz began to feel outraged. She realized the disconnect she felt was actually a lack of resonance with her husband. She could no longer adapt. She suffered from insomnia, depression, acid reflux, and was frequently ill. She was ashamed of how agitated and impatient she was with her children, but was unable to change her behavior. She came to me for solutions.

Liz had adrenal burnout and was chronically fatigued from the dynamics at home. Her energy was depleted, leaving her immune system weak and vulnerable. I helped guide her with dietary changes to revive her vitality. She began acupuncture to restore her resilience and treat her reflux. In a month, her symptoms improved.

I referred her to a therapist to heal her pattern of learned help-lessness. She had learned to feel helpless as a child and was unable to advocate for herself as an adult in her marriage. Adapting was familiar.

It was only when her hormones began to shift, that she was unable to tolerate her husband's abuse. She felt the tension between familiar adaptations and her newly felt intolerance to abuse. This was stressful for her. Her rage spilled over onto her children. In therapy, she understood her patterns and healed her wounded self-worth. She was able to process her rage and contain it, so as not to project it onto others.

In therapy, she was also able to see how she colluded with her husband against herself when she enabled his abuse towards her. This awareness empowered her. She asked him to seek therapy himself. He refused. She had the courage to file for divorce as an act of self-advocacy. By now, her symptoms had healed. She had connected with her intrinsic power. She no longer felt helpless. Liz discovered the role that learned helplessness had played in making her adapt to abuse. She needed to uncover these imprinted patterns and dismantle them. This transformed her relationship with herself and what she was willing to tolerate. She emerged, empowered and awakened through her midlife gateway.

The alchemical process of midlife

Midlife is a powerful journey that we all must take, one that transforms us from being a victim into a self-responsible adult. Dismantling the old script and replacing it with one of self-respect can be lifesaving. Our patterns can only transform when we change our behavior. This even has the power to undo the damage unhealthy imprints may have caused. Our process requires us to straddle the tension between the self-critic and self-love. This is a powerful medial place in midlife. In this tension lies the catalytic energy required for our alchemy and transformation.

The power of "No"

It is worth repeating that the most powerful word a woman can say is, "no." When spoken with conviction and sovereignty, it has the ability to change our world as we know it. It takes great courage to say "no." We risk being rejected and abandoned. We need to remind ourselves that even when we stand alone, we never are.

We are in the company of our intrinsic power. "No" activates our powerful repair work of reclamation. When we say "no" and behave from our instincts, we feel empowered and recalibrated. Saying "no" activates the Hero and the Warrior who help us to behave authentically.

We must value "no" as a sacred word, and learn to say it when directed by our feeling function. It is a word that can initiate us into connecting with our soul. It draws the line—the boundary that protects us from being dominated. This connects us to our Queen, who restores our integrity. "No" restores our will and our worth. This gives us the strength to withstand the tension between familiarity and freedom. This empowers us to become real.

"No" is a good place to begin our journey towards empowerment. We need to choose between staying unhealthy or reclaiming our health. Saying "no" to distortions requires us to remain conscious so we can dismantle these from our psyches and behaviors. We need courage and endurance to maintain our newly found position of self-worth. "No" can facilitate this.

A Woman of Wisdom and a Man with Heart

The power of choice is illustrated in this powerful story of Gawain and Lady Ragnell. This is an English tale that portrays the healing of both the wounded Masculine and Feminine. This story takes place in fourteenth century England. I first came across it in the landmark book by Maureen Murdock called *The Heroine's Journey*.

One day in late summer, Gawain, the nephew of King Arthur was with his uncle and his knights. One day, the king returned from a day of hunting and looked visibly shaken. Gawain followed him into his chambers to ask him what had happened.

While he was out hunting, Arthur had been accosted by a fearsome knight, named Sir Gromer, who sought revenge for the loss of his lands. He spared Arthur by giving him a chance to save his life by meeting him in a year at the same spot unarmed with the correct answer to the question, "What is it that women most desire above all else?" If he found the correct answer to this question, his life would be spared.

Gawain assured Arthur that together they would be able to find the correct answer to the question and during the next year, they collected answers from near and far. As the day drew near, Arthur was worried that none of the answers held the truth.

A few days before he was to meet Gromer, Arthur journeyed out to a grove of great oaks. There before him was a large grotesque woman. She was large in length and breadth and her head was mottled green and her hair was spiked with weed like protuberances and she appeared monstrous. Her name was Lady Ragnell.

Lady Ragnell told Arthur that she was on her way to meet her stepbrother, Sir Gromer, and he did not have the right answer to the question. She told him that she knew the correct answer and that she would tell it to him if Sir Gawain would agree to marry her. Arthur cried out that he couldn't do that to Gawain.

She said that she did not ask Arthur for his agreement. She wanted to see if Gawain would himself choose to marry her. "These are my terms." She told him that she would meet him at the same spot the next day, and she disappeared into the oak grove.

Arthur was disheartened because he could not imagine his nephew marrying this hideous creature in order to save Arthur's life. Gawain saw the pale and strained look on Arthur's face and he asked him what had happened. When he told Gawain about Lady Ragnell's proposal, Gawain was delighted that he could help save his uncle's life. When Arthur pleaded with him to not sacrifice himself, Gawain said, "It is my choice and my decision. I will return with you tomorrow and agree to the marriage on condition that the answer she supplies is the correct one to save your life."

Arthur and Gawain met Lady Ragnell and agreed to her conditions. The next day, Arthur rode unarmed to meet Sir Gromer and at first, he gave him all the answers that he had collected from near and far.

*Sir Gromer held up his sword to cleave Arthur in two. Arthur added,
"I have one more answer. What a woman desires above all else is the
power of sovereignty—the right to exercise her own will." Sir Gromer,
angered by the answer, knew that his stepsister had probably given
him the correct answer and swore an oath against her as he ran off
into the forest, sparing Arthur.*

*Gawain held to his promise and married Lady Ragnell when they
arrived back at the castle that day. After the wedding feast, where
all present were in shock at the horror of the monstrous bride that
Gawain had married, the newlyweds retired to the wedding chamber.
Lady Ragnell asked Gawain to kiss her. He went to her and kissed
her and when he stepped back, saw the most beautiful young woman,
smiling at him.*

*Gawain was taken aback and wary of her sorcery and asked what
had happened to her to effect such a dramatic change. She told him
that her stepbrother had always hated her and had told his mother
who had knowledge of sorcery to cast a spell on her to change her
into a monstrous creature. She could only be released by the spell if
the greatest knight in Britain would willingly choose her for his bride.
Gawain asked her why Sir Gromer hated her so much.*

*"He thought me bold and unwomanly because I defied him. I
refused his commands both for my property and my person." Gawain
smiled at her in admiration and marveled that the spell was now
broken. "Only in part," she said. "You have a choice, my dear Gawain,
which way I will be. Would you have me in this, my own shape at
night and my former shape by day? Or would you have me grotesque
at night in our chamber and my own shape in the castle by day?
Think carefully before you choose."*

*Gawain thought for a moment and knelt before her, touched her
hand and told her it was a choice that he could not make because
it was her choice only to make. He told her that whatever she chose
he would willingly support. Ragnell radiated with joy. "You have
answered well, dearest Gawain, for your answer has broken Gromer's*

evil spell forever. The last condition he set has been met! For he said that if, after marriage to the greatest knight in Britain, my husband freely gave me the power of choice, the power to exercise my own free will, the wicked enchantment would be broken forever."

Lady Ragnell and Gawain were united in sacred marriage of two equals who had made a free and conscious choice to come together. Sir Gromer had bewitched her for asserting her will and protecting her sexuality, and Gawain gave her the freedom to transform her disfiguration. She had the ability to save the king, and Gawain had the wisdom to recognize the sovereignty of the feminine. Together they found healing love and wholeness.

This story is enacted daily in our own lives when we adapt to society's dismissal of our sovereignty. "No" is commonly seen as a threat by society. To reclaim our power, we must have the courage to say it, to wander alone in "the forest" connected with only our truth. We must risk being labeled as "monstrous" or nonconformist by *not* obeying the patriarchal "power principle" of patriarchy. The healthy Masculine will always seek union with the healthy Feminine because wholeness is the natural state of health. We must first heal our unhealthy imprints before we can become whole.

Balance and wholeness are natural states of being. All life moves towards wholeness. Integration of the healthy Masculine with the Feminine always leads to wholeness. Achieving wholeness requires consciousness. It necessitates a trust in process. Living from this framework can shift our paradigm from one of illness into one of health. Reclaiming the feminine in our personal and collective psyches is a critical and urgent task. It is the only way we can heal ourselves and restore the meaning and sacredness that has been missing in our lives.

9

Reframing Health Care

Faith dares the soul to go farther than it can see.
~William Clarke

Modern health care is a reflection of our cultural myth. At its core, it functions from the "power principle," an expression of the wounded masculine. The Feminine Principle is nowhere in sight. The patient is seen as a *victim* of their illness and the physician, the *rescuer*. In this kind of relationship, the physician has "power over" the patient.

Healing is not accessible in the physician's office, where only expertise fixes. The patient arrives here expecting to be *healed*. The medical system purports to, often falling short of its promise. Advertisements that tout health and healing are mere marketing gimmicks. Actual healing does not occur within corporate health care. The Feminine Principle is not part of the patient's fifteen-minute visit. Administrators award physicians for speedy treatment and quick fixes, but not for healing. Healing is a process that takes time, presence, and framework.

Those who run this system and serve "profit over process," are under the false assumption that process compromises financial gain. This assumption drives the flawed framework of the product-driven medical model. Patients feel disillusioned and disempowered inside this system. They frequent their doctors to explore the causes for their suffering, but are dismissed with only prescriptions to manage symptoms. They are conditioned to believe that this is the best care medicine can offer, but their feelings speak otherwise. They seek healing in addition to expertise.

If physicians are to be therapeutically and cost effective, the medical system will need to balance expertise with healing (the Masculine with the Feminine Principle). Cost effectiveness is a conflict of interest for the current system, sustained by the high cost of sick care. Health care's goals when based on a profit alone, make it impossible to control costs. In addition, corporate medicine is a closed system. A closed system does not support process. Process heals, unlike fixing, which merely manages symptoms. These are dilemmas not addressed in our system today. Patients expect physicians to find *real* solutions, answers to questions that can help them make sense of their suffering. They are often ill and afraid, sometimes at the end of their lives looking for comfort and a way to die peacefully. Prescriptions and procedures do not address their deep needs. They are costly and palliate the medical system's fear of death, commonly seen as a failure. Today's system is in need of a framework that engages presence, empowers patients, and restores health. Holding space and bearing witness are sorely needed to reframe the true vision of medicine, currently distorted in favor of profit.

The disempowered patient

Physicians also suffer from the absence of the sacred feminine in health care. They are not taught to hold space for healing and mirror it back to patients. This has starved the soul of traditional medicine. They are not taught to bear witness with heart or presence. Witnessing patients in this way is an art that takes time and mentoring to cultivate. Instead, their patients frequently leave their visit with prescriptions only. These merely cover up physical symptoms that manifest from deeper "bodies." Their symptoms will not stop delivering their deliberate message, and the time between doctor visits leaves them fearful with no real solutions for restoring health.

As a result, they feel helpless and lost, anxiously dependent on only the physician's expertise they expected would make them feel whole.

Alone in their process, they feel a lack of control over their lives. Their biographies are not important to the medical framework, as it is not an area valued by traditional medicine. The patient lacks tools to explore the causes for why they are sick. They believe that illness is a random event beyond their control, and unaware, they continue to live in ways that contribute to it. The system has failed them. It has made them dependent. It has turned them into "victims waiting to be rescued." This dynamic, normalized by society, has contributed to the cultural trance that keeps patients asleep to the powerful role their choices play in their healing.

When women perceive themselves as victims of illness, they abdicate their power and second-guess their inner-wisdom. They feel physicians are the only ones with knowledge. Because their instincts are wounded, they doubt what they know. In addition, they live in a culture where they are imprinted to think there is no connection between their choices and health. In our quick-fix society, self-responsibility and empowerment are not valued; nor are the qualities of hard work and endurance needed for reclaiming and restoring health. Traditional medicine itself does not value these quailities. Women feel helpless when their process is ignored. They feel abandoned by the system, left to seek answers on their own.

Imagine a medical system where its framework included the exploration of the Four Body System™. Imagine it was committed to transformation, healing, and supporting process *in addition to* expertise. This system would be passionate about educating patients to be healthy, and as a result, have better outcomes at lower cost. It would seek the causes of illness to restore health. Imagine what it would feel like to make choices that supported health; where physicians served as teachers, coaches, and healers who empowered patients with both their expertise and presence. It would transform the current system into one where trust is possible. This could even reframe society into one that values self-responsibility and consciousness.

In this system, *health* would be normalized rather than illness. From this framework, we could teach our children to dismantle the unhealthy and adapted patterns we unconsciously modeled for them. By seeking the deeper levels that actually cause disease, we could model a healthier way of living. We could trust in our process and live and die consciously. We could end needless suffering. This could be a solution for transforming health care from a closed into an open system.

The price of fear

Fear is bad for our health. Studies have shown that fear has a negative effect on our immune system—it weakens it. It drives our unconscious patterns that impact our health. It is the reason underneath anxiety and depression. It disconnects us from our intrinsic power. Fear drives our need to eat comfort foods to self-medicate. Comfort foods harm our cell structure. Their soothing is temporary and they leave cells stymied and weak. Comfort foods are inflammatory, making them toxic at all levels.

When midlife women use comfort foods to medicate, their symptoms worsen. When patients with cancer use these foods to medicate, they feed cancer cells. This is how fear can impact health.

Physician's are not taught to value their patients' perspective or the effects that fear and empowerment have on healing. In fact, fear is very much a part of their medical training. They are imprinted to interact in ways that evoke fear in patients. Physicians adapt to what is mentored for them by the closed system of medicine. Patients consider them as a "high priest" or "priestess," an exclusive expert, as they make predictions about life and death. An example of this is during the diagnosis and treatment of cancer. Our culture associates cancer with death. We spend billions of dollars on "cancer research," that focuses only at the level of the Physical body. A cure requires us to understand the causes of cancer at all levels of the body. It requires us to explore solutions for restoring balance at all levels as well. "Waging war" on the Physical body with medications or surgery alone does not cure cancer. It never has. It only palliates it, leaving patients fearful of its recurrence, as many of them are.

It is difficult for patients to overcome a negative prognosis from the expert. When delivered, it permeates their very being, activating their fear, damaging their personal power, and weakening their immune system. It also triggers feelings of hopelessness, depression, and anxiety. Patient's put up "a fight," but for many, this is an uphill battle. Without the understanding of cause, they lack the knowledge needed for healing. Robert Johnson's statement, "The right treatment at the wrong level is ineffective," is the reason patients are fearful. They fear not knowing if their treatments will heal them at the deeper levels of cause. They depend on the medical system for their survival. Since it ignores these levels, patients live in fear of cancer recurrence. Fear does not leave them even when a remission is proclaimed. Then they are merely "cancer survivors."

When fear of recurrence looms, it sabotages a patient's ability to use cancer as the powerful catalyst it can be.

It has been shown that those who do not accept their negative prognoses, live longer with a better quality of life. Traditional medicine calls them "case reports," or "anecdotes." They are the ones worthy of study. They heal because they refuse the fear offered. They also refuse to let cancer define them. They use cancer to deepen their perspective of life. People who view cancer from this larger context, experience life more fully. They honor and value the power of self-responsibility and make conscious choices. Cancer can be a great teacher. Paradoxically, it can even facilitate the reclamation of health.

Empowered patients do not rely solely on the expertise of the medical system. They use what it offers, enhancing it with therapies that heal at deeper levels. They seek, therefore they heal. They are regenerative and resilient. Both the Masculine and Feminine Principles are engaged in their pursuit of health.

They are living examples of warriorship. They may have an "incurable" wound, but thwart its power by seeking its cause. Their healing is intrinsic and alchemical. They are able to transform the Victim into the Warrior. They are not "cancer survivors." They have transcended survivorship and truly healed.

Every cancer patient deserves to be empowered and offered this larger context for healing. We must be open to this in health care.

Physicians also need to be aware that the statistical prognoses they share with patients lack accuracy. Statistical prognoses are averages. On either side of the statistical middle is an extreme. On one extreme is success, and on the other, failure. It would benefit all to focus on the side of success to maximize healing. Patients who seek are more likely to heal. Physicians must explore ways to activate the seeker in patients to improve their outcomes. This can support healing for all.

One ill patient cannot be compared to another. Everyone's health and illness is greatly influenced by their biology, biography, lifestyle, and perspective. Physicians are trained in ways that take away hope and disempower patients. This is a critical issue that must be addressed. Physicians always need to be aware of the fear they evoke in patients and empower them instead. The elements of the Feminine Principle must be incorporated into both the medical system itself and the physician-patient encounter. Prognoses must be delivered in a way that supports a patient's intrinsic power. This approach must be rewoven back into the practice of medicine.

The medical system has a responsibility to educate patients and empower them to make and sustain healthy choices, as well as engage them in their healing process. Hope must replace fear. Fear paralyzes the immune system, sabotaging health. It also triggers unhealthy patterns patients may engage for comfort—even old ones that may have initially contributed to their illness.

Our current health care system has become a part of the problem and not the solution. For patients and physicians to restore any level of meaning to the practice of medicine, these patterns must be uncovered and transformed. Our system must evolve into an open one free of fear so it can evoke health.

The inner life of the doctor

When health care became a closed system, both patients and physicians suffered. The intention of physicians is to help and heal. They cannot practice effectively within the dynamics of a closed system. Their medical decision making and creative process is now regulated to follow policies for productivity rather than care. Productivity is valued over process and administrators regulate their monetary performance. They are allowed fifteen minutes to fix their patients with negative consequences for longer encounters. They are trained to perform like Pavlov's dog. Many feel saccharine accomplishment and find superficial solace inside the closed system to which they are feared into "belonging."

Physicians attempt to normalize this way of practice. But feelings don't lie, and month after month, year after year, the compromises felt within them deepen as the inner chasm widens. They feel trapped by the superficial framework of the profit-driven, administratively-regulated health care system that constricts their ability to practice from soul. Health care itself has become superficial, mechanical and soulless. Physicians seek ways to comfort their emptiness. Their collective wound is *the lack of meaning in their work.* When they adapt to survive, they become disconnected from the soul of medicine's vocation.

The office visit revisited

The patient in midlife seeks healing of a deeper nature. After half a lifetime, the tension between the adapted and real selves surfaces in feelings and symptoms. Lacking framework and direction, patients access the medical system for healing and guidance. They seek a safe space to dismantle their adapted selves. When symptoms are frightening, they seek validation. Physicians need to provide the comfort and safety that only their presence can offer. Presence carries expertise as well as empathy. It offers safety. It sees into and beyond symptoms. Presence alone can often heal. Presence requires one to be authentic. Authenticity builds trust. To engage presence requires personal growth.

There is an old saying, "What happens to a person in your presence is more a matter of who you are than what you know." This truth is not taught in medical schools. Physicians are taught to become experts at the cost of their feeling function. This prevents them from being able to truly heal. Healing requires empathy. Without it, physicians risk invalidating and dismissing what patients feel. Feelings are seen as "touchy-feely" by the medical system.They are not valued as important.

The office visit has the potential to heal the patient's invalidated and wounded feeling function. A safe space allows repressed feelings to emerge, bringing balance to the Emotional body. It also facilitates transformation. A physician's ability to bear witness with the power of their presence can even transform illness into health. Prescriptions alone cannot offer this form of "medicine." Being validated can sometimes be enough for a patient to reclaim their worth. Feeling like they matter can even restore their will to live.

For a patient this fosters trust. Trust is needed for her to feel safe with her questions that hold clues to her healing. A nurturing partnership between the patient and physician can heal her loneliness and empower her process. It can activate the courage needed for her to transform. It can support her health. It can heal the chaos her illness caused by reframing it as a catalyst to restore order and harmony.

This partnership is powerful enough to heal her shame and

promote self-responsibility to uncover the ways in which a patient's choices may have contributed to her illness. This can evoke her consciousness, which will help her to seek answers to life's questions that may have eluded her before. In this partnership, she can reframe herself from a Victim into a Warrior. The Warrior can restore her will to heal.

How powerful would an office visit like this be for both the physician and patient? This is a question worth asking and imagining. Without this, we fall short of the potential for deep healing. Patient encounters are bereft of this level and adapted physicians treat adapted patients from familiar dynamics. Only authenticity offers safety. This is missing in health care today.

The Feminine and Masculine Principles revisited

It is worth restating that the elements of the Feminine Principle are creative and fecund. The nature of incubation is fecundity. Fecundity is essential for creativity.

The elements of Masculine Principle analyze and fix. The Feminine when balanced with the Masculine promotes wholeness. One without the other causes imbalance. Creativity without action manifests nothing. Fixing without process does not heal. Adding qualities of listening, validating, and empowering offer a greater chance for healing. The understanding of cause is critical for cure. A context based in wholeness is the only way that healing can be evoked.

Anxiety is often the result of disempowerment caused by fear. Patients lack strategies to find order in the chaos caused by illness. Physicians must offer these. This can reframe it as a catalyst for growth. Medicine, when practiced this way, can awaken consciousness. When questions are asked and answers explored, meaning emerges. This can transform "pain into medicine." This framework is both sacred and powerful. It is inclusive and open. It combines expertise with presence and is committed to process. The closed system of medicine does not support this. Physicians have not been trained to engage this. As a result, patients feel neglected and forgotten. They feel abandoned in their process.

A failing business model

Currently, we are a three trillion dollar health care system that has more debt than worth. The medical system as it exists, is failing both as a vocation and a business. Both patients and physicians are disillusioned. Country clubs, golf outings, and pharmaceutical dinners add nothing of value to their souls. Fear is abundant and escalating. Policies and administrative mandates override patient care. Physician burnout coupled with an increase in alcohol and drug abuse are symptoms of corporate illness. The feminine is buried and all of us suffer from her absence. As long we adapt to how things are, the current closed system of health care will continue to pursue profit over process. Administrators are disconnected from medicine's sacred mission. Betraying it in favor of greed desecrates its real purpose. It must be served authentically to restore its true intent.

Connection with feeling function is essential for healing

Emotion, energy in motion, engages imagination in the creative process. These elements of the Feminine Principle need to be accessed for the current medical paradigm to be effective.

> He who is badly wounded in his feeling function
> will not be happy over anything.
> ~Robert Johnson

Feeling function makes any system committed to health and healing more effective. Without it, the possibility for healing is lost. Our collective instinct and feeling function are wounded. Patients and physicians are unhappy. Our system itself needs healing. Palliating the closed system of health care with the current version of health care reform will not heal it in the long run. It will not save money and will not serve the vocation of medicine. Until health care itself transforms into a more conscious, integrative, and open system neither health nor healing are possible.

Integrative Medicine revisited

The solution to our health care crisis can only occur through transforming the current medical system into one that is truly integrative; not a potpourri of traditional and complementary modalities that only physicians deliver. Integrative medicine cannot be used as yet another method for symptom management or a gimmick for market share like it currently is. It must engage medicine's core intent to heal. It must use scientific method with the highest standard-of-care, engaging science at every step. It must use a framework like the Four Body System™ to explore the causes of illness. This is the only way it can restore healing and meaning to both physicians and patients.

Proscutes is a mythological character who cuts off the feet and head of his guests to accommodate the size of his bed. This is what the current health care system does to Integrative Medicine. It attempts to fit this open system into its closed system box. Integrative Medicine is not a separate specialty. On the contrary, it is a more expanded version of traditional medicine. It combines process with expertise. It is the solution to today's limited framework of traditional medicine. For it to endure, it must uphold high standards. It is ultimately the medicine that can heal the failing system itself.

Adding investigative depth is critical to solving the therapeutic limitations of health care. Corporate health care views Integrative Medicine as a separate specialty. When present, an integrative consult is more expensive than a traditional one, limiting access to only those with financial means. It is not yet the expanded framework that it needs to be, limiting its ability as an affordable and viable method of care and healing. Corporate health care today uses integrative methods merely to attract market share, leaving patients disillusioned, mistaking this charade for true Integrative Medicine. The closed system of health care uses words like 'integrative' to generate profit. When incorporated into actual practice, it is marginalized and not supported. In this position, Integrative Medicine is distorted and rendered ineffective, mistaken as holistic and scientifically invalid.

Complementary practitioners do not enjoy the credibility that physicians within the health care system do. Physicians hold a superior status. Moreover, many physicians learn complementary methods with limited training and call themselves 'integrative', undermining the training process engaged for certification by complementary practitioners. Instead of competing with them, physicians need to collaborate to optimize therapeutic success. This is the only way to facilitate health while upholding high standards of medicine. It is also a way to broaden its context from merely fixing to healing. Collaboration would be a step forward in the evolution of health care. It would also be a way to to truly integrate the Feminine Principle into its existing framework without compromising expertise.

The Handless Maiden

I discovered the story of "The Handless Maiden" after she appeared to me in a dream. As I explored its meaning, I was struck by its power and symbolic significance when applied to the practice of medicine in its current state. It describes the wounding that physicians and the vocation of medicine suffer within corporate health care.

There was once a miller who had fallen on hard times. All he had left was a millstone and a large apple tree behind his mill. One day he was in the forest cutting deadwood and he came upon a charming man who said to him, "Why are you wasting your time cutting deadwood? I will make you wealthy beyond your wildest dreams and will come to claim what is behind your mill in three years." He then disappeared into the woods.

The miller thought nothing of it and wandered home. To his awe, he saw that his house was converted into a mansion with royal linens and draperies, the finest furniture and china. The miller's wife was overcome. "How did this happen?" she asked.

"I came upon a man in a black robe in the forest who promised me wealth and a life of ease in exchange for what is behind the mill. Surely we can plant another apple tree when he takes the one growing there now."

"Oh! Behind the mill is indeed an apple tree, but our daughter is there also, sweeping the yard. The man you met is the Devil."

The forlorn parents were devastated. The daughter did not marry for three years, and the day that the Devil came to collect her, she put on a white robe after she bathed and waited for him to take her.

When the Devil came to collect her, he began to scream, "She must not bathe or I cannot come near her." She then did not bathe for weeks and reeked of uncleanliness with matted hair and dirty clothes.

As the days passed, she began more and more to resemble a wild beast. But she wept hot tears that ran down her arms which cleared the dirt and left them white and clean.

When the Devil came to collect her, he was furious, "Chop off her hands, or I cannot come near her," he screamed. "If you don't, everything in your life will die."

The father was so frightened that he obeyed the Devil. He brought out his silver axe, and weeping and shaking, he begged forgiveness of his daughter and chopped off her hands. There was much crying out and the girl's life as she had known it had ended forever.

When the Devil returned to collect his bounty, the girl had cried so deeply that her stumps were clean and white as snow. The Devil was infuriated and could not take her away as her stumps were clean and he only wanted a dirty maiden.

The maiden then pleaded to her parents to let her leave and beg *for food, and she went out wandering in the forest. It was a moonlit night and she wandered with her disheveled body and matted hair with the appearance of a wild beast with stumps wrapped in white gauze. She had left her parent's house and wandered into the woods to seek her destiny as the handless maiden. Pretty soon, she came upon a royal orchard where the pears on the trees shone silver in the moonlight. She knew that each was carefully counted, but she was so hungry that she begged the spirits of the tree for some fruit. A branch bent down for her and offered her a perfect pear. She ate it gratefully and returned to the forest to rest. The next day, the king came to his orchard and noticed a missing pear. He questioned the gardener who told him, "Last night, a girl without hands appeared and the tree offered her a pear as I watched."*

The king brought his magician with him to watch if she would return that night. Indeed she returned at midnight and the tree again offered a branch to the handless maiden so she could eat the pear. The king was overcome by her beauty in the moonlight. He stepped out and declared himself to her and promised to care for her through all the days of her life. So the king married the handless maiden. He made her a set of silver hands to replace her absent hands.

A few years later, when the maiden was with child, the king had to go far away to wage a war and he left his mother in charge of her. He asked to be informed if the child was born in his absence. When the maiden gave birth, a messenger was sent to inform the king of the birth of the child. The messenger came to a river and stopped by the side of the water for a nap, as he felt tired. When he was asleep by the side of the river, the Devil switched the message, informing the king that the child was half beast. The king was horrified and sent a message back of love and caring for his wife and the deformed child. Again, the messenger fell asleep by the river and the Devil switched the message to read, "Kill the queen and her child." The Queen mother was devastated by this request and rather than follow the king's directive, strapped the baby on his mother's breast and bid her farewell, sending her into the forest.

The young queen wandered through the forest until she came upon a river. As she was parched and thirsty, she leaned forward to take a drink and her baby slipped out from its harness and fell into the river. The queen overcome by fright and love for her baby, suddenly thrust her stumps into the river and her hands instantly grew back. They grasped her baby and pulled him out of the river.

When the king got word that his queen had been sent out into the woods and that the messages had been changed through trickery, he went out into the deep woods to look for his queen and his child. He found them by the river and as they reunited, he rejoiced at their coming together again. They returned to the castle and lived a beautiful and fruitful life.

Despite all his efforts, the Devil was not able to destroy what was cleansed by tears and love.

This story is symbolic of the current state of health care in our country. The health care system can be compared to the mill that processes raw material in the story. The mill is not working, as its core mission that values process is not being served. Of course, this is how the system stays ill. Bypassing process leads to a loss of life force, sabotaging the real work of medicine. In our current system, creativity is at a standstill and true abundance has dried up. Safety is sacrificed when instinct is cut off. Once we are wounded, we are vulnerable to the promise of gold in exchange for grief, common in corporate medicine. We lose contact with the truth of our purpose and the meaning of our work.

Today, those who chose medicine as their vocation find themselves running on a treadmill with no way off, working for system that has lost its heart. Physicians cope by adapting to the way things are. They are not able to offer their presence with expertise. In fact they are rewarded for discarding elements of the Feminine Principle in favor of patient numbers. This form of practice wounds both physicians and patients alike.

Because of this, patients lose the opportunity to experience their physician's pure intent. Connection with instinct evades the 15-minute patient visit. Under pressure, physicians miss engaging their ability to heal (what they longed for before joining medicine's closed system). In its absence, chances for error are heightened. Adapting to methods that compromise the feminine wound both physicians and patients. When connection is not valued, the patient encounter loses fecundity. Fear is present when feelings are not. In a system that lacks balance, the sacred contract between physician and patient is not honored. The "hands" of the system are amputated.

Nearly twenty years ago, physicians made a Devil's bargain. The fathering function (protector or vision-keeper aspect) struck a Devil's bargain to manage the business of health care and, unknowingly, betrayed the heart of its mission. When physicians handed over the business aspects to the corporate world, they lacked discernment. They did not realize the sorrow and anguish this would cause. When the protector function is ignorant of the compromises expected, it risks betraying itself, resulting in the loss of feeling and creativity. Hands touch and sensate. They communicate love. A baby who is not touched fails to thrive. Healing is not possible without touch from the hands and heart.

Physicians cut off their feeling function by adapting to the mission of administrators. They are given "silver hands." They abdicate their creativity in exchange for financial promise. They compromise their sovereignty while sacrificing the soul of their vocation. They are not aware this will wound them in ways that it does. Adaptation comes with a grave price.

The system grinds forward in the name of "health care," and projects its *illusion* through millions spent in advertising. It is promoting neither *health* nor *care*. A physician worth is determined by insurance companies who value only procedures, not process. Primary care no longer has value. It carries neither purpose nor security. It's mission for healing is undermined. Specialities are top heavy in health care today. The promotion of *true* health has suffered and we all feel its loss.

Our system is broken and no matter how shiny the silver hands are, they are not real. *Real* hands are needed to sense and feel. We are expected to suppress the pain of being amputated and adapt to the current system. No matter how much the masculine (the expert) is engaged, without the feminine (feeling), healing is simply not possible.

Even science, in its truest sense, is no longer practiced in medicine today. It has become a "crap-shoot" where medications are prescribed without scientific method in the interest of time. Pharmaceutical companies gladly participate to fulfill their agendas and control physicians for corporate profit.

The system, at this juncture, is wandering in the forest with its stumps wrapped in gauze, holding its pure vocational seed against its chest, looking for relief, for a drink of pure river water.

Current health care reform will not provide this. For it to do so, the Feminine Principle must be honored with all of its elements. With patients, the skills of listening and feeling by weaving stories with symptoms must be valued. The patient's pain and suffering must matter again, and heartfulness must make its way back to the exam room so patients can truly heal.

The Devil must never be trusted. There is no real success without joyful feeling function. There is no joy in health care today. If the reward we seek is merely money, we risk all that is of *real* value. Physicians can no longer live with silver hands. They now want what is real, where what they do matters and makes a difference in the world. They now want what feeds their soul.

What shock forces them to thrust their "stumps" in the river is anybody's guess. But it will happen, as the story predicts the inevitable outcome. Their longing to heal may be the very catalyst needed for the system's alchemy.

The Devil will continue his efforts at illusion, enraged by the power of the feminine as she takes her rightful place in our ailing system of health care.

Health care is currently in crisis. For it to heal, physicians need to reevaluate who they are, what they represent and for how long they will wander, holding what they consider sacred and love deeply close to their hearts. For as long as physicians adapt to the conditions that the closed system dictates, they will be lost in the forest, very far from the healing river. No system can thrive without soul, especially a system that purports to heal.

The illusion of health care is crumbling. Patients are going elsewhere for their healing. Physicians must awaken to this loss. They have invested all that they are into their craft. Only physicians and patients can transform health care. It will take great courage for them to individuate together. Understanding and strategy will be needed to reclaim medicine's lost mission. Health care itself needs healing. It needs to re-connect and re-member the sacred feminine so it can be whole again. Replacing illusion with authenticity is what it needs to reclaim integrity. Patients should settle for nothing less. Physicians must acknowledge the resonance between adaptation and complicity.

We need physicians who are courageous, creative, and able to acknowledge the emptiness they feel when expected to adapt to what is not real in their work. Their compliance serves no one. Instead, it forfeits their ability to connect with patients in the many ways they had dreamed. In health care today, laptop computers sabotage the physician's presence. The fear of errors in data entry interferes with their ability to listen and diagnose. What has happened to sacred vision once held by medicine? The accelerated pace with which the Feminine Principle is oppressed under the weight of red tape is nothing short of outrageous. This beckons a deeper need for the system to transform through its much awaited death and eventual rebirth. There is no doubt the sacred feminine will move the system in this direction to restore balance as well as wholeness.

Wholeness is the natural order of things. All of life moves towards wholeness. Even illness is a stage in wholeness. Our medical system is currently ill. We must trust the wisdom of its death-rebirth process as it makes its way to becoming whole.

Physicians themselves dismiss the value of the Feminine Principle. After years of conditioning and adaptation, learned helplessness makes them vulnerable to the collective beliefs the system values. They must remember that only the masculine with the feminine can heal health care at a level that is both personal and collective. Consciousness is critical for this course correction. Courage is needed to heal medicine's sacred vision. Only through the Feminine Principle can meaning and healing be restored to physicians and their patients. Individuation beckons at this critical threshold. This will take our collective effort.

Our system based in fear and greed has wandered so far from what is real. The healer and healed must expect nothing less than its sacred mission. They must not enable the mill that health care has become. If this continues, the shock of remembering medicine's true mission will arrive as a crisis of collapse. In Carl Jung's words, "what is not brought to consciousness comes to us as fate." Crisis is inevitable when we remain unconscious.

Women's Health and the current medical model

When the Feminine Principle is absent in health care, women accessing it are neither honored or served. Their cries and longings are not heeded. They are silenced as the feminine elements of listening, receiving, healing, and process are ignored. Women are abandoned by the system and shamed for their feeling function. They are left repressed and regressed, without being guided through their midlife gateway.

Women at this medial juncture are transitioning from mother to crone. This is needed for them to become leaders, teachers, mentors, and wisdomkeepers. Without a framework to help them, they risk living their remaining days feeling empty and betrayed by their changing bodies, wishing for nature to turn back their clocks. They risk aging without grace, joy, wisdom, or consciousness. The medical system has a sacred task to help them individuate, so they can experience health and meaning in the second half of their lives. A lack of meaning is what is at stake. Our culture has betrayed what is real. We, as a collective, are sicker because of this. We struck a Devil's bargain, replacing what is real, soulful and creative with silver hands. We believed material success and corporate profit could fill the void left by soul loss. Nothing could be further from the truth.

When corporations replace their true mission with a compulsion for profit, people working for them are not honored. Material greed replaces human value. Corporate health care is no different. Our systems today have lost their way. They serve what is not real.

Only we are the ones who can change this. It is up to us to find intrinsic solutions to redefine and reframe what we have lost. Restoring elements of the Feminine Principle can heal this. Expecting a leader or a president to fix this will place us again in the role of the "victim waiting to be rescued." This is our task and we need to grow up, wake up, and rewrite our current story to give it a happy ending. We need to understand the price we have paid for adapting and abdicating responsibility for our sovereignty and power to a broken system that is governed by greed.

It is up to us to be authentic and use our voices to reclaim our birthright for wholeness, health, and for what is true. Only then will we begin to heal. We must all participate in the process needed for death and rebirth. If we don't, we will continue to perpetuate our conditioned patterns of learned helplessness and remain disempowered.

Healing the health care system

As midlife women, we need to empower ourselves with the voice of our "double." It is strong and fierce and uncovers the truth in all things. When we connect with Her to become who we really are, we will gain the insight and strategy needed to facilitate our healing by understanding the causes for our personal and collective illness.

Today, women are the main consumers of health care. The midlife woman, who is connected with what is real, demands what is her right and privilege from the health care system. If her needs are not met, she leaves and looks elsewhere for what she seeks. Her needs are simple and the framework she craves is one that can orient her in her life's gateway to a deeper and richer relationship with herself. If we, in midlife, do not answer this call, we will have betrayed our sacred responsibility to transform our lives and our world. We must all do our part. We must support and love each other into doing this.

Health care needs to be examined from the inside out, from the top down and the bottom up. There must not be any stone left unturned. When physicians analyze the current system in the same way they were trained to analyze the body, they will be able to iden- tify the pathology that keeps it sick. They will have to reach deep inside and stand in the face of criticism and rejection, with courage and heart, to heal their system that has lost its soul.

For patients, it will mean finding physicians who can meet their needs and serve them with both expertise and presence. It will also mean having their truth be honored while they are educated and healed with standard-of-care medicine. It will mean not settling for anything less than a safe space where they are held and honored, where health is fostered and hope restored.

For physicians, it will mean practicing medicine from both expertise and presence. Without the system's support, it will mean practicing alone. It will mean creating an open system, where the context of medicine transcends, yet includes traditional ways. It will mean practicing with a framework that honors expertise and presence and being open to what can truly heal. This is the only hope for solving the crisis plaguing health care today.

Not surprisingly, lobbyists and politicians try to wish our problems away. They offer rhetorical and superficial solutions for only symptomatic relief. They perpetuate the illusion of change through quick fixes and cover-ups that are short-lived yet skin-deep. Their intent and focus is once again to merely palliate the bipartisan struggles, where true intent is compromised for personal gain and party support. The soul of our system can only be healed by physicians and patients and by no one else.

The health care system itself, top heavy with many layers of administration and red tape, overcharges its patients and over controls its physicians. Its advertisements promote the *illusion* of wellness, healing, and well-being, thinking that the public will naively believe the sincerity of its efforts. But today's public consists of a vast number of midlife women who cannot be fooled into supporting a system whose mission is not real.

As we commit our lives to what is real, our world will no doubt be transformed for the better. In my least optimistic moments, when I worry about what my children will inherit, I gain solace in knowing that in our world, close to one billion midlife women are in process. They are hungry for a better world. They are hungry for what is real. Their appetites will not be satisfied by anything less than what resonates with truth and integrity. These are the ones who will change the face of health care and all organizations left limping along without the Feminine Principle.

These are the ones we can count on to transmute the mess of our world into one with depth and wisdom, honor and love. We each have a powerful feeling function that knows the language of truth. We *feel* when we are being fooled, and we feel when we are being served. We will feel our way into behaving in ways that will create a better world. We are now called to become our "double." She has awakened within our voices and our hearts. We have come to the end of a time when we cannot continue to adapt out of fear. The time has come for us to stand in the heat of transformation until we become whole.

The solutions to our problems are not complicated. They are very simple. We are called to open our hearts and our minds, and with that our systems, into a new paradigm of health care and Women's Health, one that functions from truth, meaning, love, creativity, expertise, and presence. Health care itself needs to heed the call of its "double." She is the one who has been waiting to restore its soul, the one who is restless and will not rest until the system is transformed into one of authenticity and truth—one whose healing beckons and whose time has come.

I invite you all to explore these questions and to question what is presented to you by today's health care system, and most importantly, to trust in your feeling function. Your "double" is ever present, waiting for your connection to be lived from the true, authentic you. She has wisdom and instinct and She is always right. She is the voice of transformation and truth and will connect you with what is real. I invite you all to live from Her, and in doing so, we will surely transform our world.

Bibliography

Alkhalaf, M. et al. *Growth Inhibition of MCF-7 human breast cancer cells by progesterone is associated with cell differentiation and phosphorelation of Akt protein.* European Journal of Cancer Prevention, 2002 Oct; 11(5):481–8.

Beinfield, Harriet and Korngold, Efrem. *Between Heaven and Earth.* New York: Ballantine Books, 1991.

Campbell, Joseph. *The Hero with a Thousand Faces.* New Jersey: Princeton University Press, 1973.

Childre, Doc and Deborah Rozman. *Transforming Stress: The Heartmath Solution for Relieving Worry, Fatigue and Tension.* California: New Harbinger Publications. 2005.

Colditz, Graham A, et.al. *The Use of Estrogens and Progestins and the Risk of Breast Cancer in Postmenopausal Women.* The New England Journal of Medicine. 1995. Vol. 332(24): 1589–93.

Estes, Clarissa Pinkole. *Mother Night. Myths, Stories, and Teachings for Learning to See in the Dark.* Sounds True, Inc., 2010.

Estes, Clarissa Pinkole. *Women Who Run With the Wolves.* New York, Ballantine Books: 1992.

Hersmeyer, K., et al. *Reactivity-based coronary vasospasm independent of atherosclerosis in rhesus monkeys.* Journal of the American College of Cardiology. 1997. 29 (March 1): 671.

Holford, Patrick. *The New Optimum Nutrition Bible.* Berkeley, CA: The Crossings Press, 2004.

Johnson, Robert A. *We, Understanding the Psychology of Romantic Love.* San Francisco: HarperCollins Publishers, 1983.

Johnson, Robert, A. *Transformation, Understanding the Three Levels of Masculine Consciousness.* San Francisco: HarperCollins Publishers, 1991.

Judith, Anodea. *Eastern Body Western Mind.* Berkeley, CA: Celestial Arts Publishing, 1996.

Jung, Carl G. *Collected Works of C.G. Jung. Translated by R.F.C. Hull.* Princeton: Princeton University Press, 1972.

Lee, John and Hopkins, Virginia. *Dr. John Lee's Hormone Balance Made Simple.* New York: Wellness Central Hachette Book Group, 2006.

Lee, John and Hopkins, V. *What Your Doctor May Not Tell You About Menopause.* New York: Wellness Central Hachette Book Group, 2004.

Murdock, Maureen. *The Heroine's Journey.* Boston, MA: Shambala Publications, 1990.

Satir, Virginia. *Peoplemaking.* CA: Science and Behavior Books Inc., 1972.

Stein, Murray (editor). *Jungian Psychoanalysis.* Illinois: Opencourt Books, 2010.

Tool. Vicarious. *10,000 days.* Volcano Records. 2006.

Women's Health Initiative Study. *Risks and Benefits of Estrogen Plus Progestin in Healthy Postmenopausal Women.* JAMA, July 17, 2002.

Xiao, Ou Shu et.al. *Soy Food Intake and Breast Cancer Survival.* JAMA 2009: 302(22): 2437–2443.

Index

Energy body 116, 124,
125, 126, 129, 130, 131,
132, 134, 135, 136, 137,
138, 139, 144, 147, 168,
170, 198, 212
E/P ratio 56, 70, 71
Estés, Clarissa Pinkola 17
estradiol 48, 49, 50, 56,
57, 58, 61, 71, 72, 73
estriol 48, 49, 72, 73
estrogen 48, 49, 50, 51,
52, 53, 54, 55, 57, 58, 59,
60, 61, 62, 63, 64, 65, 66,
67, 68, 69, 70, 71, 72, 73,
74, 81, 82, 83, 84, 85,
89, 95, 96, 99, 100, 101,
102, 103
estrogen dominance 53,
54, 55, 57, 59, 60, 61, 62,
64, 65, 66, 68, 69, 70, 71,
74, 81, 82, 83, 84, 89, 96,
99, 100, 101, 102
estrone 48, 61, 71
exercise 66, 81, 82, 89, 93,
99, 106, 172, 215, 222,
223
fat 48, 59, 63, 68, 69, 71,
78, 79, 82, 87, 88, 89, 90,
93, 96, 99, 104, 105, 146
fatigue 51, 55, 60, 61, 62,
70, 71, 72, 73, 74, 79, 89,
91, 95, 97, 101, 120, 131,
145, 170, 180
feeling function 18, 19,
21, 25, 31, 33, 34, 35,
36, 39, 40, 42, 44, 105,
107, 109, 112, 114, 115,
116, 118, 119, 121, 122,
125, 147, 149, 156, 159,
161, 163, 164, 166, 167,
168, 169, 170, 174, 190,
197, 199, 201, 209, 210,
212, 213, 215, 217, 220,
232, 234, 240, 241, 243,
246, 247
Feminine Principle 1, 3,
4, 5, 6, 11, 13, 15, 16, 21,
35, 44, 117, 147, 175,

194, 198, 204, 207, 208,
209, 210, 211, 213, 214,
225, 226, 230, 233, 234,
236, 239, 241, 242, 243,
244, 246
fibrocystic 60
fibromyalgia 61, 131
flax 92, 103, 104
flower-essence therapy
129–132
foggy thinking 60, 70,
81, 138
Follicle Stimulating
Hormone 51
follicular phase 51, 52, 57
Four Body System™ 20,
113, 116, 124, 125, 126,
139, 143, 147, 150, 151,
152, 172, 175, 212, 227,
235
free T3 (fT3) 74
free T4 (fT4) 74
free testosterone 58
frustration 128, 155
gastric reflux 131
Gawain 220–223
gel 58, 70
genetically modified food
(GMO) 78, 84, 86,
90–92
gluten 80, 81, 84, 87, 90,
91, 93, 136
grief 32, 33, 34, 39, 47,
114, 122, 140, 153, 184,
188, 198, 239
hair loss 62
headaches 47, 60, 63, 71,
90, 95, 101, 131, 145
healthy love 16, 156, 157,
163, 166, 167, 169, 170,
173, 174
heart attack 83, 170, 206
heart disease 66, 81, 82,
89, 99, 102, 131, 177,
210
heroine 42
high heart rate variability
127, 128

holistic 5, 236
homeopathy 132, 133,
134, 136, 137
hormone 18, 36, 48, 49,
51, 53, 54, 56, 58, 59, 61,
64, 65, 66, 67, 68, 69, 71,
72, 73, 74, 75, 81, 82, 83,
84, 88, 92, 99, 100, 119,
121, 145, 183, 198
hormone balance 56, 65,
66, 69, 71, 99
Hormone Replacement
Therapy (HRT) 53
hot flashes 42, 43, 47, 49,
57, 61, 62, 63, 64, 72, 81,
94, 97, 99, 101, 102, 145,
146, 170, 199
hypertension 50, 55, 60,
63, 81, 89, 95, 97, 105,
118, 131, 145, 206
hypothyroid 81, 89
hysterectomy 68, 72, 181,
198
identity 14, 15, 181, 185,
187, 188, 217
individuation 29, 30, 35,
38, 41, 176, 190, 199,
200, 217, 218
initiation 17, 29, 43, 44,
180, 200
inner-critic 109, 110, 111,
115, 196, 201
insomnia 47, 60, 62, 72,
123, 124, 130, 131, 145,
146, 166, 170, 205, 218
insulin 60, 70, 81, 88, 89,
100
insulin resistance 60,
81, 89
Integrative Medicine 4,
113, 114, 116, 125, 141,
151, 152, 235, 236
intrinsic power 7, 11, 15,
26, 29, 35, 39, 43, 106,
110, 148, 160, 169, 176,
177, 180, 182, 183, 184,
185, 186, 188, 190, 191,
192, 193, 195, 196, 197,

Kalpana (Rose) M. Kumar, M.D. is board-certified in internal medicine. She graduated from The Albert Einstein College of Medicine and completed her internship and residency in internal medicine at The University of California San Francisco and Stanford University Medical Center.

Her groundbreaking integrative medical framework has facilitated true healing for thousands of patients over the past twenty years. She is the founder and medical director of The Ommani Center for Integrative Medicine in Pewaukee, Wisconsin.

Dr. Kumar is an expert in the fields of Integrative Medicine, Women's Health, and Executive Stress Reduction. She is a national speaker and health care consultant. She is a futurist and visionary who has developed innovative solutions to our current health care crisis.

She can be contacted at:

The Ommani Center for Integrative Medicine
www.ommanicenter.com